Trap the U-Boats!

STORMING THE MOLE

Trap the U-Boats!
The Zeebrugge Raid April 23rd 1918

Alfred F. B. Carpenter

The Zeebrugge Raid a Short Account
by Arthur H. Pollen

LEONAUR

Trap the U-Boats!
The Zeebrugge Raid April 23rd 1918
by Alfred F. B. Carpenter
The Zeebrugge Raid a Short Account
by Arthur H. Pollen

FIRST EDITION

Leonaur is an imprint of Oakpast Ltd

Copyright in this form © 2015 Oakpast Ltd

ISBN: 978-1-78282-467-1 (hardcover)
ISBN: 978-1-78282-468-8 (softcover)

http://www.leonaur.com

Publisher's Notes

Contents

To

THE MAN-IN-THE-STREET

Introduction

By Admiral Earl Beatty

In appreciating the military reasons which directed the operations connected with the blocking of Zeebrugge, it is desirable to recall to mind the general naval situation at the beginning of 1918.

Briefly stated, the German High Seas Fleet was contained within the waters of the Heligoland Bight by the British Grand Fleet, whilst German submarines were engaged on vast operations, having for their object the stoppage of the trade of Great Britain, and interference with our lines of communication.

In the face of such an attack, the aim of Great Britain was either to destroy the enemy submarines, or, failing destruction, to prevent their egress from their bases. Convoy operations, patrol operations, and mining operations in all seas were carried out to achieve the former aim, and accomplished great results.

But enemy submarines continued to be built almost as rapidly as they were destroyed. It was essential, therefore, to take what measures were possible to render useless their bases and interfere with their freedom of exit, and it was with this military object that plans for the blocking of Zeebrugge were initiated.

Emphasis has been laid on the military reason which underlay this operation, because an erroneous impression has existed in some quarters that the Zeebrugge operations were more in the nature of an offensive designed to lower the morale of the enemy and enhance that of the British Navy, which, as a whole, had little opportunity of coming to grips with the enemy.

Whilst these moral results undoubtedly were felt after the operation, they were not the military reasons, reasons alone which justified so complex and difficult an undertaking, reasons which were never lost sight of during the planning and carrying out of the operations.

The plan was surely laid; simple in general design, details were worked out with foresight and exactitude. The factors of surprise, mystification, and diversion were utilised to the utmost. The resources of science were given full scope. Training to carry out the plan proceeded with energy and understanding, co-ordination and co-operation being apparent throughout. It was carried out with determination.

In Captain Carpenter's book we are let into the full secret, and are led step by step through the various phases referred to above, which were to be crowned by the glorious achievement of St. George's Day, 1918. His pages bring out once again the moral and military virtues of the British Navy, Officers and Men. They demonstrate that the spirit which existed in our Naval Wars of past centuries, wars which laid the foundation of the Empire, remains undiminished in the naval personnel of today.

It is for us to ensure that these glorious traditions are understood by all, and in being understood are handed on to those who come after us. This book, in placing on record the matchless qualities displayed by all concerned in the blocking of Zeebrugge, I welcome for this purpose.

Beatty
Admiral of the Fleet

19th July, 1921

Appreciations

By Marshal Foch

C'est dans un sentiment de solidarité que s'est réalisée l'union des Alliés, en 1914, quand la cause de la Civilisation s'est trouvée menacée.

A tous les moments critiques de la guerre, l'union s'est ainsi resserrée devant le danger, et lorsqu'il s'est agi de fermer un des repaires d'où les sous-marins ennemis menaçaient les communications vitales des Alliés, dans une manoeuvre splendide, avec un esprit commun de sacrifice absolu, le port de Zeebrugge a été attaqué et définitivement fermé.

Le Commandant du Vindictive a tenu à rappeler les détails de l'opération dans laquelle il a joué un rôle si brillant, et son livre constituera un précieux enseignement et donnera aux générations futures un exemple splendide.

F. Foch

(When in 1914 the cause of civilisation was menaced, it was the instinct of solidarity that brought about the Union of the Allies.

At every critical moment of the war, in the face of peril, this bond was renewed; and when it became a question of closing one of the lairs from which the enemy submarines threatened the vital communications of the Allies, the port of Zeebrugge was attacked and closed once and for all by a superb manoeuvre involving a common spirit of supreme sacrifice.

The captain of the *Vindictive* has undertaken to tell in detail the story of the action in which he played so brilliant a part, and his book will afford a valuable record and set forth a fine example to future generations).

By Rear-Admiral Sims, U.S.N.

Few incidents of the Great War had a greater influence in inspiring enthusiasm in the fighting forces and increasing their morale than

11

the successful attack upon Zeebrugge; and it will long remain as an example of what can be accomplished by the thorough co-ordination of the elements of a sound plan with the various limiting conditions of place, time, state of sea and air, and the material equipment suitable and available.

The reader of this volume will at once be struck by the painstaking care with which it was necessary that each detail be worked out, and each unit assigned its particular task to be executed at a specified time and place. Also that the amount of detail was necessarily so great, and their dependence one upon another so vital to ultimate success, that the whole may be compared to a complicated mechanism so designed to meet peculiar conditions that the failure of any part—any unit or group—or a material change in any of the conditions, would have deranged essential elements of the plan and might have jeopardised the success of the expedition.

But the principal lesson to be learned from the attack is not so much the thoroughness of the preparation and training and the efficiency of the weapons, essential as they of course were, as it is the influence of the spirit and the initiative and loyalty of the personnel that carried it out. These elements supplied the "steam," the flexibility, and the lubrication that ensured the harmonious working of the whole mechanism of which they were the soul. The basic principle was the splendid morale of the personnel inspired by the high character of its leaders.

Apart from the great interest of this narrative to the laymen, as a military exploit of the most brilliant character, and an inspiring story of heroism in war, it will always prove of great value to those military men of both branches of the service who realise the tremendous influence of the morale of their forces—the confidence in the ability of the leader which encourages initiative and inspires the highest type of loyalty.

Wm. S. Sims

By Count Visart (Burgomaster of Bruges)

Ainsi que tous mes concitoyens j'ai appris avec une grande satisfaction que la fameuse attaque de Zeebrugge par le Vindictiveallait faire le sujet d'un livre publié prochainement par Capitaine Alfred F. B. Carpenter, un des héros qui ont pris une part glorieuse à cet exploit.

Cette entreprise de la Marine de Guerre Anglaise a été assurément une des faits de guerre les plus extraordinaires des temps anciens et modernes. Elle a été accomplie avec une énergie et une audace qui a déjoué toutes les prévisions des Allemands.

Ainsi en dépit de toutes les difficultés, de tous les dangers, et de pertes cruelles, l'assaut prodigieux du mole a jeté l'épouvante parmi les ennemis et en même temps le Vindictive et les bateaux qui le suivaient ont embouteillé dans leur repaire les abominables U.B.

La cannonade entendue à Bruges nous avait déjà donné l'éveil et bientôt les rumeurs que les Allemands n'avaient pu intercepter et la consternation qu'ils tentaient vainement de dissimuler nous ont appris que l'Angleterre avait frappé un grand coup. Un tel événement releva tous nos courages.

Nous espérons qu'à Zeebrugge, sur le territoire de Bruges, un magnifique monument immortalisera ce fait inoui, mais c'est avec le plus grand intérêt que nous connaîtrons par le livre de Capitaine Carpenter toutes les circonstances de cette histoire héroïque et les noms des hommes qui ont donné une nouvelle gloire à la Marine Anglaise.

Amider Visart
Bourgemestre de Bruges

(It was with great satisfaction that I and all my fellow citizens learned that the famous attack on Zeebrugge by the *Vindictive* was to be the subject of a book, to be published in the near future, written by Captain Alfred F. B. Carpenter, one of the heroes who took a glorious part in that exploit.

This enterprise of the British Navy was assuredly one of the most extraordinary feats of war in both ancient and modern times. It was accomplished with such energy and audacity as to baffle all the German plans.

In spite of all the difficulties, dangers, and cruel losses, the wonderful assault on the mole created consternation amongst the enemy; and the ships which followed the *Vindictive* bottled up the abominable submarines in their base.

The sound of heavy firing heard in Bruges had already warned us; later, the receipt of rumours which the Germans had been unable to intercept, and their consternation which they were vainly endeavouring to conceal, proved to us that England had struck a mighty blow. Such an event renewed our courage.

We hope that at Zeebrugge, which is within the territory of Bruges, a magnificent memorial will eventually immortalise this unprecedented action, and it is with the greatest interest that we shall learn from Captain Carpenter's book all the circumstances of this heroic episode and the names of the men who added this new glory to the British Navy).

13

Author's Preface

As a result of having delivered many lectures, under official auspices and in compliance with private invitations, on *The Blocking of Zeebrugge*, the author has received several requests to record the story in more permanent form. Underlying these requests there appears to be a feeling that first-hand accounts of enterprises in the Great War should be of some value towards preserving that spirit which rallied all classes of individuals in the British Empire, in the Allied Countries, and in the United States of America, to the common cause of upholding civilisation in the face of danger. That opinion, indeed, has been openly stated to the author in Great Britain, by leading members of the educational profession and of the Church, by naval and military officers and others. Opinions of a similar type also have been received from the United States, where, during a recent series of visits to many of the larger cities, the author personally experienced that solid friendship for Great Britain which is sometimes hidden beneath surface irritations of a political nature.

Misunderstandings must occasionally arise between communities and between the members of any single community; they readily take root and develop into serious argument where the existence of a *common cause* is forgotten. For that reason the author feels that the above-mentioned opinions are not without foundation. Whilst attempting to show that co-operation between the several units of a fighting force and confidence between superiors and subordinates are important factors towards success in war, he has made this humble endeavour to induce the belief that co-operation and confidence in other walks of life are no less necessary.

There is danger of this blocking enterprise being allotted a false position in the contemporary histories of the late war owing to the somewhat prevalent custom of describing war operations with little reference to the various considerations, factors, and events which gave them birth.

The man-in-the-street is sometimes carried away by enthusiasm or despondency, as the case may be, when unexpected events occur during hostilities; he is apt to give little thought to the "why" and "wherefore" of the occurrences. That fact has been exemplified clearly enough with respect to this particular event, for, on all sides, one heard the public verdict, given in the colloquial vulgarism of the period, that the affair was a fine "stunt." The word "stunt," as unmusical to the ear as it was offensive to those concerned in the operations, has been defined as "a voluntary act, spectacular, usually unnecessary, sometimes involving risk, and designed to attract attention." However, the man-in-the-street meant well, and, after all, could justifiably plead that his lack of education on naval matters was to blame. The author has therefore addressed this book to the man-in-the-street, and has endeavoured to "put him wise," as our cousins across the water are in the habit of remarking.

The official despatches dealing with the blocking operations on the Flanders coast were published early in 1919, and, as far as despatches can go, gave a splendid account of the enterprise forming the subject of this book. But despatches are strictly limited in length and necessarily deal more with cold-blooded statements of fact than with psychological aspects. When one reads despatches of the great leaders of the past concerning the operations in their campaigns one cannot fail to notice the almost complete absence of any reference to the moral factor in war. Yet Napoleon himself declared, "*The moral is to the physical as three is to one.*" Material results can easily be gauged under peace conditions, whereas moral effect on human nature in war is only discoverable from one's own war experiences, which are necessarily limited, and from the experiences of others as set forth in the historical records of past wars. It was partly for that reason, presumably, that Napoleon studied the campaigns of Cæsar and Hannibal although their instruments of war were long since out of date.

The usual reasons for the omission of the moral factors from despatches are twofold. Firstly, the leader from whom the despatch emanates may consider it inadvisable to publish his preconceived ideas as to the eventual effect of the operations on the morale of the enemy; this concealment is especially necessary if the despatch is published before the declaration of peace. Secondly, the writer of the despatch is often unaware, at the time of writing, of the effect already obtained

16

against the enemy's morale; such effects may not be discoverable for many months after the operations have been concluded. Under certain circumstances it may also be temporarily inadvisable to present to the enemy, through the medium of despatches, information concerning psychological effects on one's own personnel. These omissions, therefore, must not be taken to infer that the moral factors were ignored. It is clear, then, that post-war accounts of operations may be far from superfluous whether considered from the point of view of the man-in-the-street or that of the student of war.

Without some conception of the strategical situation arising from the German occupation of the Flanders coast it would be difficult to grasp the true nature of the enterprise described herein. An examination of the strategical outlook alone, however, would be insufficient. The geographical and hydrographical, and even the meteorological, situations largely influenced the choice of tactical methods to be pursued for the attainment of the object in view. It is therefore important to consider the situation from these various standpoints in some detail.

The book has been divided into two parts. Part 1 deals with the Situation, the Object, the General Plan for the attainment of the Object, the Preparatory Work involved, and the various occurrences up to the eve of the Attack. Part 2 describes the events which occurred during the operation itself, and includes some consideration of both the material and moral results of the enterprise and the lessons to be drawn therefrom.

For the illustrations the author is much indebted to the Admiralty, Air Ministry, Imperial War Museum, and Press, to whom he makes this grateful acknowledgment.

With regard to the personal side of the story, it may be as well to point out that many of the officers and men concerned were mentioned in the official despatch; that fact lessens one of the difficulties attached to the author's task. A compromise between the purely impersonal attitude and the very natural desire to render full justice to each individual, regardless of the reader's patience, has been aimed at.

The author trusts that the reader will be tolerant of omission and repetition, and will forgive the rather obvious shortcomings of a literary nature which, alas, appear all too frequently in the book.

Alfred F. B. Carpenter

8th March, 1921

PART 1: THE BLOCKING OF ZEEBRUGGE

CHAPTER 1

The Strategical Situation

The main function of a navy in war is that of obtaining the command of the sea. The purpose for which such "command" is desired is the utilisation of the sea-lines of communication and the denial of the same to the enemy.

Soon after the commencement of the war in 1914 the sea-lines of communication across the English Channel assumed considerable, if not paramount, importance for the transfer of personnel and material from Britain to the Allied forces in France. It was equally incumbent on the navy to maintain the trans-Atlantic and other lines of communication along which the necessities of life and war were carried to the Allies in all theatres of war.

The first step towards obtaining "command of the sea" is the removal of the obstacles which stand in one's way. In this particular case the main obstacle (admittedly constructed for the purpose) was the German High Seas Fleet. Thus the first duty of the British Grand Fleet was that of destroying the so-called High Seas Fleet, or, if destruction was found to be impracticable, of reducing it to inactivity. The German Fleet was fully alive to that fact, and, almost throughout the war, hid themselves away in their naval bases under the protection of their coast defences. Thus, as events showed, the High Seas Fleet did not prove to be a very serious obstacle to our command of the sea; but, and this fact is easily forgotten, we could not *foresee* the continuance of their ineptitude and lack of spirit. The German submarines, however, were a formidable obstacle, indeed. It is unnecessary to reiterate what is already common knowledge on that point.

Submarines, by their nature, have certain limitations. Except in the case of the submarine cruisers, which only materialised in the latter part of the war, such craft are considerably hampered in their move-

19

ments by their comparatively small radius of action. Owing to the geographical situation of Germany, her submarines were forced to expend an important percentage of their fuel during the outward and homeward voyages between their bases and the trade routes. This expenditure cannot merely be judged by the distances which had to be traversed; the expenditure of fuel in the submarine bears some relation to the *whole circumstances* of the voyage.

The endurance of the personnel is another important factor, and is similarly affected by the circumstances under which they are employed. For instance, in waters patrolled by enemy vessels, high speed must always be readily available and the strain on the personnel, consequent on the danger of sudden attack from surface craft, aircraft, or other submarines, to say nothing of the presence of mine-fields, is increased. Thus the longer the passage that the German submarines were forced to undertake in comparatively narrow and dangerous waters—such as the North Sea—the less work could they do on our more important trade routes. That statement is closely connected with the subject of this book.

It did not require very much intelligence on the part of the German Admiralty to realise that the possession of bases on the Flanders coast would greatly facilitate their submarine campaign owing to the consequent reduction of the voyages to and from the trans-Atlantic, or Channel, trade routes. Flanders was therefore used, as will be explained later in detail, to provide advanced bases for German submarines.

The coast of Flanders lent itself to other naval uses. In addition to the *guerre-de-course* tactics of the enemy—*i.e.,* the direct attack on Allied merchant vessels—it was always open to Germany to take their whole main fleet to sea for the purpose of seeking advantageous conditions for bringing a portion of our Grand Fleet to action.

Movements of modern fleets under war conditions necessitate the use of various types of small craft to precede them—e.g., mine-sweepers for clearing channels for the fleet to pass through, destroyers for supporting the mine-sweepers and for driving back the enemy's small craft, light cruisers for scouting purposes, etc. Mine-sweepers and torpedo craft, by virtue of their small size, are unable to keep the sea for long periods. It will therefore be realised that, in the event of the High Seas Fleet putting to sea for operations in southern waters, the Flanders coast provided Germany with an advanced base from which their light craft could operate.

The German torpedo craft based in Flanders, therefore, would be able to serve a double purpose, *viz.*, that already mentioned and that of attacking our patrol craft, our coast and our merchant vessels when opportunity offered. The mine-sweepers could also serve a double purpose in that they were required to sweep channels for the ingress and egress of submarines based in Flanders whilst being suitably placed for sweeping duties in advance of the main fleet. That Flanders was also suitable for aircraft bases is as well known as it is obvious; but it may not be generally understood that such aircraft would also be of special value to the main fleet under the conditions stated above. Thus, to sum up, the occupation of the Flanders coast by the German sea forces would be of treble value—to provide, firstly, a base for the submarines employed on commerce destruction; secondly, a base for the advanced flotillas and aircraft operating in conjunction with the main fleet in the event of the latter coming south; and, thirdly, a base from which to attack our southern coasts or sea-patrols and from which to indulge in air raids against British and French territory.

The foregoing consideration of the possible uses of Flanders to the German Navy shows the inherent value of an advanced base in that locality; the intrinsic value obviously depended upon the existence of suitable harbours for use as bases. Let us now examine the geographical situation.

In the latter part of 1917 the Flanders coast, as far westward as Nieuport, was in the possession of the Germans. The northern extremity of the line separating the German and Allied armies was situated approximately on the Yser Canal, which emanates from Nieuport harbour. The latter was dominated by the gunfire of both armies; its use was, therefore, denied to both. The only other harbours on the coast of Flanders were Ostende, Blankenberghe, and Zeebrugge. These will be described in some detail presently.

The Flanders coast consists mainly of flat country barely elevated above the level of the sea. Sand-hills along the shore act as a barrier between the sea and the land. Parallel to the shore the tidal current runs to and fro with considerable velocity. The tendency for the tidal current to wash away the sand from the shore is partially countered by the use of *groynes*, such as are similarly used to maintain our own coastline in many parts of England. Although the *groynes* on the Flanders coast are carried well out into the sea—they are often 100 yards in length—the movement of sand along the coast is very considerable, and, as will be explained later, has a strong influence on the harbour situation in that locality.

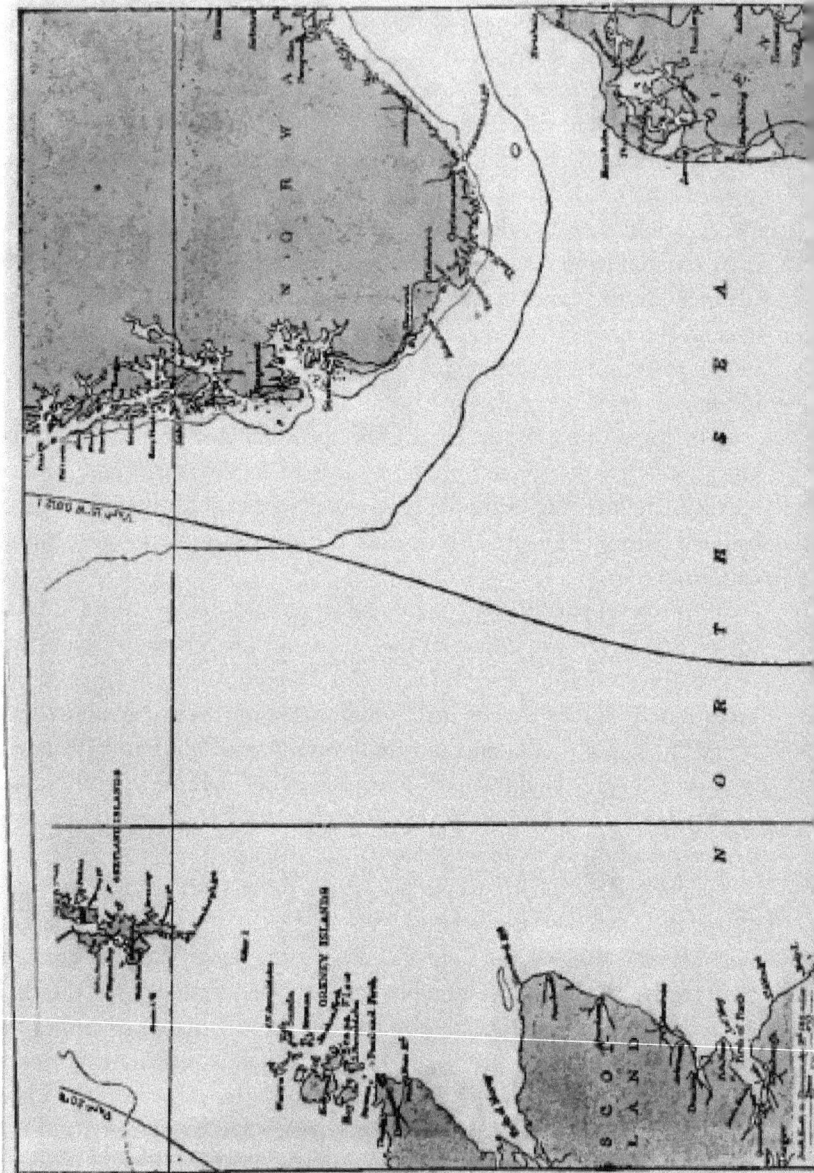

CHART SHOWING THE RELATIVE POSITIONS OF DOVER, ZEEBRUGGE

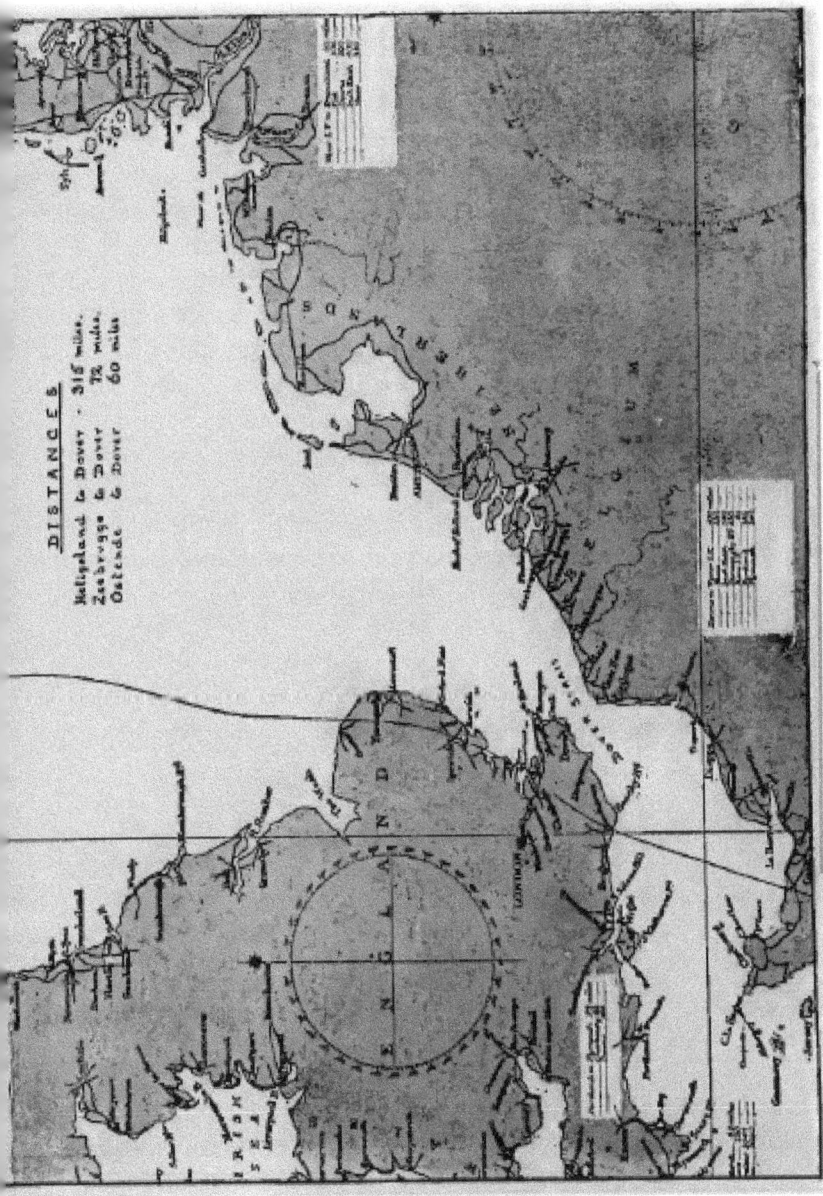

HELIGOLAND, AND THE EXITS FROM THE NORTH SEA.

The approaches to the coast are beset with shoals reaching to a distance of eight miles from the land. These shoals have always provided serious obstacles to navigation. During times of peace the charts of this locality had been kept corrected by virtue of continual surveying. The shoals were frequently moving and new shoals appeared from time to time. The channels required almost constant dredging. For obvious reasons during the occupation of Flanders by the Germans it was not possible for the Allies to continue either the surveying or the dredging.

Before the war navigation off this coast required the use of many facilities such as buoys and lighthouses. At the best of times buoys are not very dependable as navigational aids owing to their tendency to break away in heavy weather or to drag their anchors along the bottom. Their positions need to be "fixed" from time to time by means of angles to shore objects, or by methods of astronomical observation, and then compared with the positions shown on the charts. Lighthouses, however, unless they are of the small type without lighthouse-keepers, are more efficient aids to the navigator. During the war the lighthouses east of Nieuport were only used by the Germans during short periods when specially required for their own craft; the majority of the buoys were withdrawn and the remainder were moved to new positions which were frequently altered to prevent the Allies from making use of them. Thus, during the war, the charts available to the Allies were very soon obsolete; no others were obtainable. Navigation off the Flanders coast, for Allied vessels of any size, therefore, became decidedly hazardous.

The tides on the coasts, in addition to running alternately eastward and westward with considerable velocity, also caused large differences in sea-level amounting to fifteen feet between the highest and lowest states of the tide.

Mention has already been made that the only harbours on the coast eastward of Nieuport were situated at Ostende, Blankenberghe, and Zeebrugge. But these were not natural harbours. They had been artificially cut out of the coast-line by means of dredging. The entrance channels were preserved by piers built out into the sea and by dredging operations designed to retain the desired depths of water.

Ostende, before the war, had been much used as a commercial harbour, and was therefore provided with numerous wharves, basins, and docks. It was a suitable harbour for all classes of submarines and torpedo craft. Blankenberghe was a little harbour about nine miles

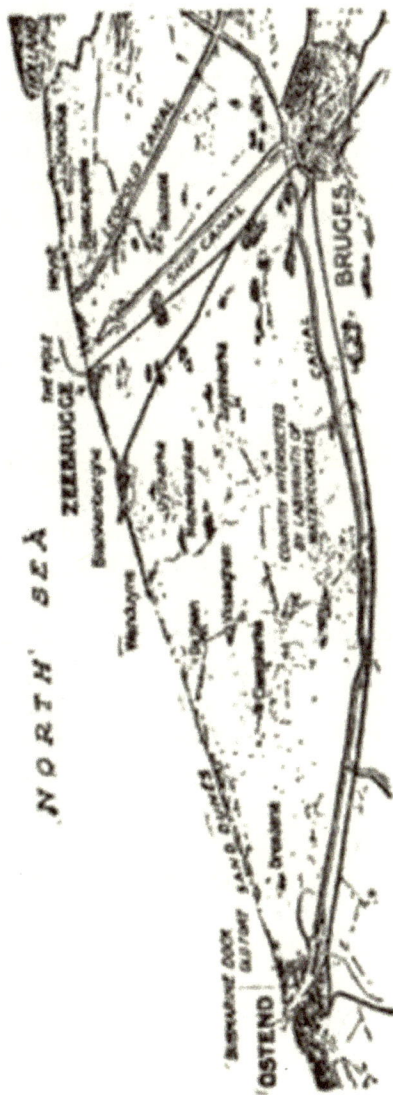

NORTH SEA

ZEEBRUGGE

BRUGES

OSTEND

BIRD'S–EYE VIEW OF CANALS

east of Ostende and three miles west of Zeebrugge. Its depth was exceedingly small; it could, therefore, only be used for shallow draught vessels such as fishing boats, motor boats, and the like. It was true that the rise of tide, amounting to approximately fifteen feet, would enable larger vessels to enter or leave near the time of high water, but any naval vessel stationed in a harbour from which it can only proceed to sea during a limited portion of the twenty-four hours at once loses much of its value. Zeebrugge could accommodate vessels up to a considerable size: the harbour works and depths will be described in detail presently. Although these three places provided the only harbours on the coast, there was a harbour of great importance at Bruges, about eight miles inland from Zeebrugge.

Bruges harbour was also entirely artificial, consisting of locks, basins, and waterways built on the canal system. Bruges was connected to the sea by means of canals running to Zeebrugge and Ostende, these canals converging on the waterways of Bruges in such a manner that vessels of a certain limited size could pass from Ostende to Zeebrugge, and *vice versa*, without actually proceeding into the open sea. A series of small canals also connected Bruges to Antwerp, *via* Ghent, but this canal system, being only constructed to accommodate barges, did not materially add to the value of Bruges as a harbour for sea-going vessels.

Of the three canal systems connecting at Bruges, the canal to Zeebrugge easily held first place in importance. This canal was built by the Belgians. It was commenced in 1896 and completed in 1907. Six and a quarter miles in length, it was almost entirely straight throughout. It could accommodate torpedo-boat destroyers or submarines, both of the largest size, and could, if required, have been used by light cruisers.

At the seaward end of the Ostende and Zeebrugge canals, locks were constructed so that vessels could pass from the canals to the sea, or the reverse, at any state of the tide, without lowering the level of the water in the canal.

The above-mentioned harbours were used for naval purposes by Germany as follows. Bruges was chosen as the main naval base. Shelters for protecting submarines from aerial attack, floating docks, repair workshops, all the other facilities which go to make a modern dockyard for small vessels, and the necessary stores and ammunition, were to be found there. The number of naval craft based on Flanders appeared to vary considerably; but, at the beginning of 1918, approximately eighteen submarines and twenty-five destroyers or torpedo-boats would be at Bruges on an average day. The submarines lay in the special shelters which were covered by roofs of re-enforced concrete several feet in thickness. Bruges, then, was not only the dockyard but also the resting-place of practically all the German naval craft based on Flanders.

The sea exits from Bruges, as already mentioned, were situated at Ostende and Zeebrugge. There was some doubt, however, whether the Bruges-Ostende canal could be used for the passage of anything larger than very shallow draught vessels such as motor boats or barges. The Ostende canal was known to be narrow, tortuous, and shallow; it had been constructed many years earlier than the Zeebrugge canal.

At Zeebrugge and Ostende a few German craft were usually stationed for duties of an immediate nature such as mine-sweeping, patrolling, and duties connected with the defence of the coast. These harbours were specially useful as taking-off places for vessels which had concentrated in readiness for operations at sea, or as bolt-holes for the same craft when pursued by our patrol vessels. Both harbours were open to bombardment from the sea; that reason, more than any other, probably influenced the Germans to use Bruges for their main base. Ostende, being more open to attack from the sea and air than was Zeebrugge, was the less important harbour of the two.

Blankenberghe harbour, owing to its small size and shallow depth, was used as a base for the German armed motor boats; it is believed that about thirty were stationed there. This harbour, being unconnected with the canal system, was not in direct inland communication with Bruges by water.

In addition to the submarines and torpedo craft already mentioned, the Germans had a large number of trawlers based on the various harbours for mine-sweeping and patrol duties. At Zeebrugge they had their largest seaplane base in Flanders; another seaplane base was situated at Ostende.

In due course Flanders had become a veritable hornet's nest. Let us consider for a few moments to what extent these hornets could trouble us.

Across the English Channel, and especially in its eastern portion, we had established lines of communication of tremendous importance. It is no exaggeration to state that, every few *minutes* of the day and night, a vessel, of one sort or another, left the English shore for France with her cargo of personnel, guns, ammunition, food or fuel, etc. Day after day, night after night, for months on end, a constant stream of vessels poured across the Channel in support of the Allied armies or on the return trip to English ports with wounded, men to whom a welcome spell of leave had been granted, empties for refilling, motor transport vehicles for repair, and the like. The wounded were carried in hospital ships; but, as the world knows and can never forget, the Germans ruthlessly torpedoed them whenever the chance offered, regardless of the Geneva Convention, heedless of the damnable inhumanity of the proceeding, seeking only for opportunities for indulging in the frightfulness which formed part of their *Kultur*.

All these vessels were continually open to attack, not only from submarines but also from the surface craft and aircraft based in Flanders. At any chosen moment, preferably at night or during misty days, these hornets could emanate from Ostende or Zeebrugge on their deadly missions. Further westward our trans-Atlantic lines of communication offered innumerable opportunities for the German submarine commanders to display their brutality against comparatively defenceless merchant vessels, or to attack transports carrying munitions of war and troops from the American Continent. The passage through the English Channel afforded the most direct route for German submarines proceeding to, or returning from, their hunting-grounds.

The mercantile traffic off the southeast coast of England and in the entrance to the Thames was also within easy reach of the German bases in Flanders; so were our seaside resorts, such as Ramsgate and Margate, which provided favourable opportunities for bombardments with resultant casualty lists of innocent women and children.

Dunkerque and Calais on the French coast were the nearest seaport objectives to the Flanders coast; they both experienced frequent aerial attacks and an occasional bombardment from the sea.

As a counter to the German craft in Flanders the British Admiralty had established a force known as the "Dover Patrol." As the name implies, this force was primarily based on Dover. Their duties were mainly those of protecting the transports bound across the English Channel, preventing the German naval craft from passing through the Straits of Dover, and watching the exits from Bruges so as to obtain timely information of concentrated German forces putting to sea. The story of the Dover Patrol is of intense interest, but so many pages would be required to do it even bare justice that I can only refer the reader to books written especially on that subject. Suffice it to say here that, day and night, winter and summer, fair weather and foul, the Dover force patrolled the sea so successfully that the German attempts to use their surface craft for attacking the Allies were few and far between. The difficulties of preventing the submarines passing through the Straits of Dover were immense. We must realise that the maximum portion of a submerged submarine visible above water amounts to a periscope of a few inches in diameter. Compare that dimension to the width of the Strait which at its narrowest part is twenty miles. *A few inches in twenty miles*—if I have calculated aright that means that the visible portion of the submarine would cover little more than *one-millionth* part of the surface between Dover and Cape Grisnez. And when we also realise that the periscope would only be raised above water for a few seconds at long intervals we shall begin to understand the difficulty of the problem. Yet, as we know now, the Dover Patrol force, under the direction of Vice-Admiral Sir Roger Keyes, eventually rendered the passage through the Straits to all intents and purposes impossible for a submarine. All honour to the Dover Patrol!

A point which, until recently, unaccountably seemed to have escaped notice was that the work of the Dover Patrol was carried out on behalf of all the Allies and of the United States. It was not a British force acting solely in British interests. Though it is difficult, and perhaps invidious, to apportion the credit for protecting the Allied lines of communication, yet there is no shadow of doubt that the troops from Canada and from the United States of America owed to the Dover Patrol force a tremendous debt of gratitude for their safe passage overseas. Recognition of this fact has since been shown by the erection at New York, and on the French coast, of memorials to the Dover Patrol. When the late war has faded into history, and those of us who took part have long since "gone west," such memorials will remain to bear witness to the splendid sacrifice and unselfish gallantry of those hardy seamen who did their utmost to uphold the honour of civilisation and to destroy the forces working for its overthrow. (This opportunity of acknowledging the success of their extremely arduous efforts, humble and brief though the acknowledgment may be, partially counterbalances my regrets at not having had the chance of serving with the "Dover Patrol" except on the occasion which this book is designed to describe.)

The final closing of the Straits, however, was far from accomplished by the spring of 1918. At that time we had reason to believe that a large percentage of the total Allied losses in merchant ships was caused by the Flanders submarines, and that the percentage was on the increase.

CAPTAIN ALFRED F. B. CARPENTER, V.C., R.N.

Now patrol work of the type described above is essentially defensive in its nature. This statement is not intended to imply that the Dover Patrol force were always employed on defensive tactics; such was by no means the case. Our monitors frequently bombarded the coast defences and the harbour works at Ostende and Zeebrugge; our motor boats were continually patrolling close off the three coast harbours, watching for opportunities to torpedo any German vessels which ventured to sea; our mine-laying craft were employed, night after night, in laying mines to the detriment of the German submarines. But from time to time various suggestions had been made that we should adopt still more offensive measures against the enemy. It is a very simple matter to make suggestions, but by no means so simple to accompany them with a reasoned statement, based on logical deduction, which will *convince the authorities* of their value. Until a particular Plan has been put into execution it may, in the literal sense, be rightly designated a "paper scheme." It is both unreasonable and unfair to attach a derogatory sense to the term. It is equally unreasonable for authors of schemes which have not passed the paper stage to belittle operations when the latter, based on schemes which differed from their own, have actually taken place with successful results.

Whatever suggestions were made, it is clear that there could be only two radical methods of attaining our object. The most satisfactory, of course, would have been the recapture of the Flanders coast and of Bruges, with all the hornets in their nests, by means of military operations. Unfortunately that was impracticable; the Allied armies were not yet sufficiently strong. The only alternative to capture of the craft in their harbours was that of preventing them putting to sea— i.e., destroying or blocking their exits. Several schemes for blocking operations had been proposed. In tactical method they had varied from blowing up the harbour entrances, as suggested by the Halifax disaster, to "building in" the entrances under cover of poison gas. Whether such methods were considered too risky, too expensive, or too hopelessly fantastic is more than the author of this book knows.

An attack on Zeebrugge had been strongly advocated by an eminent flag officer in November, 1916, but no details were given by him as to the nature of the operation. In May, 1917, detailed proposals for an attack had been submitted to the Admiralty by another distinguished officer. This attack involved a landing on the Mole at Zeebrugge, the general idea of which was not dissimilar from that eventually followed. This particular scheme had not earned the approval of

Their Lordships, nor was it considered suitable by the vice-admiral then in command at Dover.

Many months after the blocking of Zeebrugge had become an accomplished fact two earlier schemes came to light—these having emanated from the author of that submitted in May, 1917. In November, 1917, however, the only previous proposals which were available for consideration by the Planning Division of the Staff were those of November, 1916, and May, 1917, mentioned above.

In November, 1917, Admiral Sir John Jellicoe was First Sea Lord and Chief of the Naval Staff. He had requested the Director of Plans to consider, amongst many other things, the possibility of blocking the Belgian ports.

The Plan was *evolved in the Admiralty*, being commenced on November 13th, and laid before Their Lordships on December 3rd. The Plan was accepted as feasible, and earned Their Lordships' decision to have it carried out. No previous Plan had reached that stage. The original edition of the Plan did not emanate from another country, or from civilian sources, or from any other source outside the Admiralty buildings in Whitehall except in so far as the details of one particular phase of the operation were the outcome of conversations, at the headquarters of the Air Force, with an expert on the formation of artificial fogs.

The foregoing definite fact has been purposely inserted to correct other statements which have been published elsewhere, presumably in error. I shall deal with the details of the Plan in a subsequent chapter.

Before leaving the consideration of the *origin* of the Plan, I should like to emphasise one particular point. Perhaps this can be most readily illustrated by a simple simile. An uncorked bottle, containing some noxious fluid, stands upon the table. You realise the disagreeable results which will follow on the escape of its contents. You cork the bottle. Now your action is so obviously correct that you scarcely give it another thought. If any credit was due to anybody you would probably take it to yourself; you would not apportion any particular merit to that fond parent who first initiated you into this obvious solution of the problem. In the case, therefore, of the Blocking of Zeebrugge one need not apportion credit to the person who first *suggested the mere idea*; the credit is entirely due to the man who, in spite of all the difficulties, evolved a *method* of "corking the bottle" and who, later, overcoming the great obstacles in the way, carried the method into execution.

Before we pass on to review the difficulties of blocking the exits from the German bases it would be advisable to consider the probable effects of such an operation; this being the logical sequence actually followed before the details of the Plan were formulated.

The results to be attained by blocking the exits would probably be as follows. Firstly, there would be a reduction in the number of Allied vessels sunk by mine or submarine warfare; secondly, a decrease in raid activity on the part of the enemy torpedo craft; thirdly, the loss of a convenient advanced base for small craft operating in conjunction with certain movements of the High Seas Fleet; and, fourthly, the reduction in the number of enemy vessels available for the purposes mentioned.

The first two results concerned reduction of enemy activity arising from the longer passages involved by the use of more distant bases such as Heligoland or the German rivers from which the small craft could continue their depredations. The third result speaks for itself. With regard to the fourth, it has already been stated that, on an average day, there would be many torpedo craft or submarines resting and repairing at Bruges. If the exits were blocked the use of these craft would be denied to the enemy, just as effectually as if they were sunk, for as long as the exits remained unopened. This loss to the enemy, temporary or permanent, could doubtless be described in terms of reduction of Allied losses of merchant tonnage. The Admiralty authorities could probably have calculated, within fairly correct estimates, the average loss of merchant tonnage caused to the Allies by a single enemy submarine or surface torpedo craft. Our former average loss per given period would thus be lessened in proportion to the number of enemy vessels bottled up in the canals during that period.

There would, of course, be other, less important, consequences arising from the blocking of these exits; e.g., the inconveniences caused by the necessary transfer of fuelling and repair facilities elsewhere, the extra work thrown on the escorting vessels in the Bight, and the fact that the craft already at sea and operating from the Flanders coast would be forced to curtail their current trips if they desired to arrive at their new bases with their usual reserves of fuel.

All these material gains to the Allies would be of considerable importance, but the moral effect was not unworthy of consideration. The more audacious an undertaking against an enemy the more intense will be the victor's enthusiasm consequent on success, and the greater the despondency and loss of moral to the vanquished. Attempts to block a hostile port in the face of carefully prepared defence measures may certainly be described as audacious, unless the word "impertinent," which the author is inclined to allocate to this particular event, is deemed to be more truly descriptive. If we endeavour to imagine what our own feelings would be on hearing that enemy vessels had entered one of our strongly defended harbours and blocked the entrance, we shall arrive at some idea as to the probable moral effect produced by such an enterprise. In spite of the almost entire absence of activity on the part of the High Seas Fleet, the Germans had never ceased to sing its praises with all the bombast of which their waning spirit was capable. It was not difficult, therefore, to estimate the dejection and consternation that would spread throughout Germany when the success of our efforts became known. *The loss of prestige in the German Navy would be not merely certain but perhaps of vital consequence later on.*

CHAPTER 2

The Local Situation

The village of Zeebrugge stands near the entrance to the Zeebrugge-Bruges canal. At about half a mile inland from the coast at Zeebrugge the canal lock was situated. To seaward of the lock, the entrance channel, being open to the sea, was tidal. On the eastern side of the entrance channel, about midway between the lock and the coastline, a small tidal harbour had been constructed for the use of fishing craft. This tidal harbour was of no special value for naval purposes, owing to its small depth. From the coast-line the entrance channel was continued into the sea for a distance of about two hundred and seventy yards by means of *estacades*—*i.e.,* wooden piers. These piers, curving outwards from the shore, are conspicuous in the illustrations. For the purpose of protecting the canal entrance from rough seas, which might interfere with the passage of vessels to and from the canal, the famous Zeebrugge Mole had been constructed for the Belgians. Semi-circular in shape, it emanated from the shore at a distance of about half a mile to the westward of the canal entrance; thence it curved round to the northward and eastward. This curved Mole protected a roadstead, of some three hundred acres in extent, from northerly and westerly gales. Easterly winds did not cause such heavy seas as those from the directions already named owing to the protection afforded by the Netherlands coast.

The construction of the Mole was a colossal task. There are no similar works of such magnitude in Great Britain or the United States. When lecturing in the latter country I always made a point of emphasising that fact to our American cousins; their unfailing humour never failed to appreciate this little friendly "dig."

The total length of the Mole was over one and a half miles. For purposes of description it may be divided into four portions. Com-

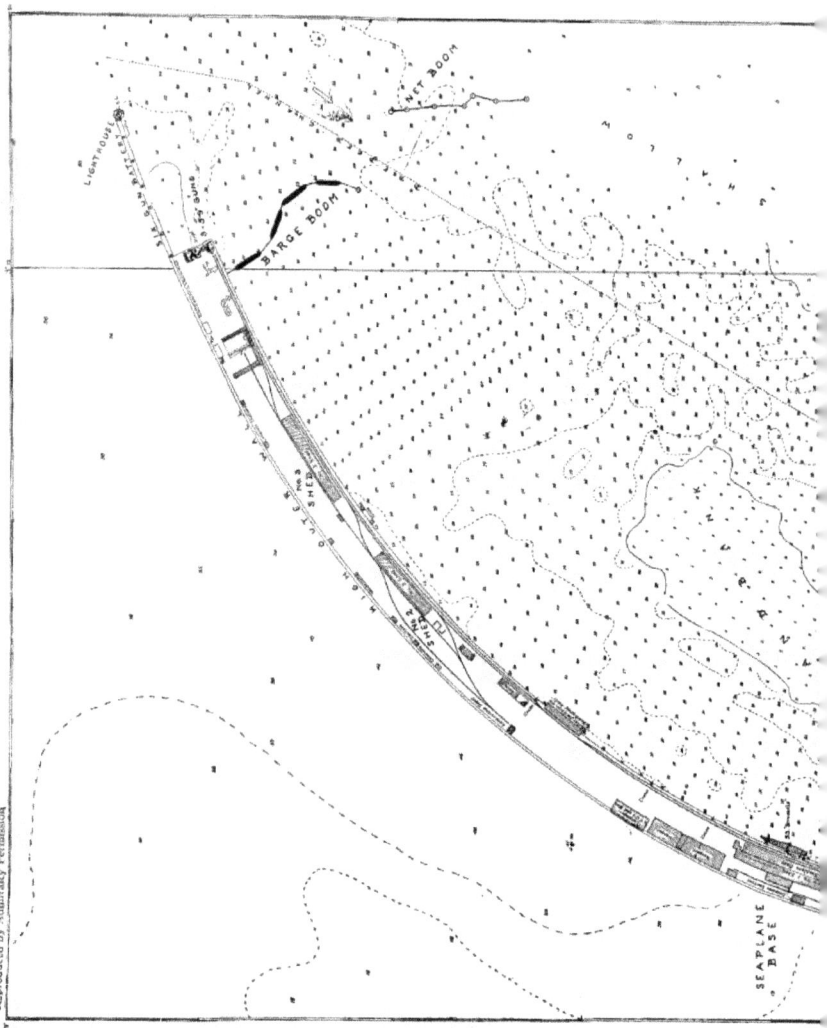

PORT OF ZEEBRUGGE

PORT OF ZEEBRUGGE.

mencing at the shoreward end, the first portion of the Mole took the form of a stone railway pier built into the sea for a distance of two hundred and fifty yards. This pier was connected to the second portion, which consisted of an iron-piled railway viaduct three hundred and thirty yards in length. This, in turn, was connected to the third portion, which formed the Mole proper. The latter was built of concrete blocks on its seaward and shore sides, the central part being filled with gravel and paved with granite. The width of this portion of the Mole was no less than eighty-one yards, and its length about eighteen hundred and seventy-five, or rather over a land mile. At its northeastern end, the fourth portion consisted of an extension piece, two hundred and sixty yards long and fifteen feet broad, with a lighthouse at its eastern extremity.

If the Mole had been constructed solid throughout its entire length, the task of keeping the channel, leading to the canal entrance, or the roadstead, at a convenient depth would have been impossible owing to silt.

Silt may be defined as the movement of sand or mud, according to the nature of the sea bottom in the locality, due to current. The bottom of the sea in this locality was sand. The current off the Flanders coast is caused by tide—it is usually spoken of as tidal stream. Tidal streams reverse their direction of movement about every six hours. Now the movement of sand caused by a tidal stream tends to deposit that sand in or against any irregularity with which it meets, whether the latter is a groove on the sea bed or an obstacle such as a wreck. This deposit first takes place from one direction, and then, when the tidal stream reverses, from the opposite direction. It will therefore be seen that, where a channel is artificially cut on the floor of the sea, silt will continually tend to fill that channel again until the bottom is level once more. And a ship which grounds in a locality affected by silt will have sand deposited against her sides much to the detriment of salvage operations. These facts are well enough known to seamen and have an important bearing on this narrative.

Suppose for a moment that the entire Mole had been built in solid formation—*i.e.,* that the tidal stream had no free passage under the viaduct. The west-going stream would tend to carry sand into the roadstead between the Mole and the canal entrance, whereas the east-going stream would be unable to remove the deposit a few hours later. Thus the roadstead would soon have become useless, and access to the canal would have been impracticable.

The sand along the whole Flanders coast was extremely susceptible to movement. Such tendency was partially countered by the extensive use of groynes. These latter, however, could not be carried very far out into the sea owing to the difficulties of construction and repair. There were, therefore, no artificial barriers to prevent the movement of the sand to the eastward or westward beyond a short distance from the shore. Hence the necessity for keeping a portion of the Mole open to allow the tidal stream to flow in both directions. Even so, a large shoal had formed in the roadstead, and reduced the acreage available for anchorage purposes.

When first designed the open viaduct was of shorter length than that eventually constructed; the alteration was considered necessary after local experience of the silt had been obtained. The iron piles, or pillars, on which the viaduct was supported were of great strength and much interlaced with steel rods to allow for severe buffeting in heavy gales and to take the strain of railway traffic. A portion was actually demolished by a gale when under construction, and the completion of the Mole was consequently delayed for many months.

When making enquiries in search of expert advice on questions of salvage, I had an interesting conversation with an individual who had had considerable experience in salving vessels in other waters. Maybe this book will remind him of our discussion. In his opinion salvage work presented no great difficulties. It was only a matter of obtaining the necessary apparatus, he thought, and any vessel—concrete-filled or otherwise—could be removed in a month or so.

"How about silt?" I asked.

"Oh, silt shouldn't make much difference," he replied, and added, "but we have no silt to speak of in that part of the world, so I cannot say for certain."

We then discussed the possibilities of salving a blockship at Zee-brugge, for he had been informed of the proposed operation. Eventually our conversation nearly resulted in a wager; that we came to no terms was perhaps due to the fact that payment might have necessitated application to a war widow.

The first and second portions of the Mole had not been materially altered by the Germans during their occupation.

The third portion of the Mole will require detailed description. In peace days the Mole had been used as a commercial wharf as well as a breakwater. Ships used to secure alongside its inner wall. All the necessary facilities, such as bollards for securing hawsers, fixed and travelling

cranes for loading or unloading cargo, and arrangements for embarking passengers, had been provided. A large railway passenger station,
nearly two hundred yards long, was situated near its southwestern
end; a goods station and a coal shed, both very large buildings, stood
further to the northeastward. The floor level of this portion of the
Mole was about nine feet above the level of high tide. On the outer
(seaward) side a high wall, of great strength and thickness, had been
constructed for the purpose of preventing rough seas from breaking
over the Mole and damaging the sheds or washing away the railway.
The top of this wall was twenty feet above the floor level of the Mole
and therefore twenty-nine feet above the level of high tide: at low tide
it towered forty-four feet above the sea.

The fourth portion of the Mole was really formed by a continuation of the outer wall, which extended beyond the third portion to
the lighthouse.

The appearance of all portions of the outer wall, as viewed by
anybody situated in a boat alongside it, was exactly similar throughout
its entire length from the lighthouse to the railway viaduct. Thus the
individual in the boat, except in the unlikely event of being able to
see over the top of the wall, would be unable to tell, at all definitely,
whereabouts his boat was situated relative to objects on the Mole. But
this fact had not been accidentally overlooked by the designer of the
Mole; there was no object in taking it into consideration, for there
was then no idea of any vessel berthing alongside the outer wall. For
instance, there were no bollards, no cranes, no capstans for working
hawsers, in fact no arrangements whatever for berthing a ship.

I have already stated that this outer wall was of great thickness,
varying from twenty-five feet on the sea bottom to ten feet in that
portion standing above the floor level of the Mole. Four feet below
the top of the wall there was a pathway, nine feet broad, running the
whole length of the wall. This pathway was known as the parapet. The
parapet was bounded on its seaward side by the four-foot wall just
mentioned; on its inner side iron railings, three feet high, were placed
to prevent anybody falling from the pathway to the floor of the Mole
sixteen feet below. Flights of steps led up from the Mole floor to the
parapet, but these flights were very few and far between.

That portion of the outer wall which formed the lighthouse extension of the Mole was broadened, above the sea level, to about seventeen feet throughout its length. The pathway was similar to that
just described, but fifteen feet in width. This portion of the Mole was

hollow, a tunnel inside it running from the third portion of the Mole to the base of the lighthouse.

The navigable channel from the open sea to the canal entrance could only be maintained in an efficient state by means of continual dredging, owing to the silt. The channel passed close to the lighthouse at the end of the Mole, and then in a fairly direct line, for a distance of three-quarters of a mile, to a position midway between the extremities of the two piers marking the canal entrance. Thence the deep water channel passed slightly to the westward of the central line between the piers. This latter portion of the channel had become exceedingly narrow by virtue of the sandbanks which had formed on either side of it and which actually uncovered at low water. A vessel drawing more than twelve feet or so was forced to keep exactly in the middle of this dredged channel to avoid grounding. Photographs taken at or near high tide gave the channel the appearance of extending from one pier to the other, at least a distance of one hundred yards; those taken near low water showed how narrow the channel really was. In the region of the two piers the silting of the sand was more rapid than elsewhere: the narrowest part of the channel was situated near the shore ends of these piers.

The Germans had not rested satisfied with either the Mole, the canal entrance, or the lock as they found them. The Mole itself had been transformed into a fortress, and further defences had been constructed for the purpose of guarding the canal.

Batteries were placed on both sides of the canal entrance. These ranged from four-inch guns to twelve-inch guns. Barbed wire entanglements were erected along the shore line; trenches, containing machine guns, were dug close behind them. It was believed that a boom of some sort, capable of being hauled across the channel or removed at will, was kept handy to the outer lock gate. The gate itself, "caisson" is the correct technical term, was withdrawn into an armoured housing, impervious to shells or bombs, when the lock was opened to allow vessels to pass through. The caisson was also provided with an armoured roof for defence against aerial bombs. The lights on the wooden piers were only lit when specially required to guide a German vessel to the entrance.

On the Mole a very large seaplane base was established with the original passenger station as its principal building. Several other buildings for housing seaplanes, fuel, or bombs, and workshops were erected by the Germans close by. A merchant steamer, the *Brussels*, formerly

A PORTION OF THE GERMAN BATTERY ON THE LIGHTHOUSE
EXTENSION OF THE MOLE

VIEW OF THE CANAL ENTRANCE WITH ITS CURVED PIERS.
This photograph was taken at high tide.
Note the Mole in the distance

commanded by the ill-fated Captain Fryatt, whom the Germans did to death so abominably, was moored alongside the station, and was believed to be used as living quarters for the personnel of the seaplane base.

The broad portion of the Mole was used as a base for submarines passing through Zeebrugge *en route* for Bruges or to the open sea; it was also used for such torpedo craft and mine-sweepers as were required for immediate duty in that locality. From the north-eastern large shed to the lighthouse the Mole had been turned into a veritable fortress. It was believed that the lighthouse was used as the Mole signal station. A battery of six or seven guns was situated on the lighthouse extension of the Mole. These guns were at first surmised to be 3.5-inch guns, but it is probable that they were larger—in fact, up to 5.9-inch guns firing a shell of approximately one hundred pounds in weight. It was believed that the guns of this battery could fire out to sea and could be turned to fire towards the shore.

Any vessel approaching from seaward and passing into the dredged channel, *en route* to the canal, would be within the danger zone of this battery, from the latter's extreme range out at sea to the canal lock, always provided that the state of the visibility allowed the vessel to be seen. Incidentally, owing to the situation of the deep channel, the vessel would be obliged to pass within *a few yards* of this battery when rounding the Mole end. A vessel endeavouring to berth alongside the outer wall would have to approach close to this battery, *i.e.*, on a westerly course. At first sight it might appear feasible to approach *from* the westward on an easterly course and thus avoid passing close to the battery, but that is not so. High tide and slack stream do not coincide on this coast. For about three hours on each side of high tide the streams run *to* the eastward: at other states of the tide there would be insufficient depths of water for a vessel to berth alongside. It would therefore be necessary to approach from the eastward, *i.e.*, to stem the tidal stream.

Now let us imagine for a few moments a duel between this battery and a warship within—say—one thousand yards. The reader probably knows that such a distance nowadays comes within the definition of "point-blank range"; *i.e.*, a range at which a gun practically cannot miss a ship. Picture, then, an average-sized vessel of three hundred feet in length. The guns could hardly miss her—in fact, the gunners could select which particular portion of her should serve as their target. The ship's guns would return the fire. The most vulnerable portions of the

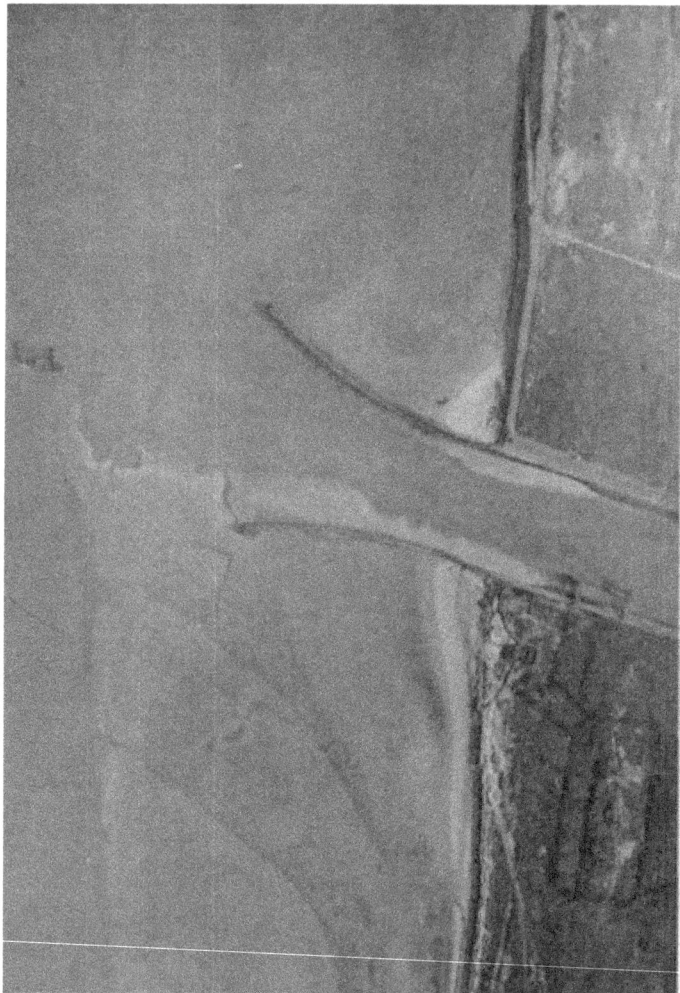

AERIAL PHOTOGRAPH OF THE CANAL ENTRANCE.

Taken shortly before the enterprise, showing the sandbanks narrowing the entrance channel.
At the top of the photograph a dredger at work indicates the position of the approach channel

battery ashore are the guns themselves. The muzzle of each gun showing just above the wall would, as viewed from the ship, cover barely one square foot in size. Now at golf we call it a "fluke" when a golfer holes out from the tee although he has attained his object. (I apologise for this to non-golfers.) Similarly, if the ship's gun *hits* the shore gun we should call it a "fluke," although that is the object forming the target. And, as already implied, if the shore gun *misses* the ship, that also will be a "fluke." On the face of it, it certainly does not look as if the ship would stand much chance, even at a distance of one thousand yards. But how if she is closer? If a thousand yards is point-blank range, how shall we designate a hundred yards?

At the eastern end of the broad part of the Mole, and on its floor level, the Germans had erected a battery of three heavy guns. These were so placed that they could fire on any incoming vessel immediately she rounded the lighthouse. Woe betide a vessel attempting to do so in the face of such guns. The latter were probably of the 5.9-inch type. Under water, immediately below this battery, we eventually found some submerged torpedo tubes, but I am not aware as to whether they were constructed before the blocking operation or not; their direction of fire was similar to that of the guns above them.

Close westward of these batteries of heavy guns and torpedoes, and standing against the high outer wall, the Germans had constructed a long shed of re-enforced concrete; this shed provided the living space for the personnel of the Mole garrison.

The total numbers of Germans on the Mole probably reached not less than a thousand. Although this number may include the personnel of the seaplane base yet they would all be available for the defence of the Mole in case of an attack.

Slightly to the westward of the garrison's quarters, trenches had been sunk in the floor of the Mole and surrounded by three complete sets of barbed wire entanglements. It was believed that the usual accessories of a coast fort—e.g., searchlights and range-finders, etc.—were placed on the outer wall parapet, and that there would probably be some small guns there also.

So much for the Mole itself. Across the channel the Germans had placed booms. One of these, consisting of four Rhine barges, was moored between the eastern end of the broad part of the Mole and a buoy situated two hundred and seventy yards to the southward. These barges were filled with stone, had nets slung beneath them, and were connected together by wire hawsers. If a surface vessel attempted to pass between the buoy and the Mole she would be brought up by this boom and probably damaged by collision with one of the barges. If a submarine attempted to dive underneath the barges she would be caught up in the nets. The other boom consisted of entanglement nets moored between a series of buoys to the southeastward of the barges. Any ship attempting to pass through them would probably have her propellers entangled, with the result that her engines would be brought to a complete stop. Thus, whichever boom was encountered by a ship, the latter would, at the least, be partially disabled and stopped. The Mole batteries could then have sunk her at their leisure by gunfire. The only route by which a vessel could pass clear of these two booms was that between the southeastern barge and the northern entanglement net; *i.e.*, within two hundred and fifty yards of the heavy gun battery on the Mole. But even if, by dint of good fortune or special good management, a vessel managed to pass the Mole batteries and the booms, she would still have to run the gantlet of the naval vessels in the anchorage and the batteries on shore before reaching the canal.

The German torpedo craft, which were available for local duty, used to berth alongside the inner side of the Mole, close to the westward of the barge boom. By virtue of their guns, torpedoes, and searchlights, and the fact that they probably kept up steam in readiness for instant action, these craft provided a valuable addition to the Mole and canal defences.

The foregoing description of the local defences at Zeebrugge has probably been sufficiently detailed to lead to the conclusion that the Germans were fully alive to the possibility of attacks on the Mole or canal. Whether or not they considered that such attacks would only form part of some more ambitious operation, such as a military landing on the coast, our enemies had left practically no stone unturned to repel them. The defence measures must have appeared, especially to those on the spot, to be more than sufficient.

It is well known that, although the possession of detailed local knowledge will usually be of great value towards the formation of plans of attack, there are occasions when local knowledge is apt to make local difficulties loom extremely large. For instance, in this particular case, the navigational difficulties caused by the strong tidal stream, the difficulty of recognising objects on the low-lying shore during darkness, the uninviting appearance of the outer Mole wall as an obstacle to be surmounted, and many other matters would prob-

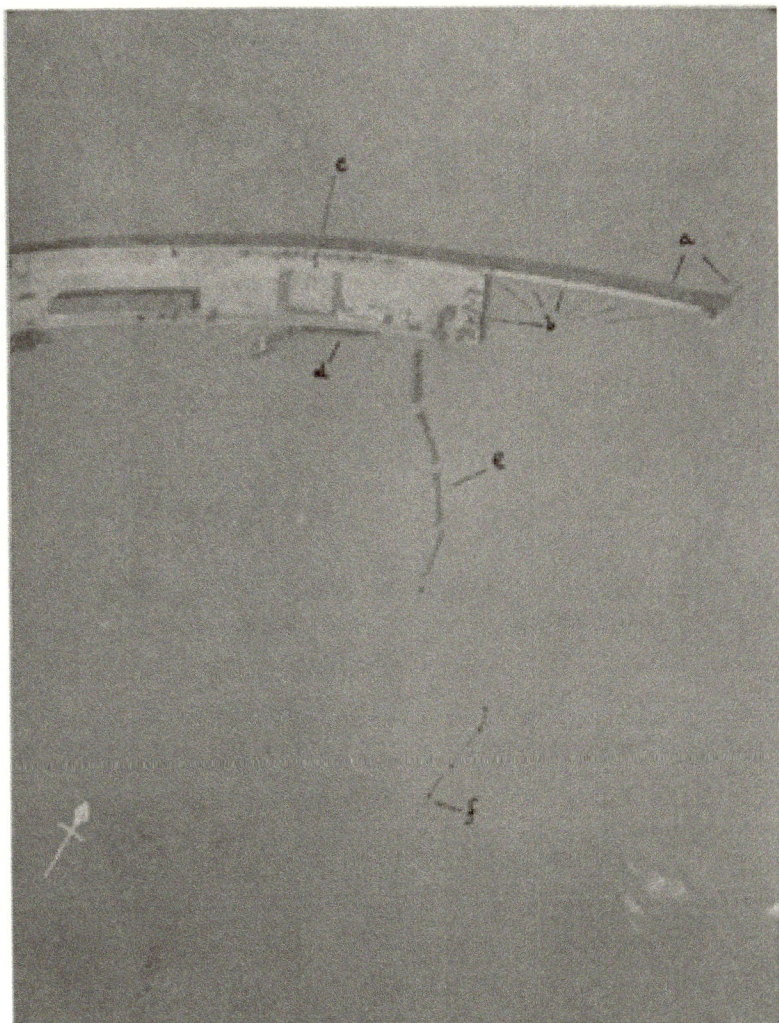

THE NORTHEASTERN END OF THE MOLE

a. The shadows of the parapet wall and of the lighthouse at its extremity
b. The Mole batteries
c. Trench system surrounded by barbed wire
d. German torpedo craft alongside Mole
e. The barge boom
f. The boom of entanglement nets

ably have induced the belief, in those who were actually acquainted with these difficulties, that such attacks would have no chance of success. There is, therefore, reason to believe that, although they realised an attack might be attempted, the Germans were perfectly satisfied that the defences could neither be improved nor penetrated.

The reader will probably have arrived at the conclusion that the Germans were devilish in their thoroughness. Yet there was still one joint left in their armour—and we penetrated it. But I must not anticipate.

CHAPTER 3

The Outlying Obstacles

Thus far I have only dealt with the local defences of Zeebrugge. But there were many other obstacles in our way—such as the coast batteries, mines, surface patrol vessels, submarines, aircraft, and the vagaries of the weather in addition to the navigational difficulties mentioned in the first chapter.

The coast-line of Flanders bristled with guns. The section of the coast from three miles west of Ostende to six miles east of Zeebrugge, approximately twenty-one miles in length, was defended by two hundred and twenty-five guns; one hundred and thirty-six of these were of the heavy type, i.e., six-inch and above, up to fifteen-inch guns.

At one period of the war, soon after the Germans first obtained possession of that locality, the coast defences had been few and far between. In those days our ships used to bombard from such short ranges as ten thousand yards. In course of time heavier guns were set up on shore so that our vessels were forced to keep at a more respectful distance. The first bombardments from ten thousand yards had been answered by the establishment of German guns having a range of fifteen thousand yards. When better weapons became available for bombardment from twenty thousand yards the Germans replied with guns firing up to twenty-five thousand yards.

And thus the duel continued. Finally, the ranges increased to upwards of forty thousand yards (twenty-three land miles). Monitors were specially constructed for this purpose and their marksmanship was wonderfully accurate. This accuracy is borne out by the fact that scarcely any damage was caused to the residential quarter, although Ostende was bombarded again and again; yet works of military importance, such as docks and railway stations, closely adjoining the residential quarter, were hit time after time.

In a straightforward gunnery duel between a ship and a fort, within the effective range of each, the former stands no chance. In these days, however, such duels savour little of the old-time broadside fighting between ships.

Even the largest and most modern coast guns are of comparatively small avail for defensive purposes unless the attacking ships are visible, or unless the firing can be controlled satisfactorily by such indirect means as the use of aircraft for observational purposes. At night the attackers must be illuminated by star-shell, flares, or searchlights. Under the ordinary fog conditions—*i.e.,* when the whole locality is obscured by fog—aircraft cannot observe the results of firing nor can the attacking forces be illuminated.

Under exceptional fog conditions—*i.e.,* when a fog (natural or artificial) lies between the shore guns and the attacking vessels, the latter being in clear weather—good co-operation between the batteries and aircraft in daylight enables the fire to be directed so accurately as to ensure destruction to vessels which remain in the danger zone.

The only alternative to directed firing is that of barrage firing, such as is used so greatly in modern land warfare. The defence guns can establish a shell barrage, for a limited period, across any zone which the attacking ship is attempting to penetrate *en route* to her objective. The vessel which steams into an efficient heavy gun barrage from modern guns is unlikely to survive.

I afterwards visited one of the large German batteries near Ostende, called the Jakobynessen battery, which mounted fifteen-inch guns and fired projectiles weighing nearly one ton each—seventeen hundredweight to be precise. They were mounted in specially constructed gun-pits amongst the sand-hills close behind the shore, and were so well hidden that they could not be seen from a distance of little more than a single gun's length. The projectiles stood over six feet high and were murderous-looking instruments of warfare. These particular guns, and there were others of a like nature, could probably have ranged up to sixty thousand yards (over thirty-four land miles).

The whole area off this section of the coast, up to about twenty miles to seaward, was included in the danger zone of the coast batteries. No vessel could maintain her position in that area, under ordinary conditions of visibility, for more than a few minutes at the outside limit. The reader may consider, however, that a ship desiring to attack the coast would merely have to approach in foggy weather or under cover of darkness. In foggy weather she would be unable to locate her objective—so that can be ruled out. At night she might conceivably arrive within a few thousand yards without being seen or heard. But immediately she was located by the defences the latter would fire their star-shell and switch on their searchlights. The whole area would thus be illuminated like daylight. The vessel discovered under such conditions would probably be blown to pieces within five minutes.

Thus it is manifest that ships cannot approach a hostile coast, in the face of modern defences, under the ordinary conditions of daylight or darkness, or in fog.

We will now consider the mine problem. The German mine-fields extended to a distance of several miles from the coast. We had reason to know of their presence; from time to time, as reported in the press, our vessels had been blown up.

Mine-fields off one's own coast provide a certain measure of defence. But they are also an embarrassment in that one's own vessels cannot pass through them, when approaching or leaving harbour, unless safe channels are kept clear for the purpose. This applied to the mine-fields under review.

The reader may possibly have jumped to the conclusion that all we had to do was to navigate calmly through the German safe channels. It certainly sounds plausible. As a matter of fact, such an idea borders on the ridiculous. Let us think this matter out carefully. Our forces could not pass through such channels unless they possessed information as to the positions of those channels. But if such information were received, the chances would be long odds on the information having been "made in Germany." Far from such information being correct, therefore, the positions mentioned would probably be those of the most dangerous mine-fields. Nevertheless, suppose we received information which, from the nature of its source and data, we had every reason to credit; and suppose we acted on such information. Well, on the voyage across the sea, or even before we actually start, the enemy discover that we intend to attack. What will they do? Their argument would be as follows: "The British are coming over to attack us; they may have discovered the positions of our safe channels; we dare not take any chances so we will mine our own safe channels immediately." Mine-layers, kept ready for instant use, would be sent to sea at once. In a very short space of time, probably an hour would be more than sufficient, the previous safe channels would have been converted into areas of the greatest danger.

There are alternative methods which the attackers may adopt.

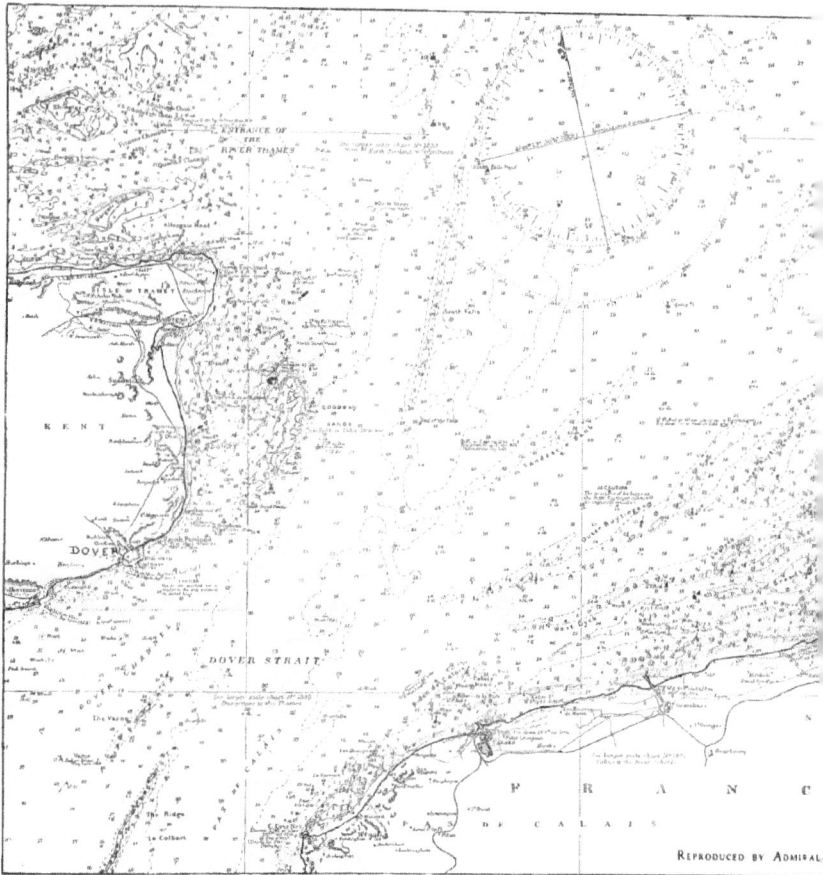

A portion of Chart 1406, showing the Dover Strait, the waters between Dover and Zeebrugge.

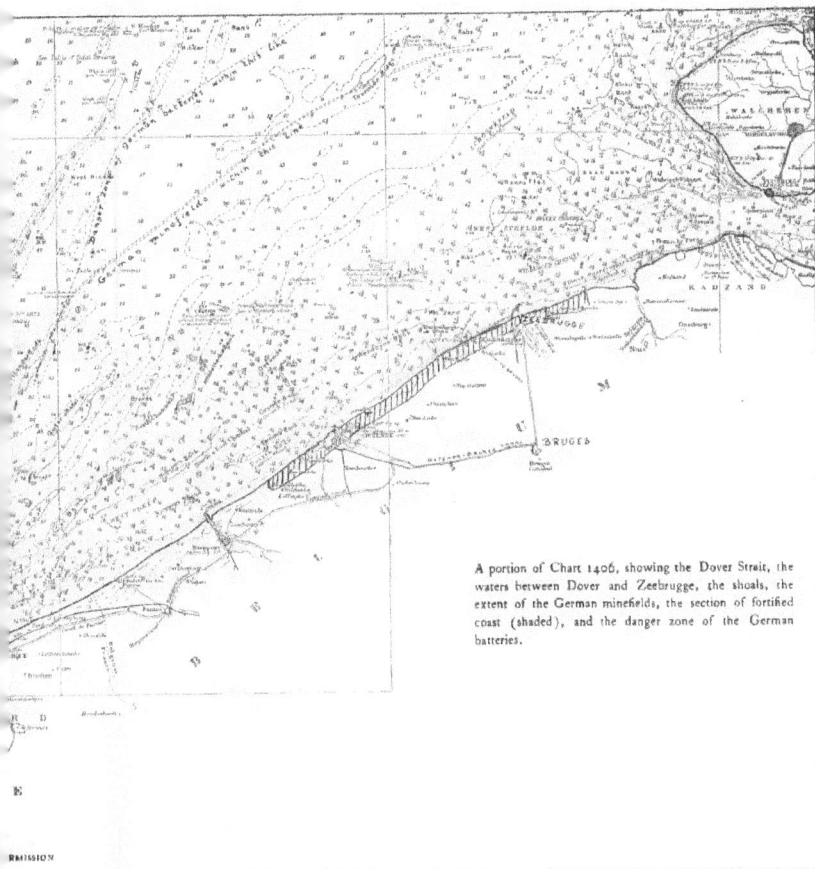

A portion of Chart 1406, showing the Dover Strait, the waters between Dover and Zeebrugge, the shoals, the extent of the German minefields, the section of fortified coast (shaded), and the danger zone of the German batteries.

...HE SHOALS, THE EXTENT OF THE GERMAN MINEFIELDS, THE SECTION OF

...ORTIFIED COAST (SHADED), AND THE DANGER ZONE OF THE GERMAN BATTERIES

Firstly, they may advance to the attack preceded by a force of mine-sweepers. Now mine-sweeping is a very slow process if it is to be carried out thoroughly. It is inconceivable that a large force of these vessels could steam about, mine-sweeping, near the enemy's coast for a considerable period without being discovered. Their discovery would give the whole show away; the enemy would know that we were approaching; the whole element of surprise would be lost.

The other method open to the attackers is that of proceeding to their objective without mine-sweepers, after having carefully weighed the probabilities of danger existing on the various alternative routes, and, on arriving at the danger area, passing through it and *chancing the result*. And that is what we did—we chanced it! But I am anticipating once more.

Outside the German mine-fields, and in any inshore areas which were unmined, German patrol craft would probably be stationed. Patrol craft, in comparatively narrow waters, are effective for discovering the approach of surface vessels in clear weather by day or night. The *minimum* harm that they could do to the attacking force would be that of reporting the latter's approach. A single alarm rocket might be sufficient. It is, therefore, almost inconceivable that the patrol vessels could be passed without the alarm being given. Any gun-firing would, of course, act as an alarm; ramming, a much more silent method, would be the best course open to the attacking craft if they encountered the patrols.

There were two other forms of patrol, however, which could provide even more serious obstacles.

Submarines, stationed on the route between the attacker's base and the objective, could patrol at periscope depth. The passing of the squadrons, viewed through the periscope of the unseen submarine would be reported by wireless telegraphy immediately the submarine could come to the surface. Thus, long before the attack commenced, the defenders would be perfectly well aware of the attacker's approach, whereas the latter would imagine that their mission was unsuspected. This use of a submarine, as a lookout, would be of infinitely greater importance, in such an event as this, than her use as a torpedo vessel.

Aircraft patrolling off the coast—say at a height of five thousand feet—would be able to see as far as the southeast coast of England, provided the atmosphere were clear. Under average conditions of visibility there would be no difficulty in discovering a naval force several miles distant. Such discovery would be immediately reported to the defences with the same result as that just described in the case of the submarine. The Germans had a strong force of seaplanes based on the Flanders coast. These machines were generally patrolling the vicinity—*provided the Allied aircraft were not about*.

We have now arrived at the stage where we can make a summary of the main obstacles in the way of a blocking enterprise at Zeebrugge. There were (*a*) the aerial patrol; (*b*) outlying submarines; (*c*) surface patrol vessels; (*d*) mines; (*e*) uncharted shoals; (*f*) lack of navigational aids; (*g*) coast defence batteries and illuminating apparatus; (*h*) the guns on the Mole; (*i*) the obstruction booms; (*j*) the harbour defence craft; (*k*) the shore batteries defending the canal; (*l*) the difficulties of seamanship in a tideway; and lastly (*m*) the vagaries of the weather.

In connection with a blocking enterprise at Ostende the same obstacles applied with the exception of those resulting from the presence of the Mole.

The list is undoubtedly formidable *though not yet complete.* The operation, on the face of it, did not seem to be altogether simple.

In writing this book I may be taken to task for concentrating on the operation at Zeebrugge and leaving the Ostende stories untold.

The latter operations, there were two, would necessitate a volume to themselves. And—this is the all-important point—I am not competent to render a first-hand account of them because I was not in the position of an eye-witness. Let us hope that the story will be written some day, so that the splendid work of poor Godsal, (Commander A. E. Godsal), who afterwards lost his life at Ostende in my old ship, and of his gallant troop may be properly recorded.

Owing to the fact that we were uncertain as to the extent to which Ostende could be utilised as an exit from Bruges, we naturally decided to assume its efficiency; *i.e.,* to assume that blocking the craft in at Bruges would necessitate blocking both Zeebrugge and Ostende.

The harbour entrance at Ostende was somewhat similar to the canal entrance at Zeebrugge. There were two piers flanking the entrance channel, the whole area being commanded by shore batteries. The only other comparison between the places which calls for mention here is as follows. Whereas the Mole at Zeebrugge provided additional obstacles against entry, it also acted as a landmark from which the canal entrance could be found. At Ostende the defence obstacles would be less complicated, but the harbour entrance would be more difficult to locate.

Now, the decision to block both exits naturally led to the conclusion that they should be blocked simultaneously if practicable. Otherwise the operation at one place would serve as a warning to the other. For instance, it would have been rather absurd for us to block Zeebrugge one night with a view to coming along on the following night to block Ostende. The absurdity would have been only slightly less in degree if we blocked one exit at—say—midnight with the idea of blocking the other at 2 a.m. For the defence batteries at the two places would naturally be in telephonic communication, and even half an hour's notice at the second exit would be sufficient to prepare a very warm reception for us. Simultaneous blocking was our aim; thus the whole operation was directed to that end, a fact which influenced the events to be related.

It has been suggested that "blocking the exit" was not the best method of preventing the egress of German vessels from the Zeebrugge canal. An alternative method, that of destroying the lock-gate by gun-fire, was referred to. The idea sounds plausible enough at first. As a matter of fact, many attempts had been made, by means of long-range bombardments, to achieve that end. They had all failed. The lock-gate appeared to have a charmed life. Huge shell had burst in its vicinity and yet it still remained intact. The suggestion was then put forward that the lock-gate should be bombarded *from close range* under cover of smoke or gas. This suggestion was accompanied by the opinion that an attempt at blocking the channel would be futile. I am much puzzled at this idea of close bombardment. For it was as obvious, as it was known to be a fact, that the Germans would withdraw the gate into its armoured recess immediately a bombardment was suspected. This would have been the work of a few moments; the outer lock-gate would have been rendered absolutely immune from destruction.

The argument that there were two lock-gates, outer and inner, and that the Germans could not withdraw both, owing to the fear of the canal running dry, also sounds plausible until it is closely examined. Firstly, however, it is clear that the canal would only run dry if both lock-gates were opened *at low tide*; secondly, an inshore operation at low tide would preclude the use of any craft other than those of shallow draught; thirdly, owing to the presence of the outer wall of the Mole, whose height would be over forty feet at low tide, the bombarding vessels could only obtain a direct line of fire at the lock from a position inside the Mole where the extensive shoals would allow very little room for manoeuvring, to say nothing of the defences on the Mole itself; fourthly, the canal, even if emptied, would refill from the rising tide within a few hours, and there was no certainty that the temporary evacuation of the water would cause serious damage; and lastly, one may assume, if there was really any substance in the idea, that the vice-admiral whose many long-range bombardments had failed to achieve their purpose would have long since attempted a short-range attack.

So, the decision to block the entrance at Zeebrugge having been reached, the best position for blocking had to be considered. It has already been shown that the narrowest portion of the channel to seaward of the lock was situated near the shore ends of the wooden piers. Another position even narrower in size was that of the lock-gateway itself. But the mere width of the position chosen was by no means the only consideration.

The actual sinking of the blockships in position did not provide the final argument; a point of great importance concerned the practicability of removing them out of the channel; it is of little use to block a channel in such a manner that it can easily be unblocked. This matter concerns the art of salvage.

Salvage is a highly technical subject, but a few remarks at this stage are necessary if the reader is to appreciate the extent to which considerations of salvage affected the problem under discussion.

Salvage operations must vary according to the circumstances of each particular case. The size of the vessel, the damage which she has sustained, the manner in which she is resting on the bottom of the sea, the nature of the ground, the tides, the depth of water, the degree of exposure to rough seas, the proximity of shelter for salvage craft, and the distance from the land are all factors of importance, but they by no means exhaust the list.

One of our main purposes in considering salvage operations was that of ascertaining the chief obstacles to salvage, so that we could provide the enemy with as many of those identical obstacles as lay in our power.

Another important object, concerning the immediate problem at Zeebrugge, was that of deciding the best type and size of vessel to be used in addition to the question of what particular damage each vessel should receive, and how she should be fitted to defy attempts at removal.

There are three principal methods of removing a sunken ship. First, bodily removal with the aid of some lifting agent. Second, dispersion by explosive means. Third, piecemeal removal by cutting away.

Regarding the first-mentioned method, a small vessel can be lifted by passing hawsers beneath her and securing the ends to salvage craft on the surface overhead. The hawsers being hauled taut at low tide, the vessel will lift off the bottom when the rise of tide lifts the salvage craft, and can then be transported bodily elsewhere. Larger vessels can be lifted by the use of compressed air, or by pumping out the vessel after closing all holes under water. Provided the ship is upright the compressed air method can leave out of account the damage sustained below the vessel's normal waterline, but the remainder of the hull must be rendered airtight. Air can then be pumped into the hull until the vessel is lifted, and she can be towed away as required.

This method has been used successfully when removing large vessels, but the practicability of rendering them airtight chiefly depends on the damage which they have sustained. The pumping-out method, comparatively speaking, is the most simple one to adopt, provided that the damage to the hull is small. The damaged portion must be repaired by divers unless the more elaborate method of building a coffer-dam—i.e., a sort of dock—around the ship, is pursued. Divers cannot work in a strong tidal current or in rough weather. The repair of holes under water is rendered extremely difficult, if not actually impossible, when the bottom of the ship is badly holed with the ship resting on the damaged portion. The ship must be made watertight, or nearly so, below the surface of the sea before she can be lifted. The word "watertight" is qualified here because, as a matter of accuracy, the ship can be pumped out and lifted, provided that the pumps can eject water at a greater rate than the latter is flowing in. Before passing on to consider the next method it may be as well to remark that special difficulty is experienced when moving sand—i.e., silt—has access to the holes in the ship.

Dispersion by means of explosive charges may, under certain circumstances, be a simple operation, but, on the other hand, there are certain conditions which put this method outside the pale of choice. For instance, in the case of a ship sunk in a narrow channel where much silt is experienced, the explosive method is almost worse than useless. For every explosion in a given section of a vessel will tend to shatter that portion into several pieces. Each piece falls to the bottom and forms a new obstruction. Silt then enormously aggravates the situation, for the sand will collect against the obstruction until it becomes a miniature sandbank. Such shoals are then difficult to remove.

A bucket-dredger—*i.e.*, a vessel fitted with an endless chain of buckets for scooping up the bottom—will break her buckets as soon as they encounter the steel kernel of the shoal. On the other hand, a suction dredger—*i.e.*, a vessel designed to suck up sand off the sea-bottom—cannot raise solid material. Neither type of dredger can remove the *cause* of the shoal; any removal of sand under such conditions is merely temporary; the sand will recommence building up the shoal as soon as the dredger ceases work. Dredging against such obstacles is of little more use than dredging against rocks.

There remains the third method, namely, piece-meal removal by means of "cutting away." Cutting away can be accomplished, in the ordinary course of events, by means of acetylene gas cutters or by pneumatic tools. Acetylene gas will cut through steel with little more effort than a knife cutting through india-rubber. But acetylene gas cannot be used under water and cannot cut through large thicknesses of cement. Pneumatic tools provide a very laborious and tedious means of cutting large quantities of steel. Work under water entails the use of divers. Thus, the removal of a ship by the piecemeal process is an exceedingly prolonged undertaking, especially as each piece must be lifted out when cut away; for reasons already stated the pieces must on no account be allowed to fall to the sea-bottom.

From the foregoing remarks we arrive at the following conclusions. The blockships should be too large to lift off the bottom by the hawser method. They should be extensively damaged and sunk in such a manner that they would rest on the damaged portion of the hull. They should be fitted to counter "cutting away" tactics, and should be sunk in positions where silt would render impracticable the explosive method of dispersion; the damage should be so situated as to give the silting sand access to the hull through the holes in the latter.

These general anti-salvage considerations, however, did not furnish us with all the data required. They required to be dealt with in greater detail, and the matter of dimensions was another important factor.

It was essential to render impossible the passage of the German naval craft out of the canal *over the top* of the sunken blockships. The tide at Zeebrugge rises fifteen feet between its low and high levels. Allowing six feet as the minimum depth required to float small naval craft, it will be seen that the upper portion of each blockship should reach to within six feet of high tide level, or, at least, nine feet above low tide level, when resting on the bottom. The height of the blockship's hull, therefore, would need to be equal to the depth of the sea at low tide level plus, at least, nine feet. Now, the choice of vessel is naturally limited. In the midst of war it is unlikely that a navy would possess many craft, if any, which were not already in use for other purposes. Thus, the dimensions just referred to would have to fall within certain limits, namely, those corresponding to the dimensions of the only vessels from which one is likely to be able to choose. That part of the total height due to the rise of tide was beyond control; it would be the same anywhere in the same locality. Thus, the position chosen for the blocking must necessarily have a low tide depth of such an amount as would make the total depth at high water correspond to the total height of the available hulls.

Then again the number of ships required would depend on the relation between their horizontal dimensions and the breadth of the channel to be blocked. For instance, a single vessel whose beam dimensions were approximately equal to the breadth of the lock gateway would be sufficient to block the latter, provided that the height of her hull also agreed with the conditions just mentioned above.

Now, it had to be borne in mind that if a vessel was sunk in the lock gateway the "cutting-away" method would be greatly facilitated by the erection of cranes and machinery, within a few feet of the vessel, on dry land. This position, being so far removed from the tidal current which runs parallel with the Belgian coast, was unaffected by silt. Thus, although the lock gateway, by reason of its small breadth, could be completely blocked by any suitable vessel sunk therein, the work of salvage would be very much less difficult here than elsewhere.

Further out, between the wooden piers at the canal entrance, the navigable channel was approximately one hundred and twenty feet in breadth; i.e., slightly over one-third of the whole distance between the piers. A vessel of one hundred and twenty feet in length, therefore, would require to be turned dead across the navigable channel before sinking if she was to block every inch of it. Obviously, a vessel of three hundred feet in length would not require to turn herself to anything like the same extent. The maximum depth in this position was believed to be about thirty-six feet at high tide level. Thus, we arrive at the conclusion that a blockship sunk between the wooden piers would need to have a hull whose height was not less than thirty feet, and to have a length of at least one hundred and twenty feet.

In this position the silt was known to be very active. That fact, taken in conjunction with the exposure to rough seas, the presence of the tidal current, and the impracticability of erecting salvage plant

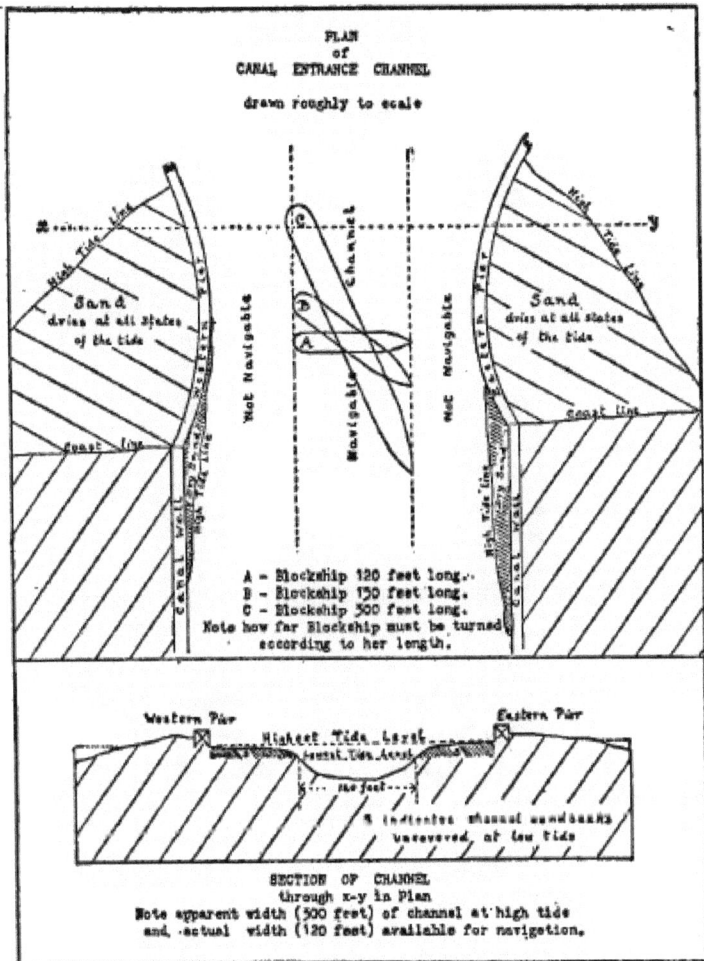

PLAN OF CANAL ENTRANCE CHANNEL

on the land within easy reach of the vessel, rendered it obvious that, all things considered, the position between the wooden piers would be the ideal blocking position if suitable vessels were available for the purpose, and if such vessels were damaged and sunk with due regard to anti-salvage considerations.

It is common knowledge that when vessels are fitted out as block-ships they usually carry a goodly cargo of cement. The general notion, however, about the use of this material is that it is merely intended to make the ships heavier and thus less capable of being lifted. That is only partially correct. There is another and more important use for ce-

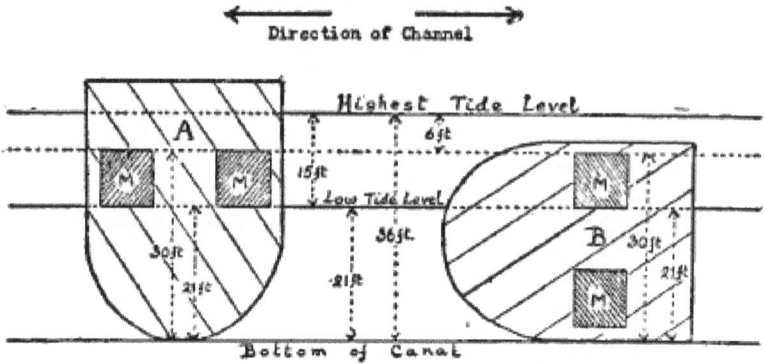

← Direction of Channel →

SECTIONAL SKETCH of SUNKEN BLOCKSHIPS

A - resting on even keel
B - resting on beam ends

Shaded areas M indicate suitable positions for
placing 'anti-cutting-away' material.

ment, namely, as a counter against the use of acetylene gas for cutting the ships to pieces. The general scheme is that of placing the cement in just those positions where cutting would be most necessary; in our case, in those portions of the ship which would be above the lowest level of the tide and up to within six feet of the highest tide level. The depth of our chosen position being twenty-one feet at low water and thirty-six feet at high water, this meant that the cement would need to be placed between the levels of twenty-one feet and thirty feet above the keel, provided that the ship was sunk in an upright position. With regard to the latter proviso, steps must be taken to guard against the eventuality of the ship resting on her beam ends on the sea-bottom as a result of capsizing when foundering. This cautionary measure necessitated placing the cement between the levels of twenty-one feet and thirty feet from her beam ends at either side of the vessel as well as between the same vertical distances from her keel. Nothing should be left to chance that can be provided for in advance.

It was clear enough that the task of ever getting the ships into the desired positions for sinking would be far from simple; having attained that object it would be the height of stupidity to sink the ships in such a manner, and so fitted, that their removal would be comparatively easy.

After the operation had been successfully completed I could not help being rather amused at a certain individual who expressed the opinion that "the Germans are so cute that they'll probably remove the blockships in a day or two." Why were some people always so ready to credit the Germans with everything that's wonderful? The reasons were not far to seek; such ideas arose partly from natural ignorance on technical matters and partly because the Germans never ceased to assure us how marvellous a nation they were. And some of us believed it! *Verb. sap.*

With all the difficulties in the way of attainment, what counter considerations were there to make the attempt worth the undertaking?

CHAPTER 4

The Chances of Success

What were the chances of success?

The lessons of personal experience and of past history are the chief guides when calculating the probability of success in any operation. He who ignores history acts unwisely. He who studies history and proposes to attempt something which has always failed hitherto either may be excessively foolish or may be aware of a new factor affecting the situation. He may be merely flying in the face of Providence or basing new proposals on a well-considered judgment of the new circumstances.

Naval history contains a few examples of operations somewhat analogous to that under investigation. The more noted are the attacks on Martinique in 1794, on Teneriffe in 1797, the attack on Ostende in 1798, the cutting out of the *Hermione* from Puerto Cabello in 1799, the sinking of the American steamer *Merrimac* at Santiago de Cuba in 1898, the Japanese attempts to block the entrance to Port Arthur in 1904, and, during the late war, the attempt to block the Rufigi River by a British collier in November, 1914.

In none of these cases were the conditions quite parallel to those at Zeebrugge and Ostende, but some features of each bore a certain similarity.

The attacks on Martinique and Puerto Cabello showed the great value of determination and initiative in the face of powerful shore defences. They also showed the disadvantage accruing to the defence force by reason of the latter's ignorance as to the true nature and object of an attack by sea forces.

The attack on Santa Cruz, Teneriffe, was led by the immortal Nelson himself. It involved the storming of the Mole which was defended by the enemy's batteries. Two attempts were made. The first was carried out in the face of adverse weather conditions which rendered "surprise" impossible; the attack was withdrawn soon after the landing parties had left their ships. The second attempt, made two days later, was also a failure, but a glorious failure indeed. Very few of the boats reached the Mole, which, however, after a desperate encounter was captured by the storming parties. The latter were unable to advance owing to the fire from the hostile batteries. Nelson, who, it will be remembered, lost his right arm in this engagement, failed in his object. This failure provided the outstanding interruption to the long list of victories gained by our greatest naval hero of all time; Nelson himself expressed his feelings of disappointment and physical incapacity with the words "I go hence and am no more seen."

The attack on Ostende in May, 1798, was directed against the lock gates for the purpose of interfering with the concentration of the flotillas destined for the invasion of England. This attack had originally included a blocking operation, but that idea was apparently abandoned. The attack, carried out in the face of a rather feeble defence, was completely successful, but a severe gale prevented the re-embarkation of the forces, with the result that over one hundred and sixty were killed or wounded and nearly eleven hundred and fifty were taken prisoners—an interesting point in view of the fact that only about half a dozen casualties occurred during the attack itself. The embodiment of the main principles of fighting led to success on that occasion as they will usually do under similar conditions. The moral effect in England, in spite of the heavy losses, is recorded as having been most beneficial.

The blocking attempts at Santiago and Port Arthur, carried through with complete indifference to danger in each case, were failures.

The main difficulties with which blockships must contend may be briefly stated as follows:

(*a*) That of *locating the destination* in darkness, increased by the absence of the usual local navigational aids such as lighthouses, buoys, etc.

(*b*) That of *reaching the destination*, when located, in the face of the enemy's opposition.

(*c*) That of *turning and sinking the vessel*, after reaching the destination, so that the channel will be efficiently blocked.

Dealing with these difficulties in detail, the reader is probably aware of the fact that navigation is by no means an exact science. On the open sea a captain is usually satisfied if he knows his position to within three or four miles. When approaching the coast this wide margin of safety must be considerably reduced—hence the need of lighthouses, buoys, fog signals, and so forth. The upkeep of such aids is naturally in the hands of the power which occupies the coast concerned. Thus, under war conditions, one aims at removing all navigational aids, as far as one's own requirements will allow, which may assist the enemy. By this means, the enemy when approaching one's coast, must either trust to the rather inexact methods used in the open sea or they must establish their own navigational aids beforehand. The objection to the latter is manifest; craft sent ahead to lay down buoys, etc., are apt to give one's intentions away, and it is open to the enemy to remove such aids as soon as they are placed.

With regard to the second main difficulty, namely, that of reaching the destination, when located, in the face of the enemy's opposition, the difficulty here is so obvious as to render detailed remarks unnecessary.

With regard to the difficulty of turning and sinking the vessel satisfactorily, this is largely a matter of seamanship. With wind and tide both affecting a vessel it is seldom possible either to keep her stationary over a particular position or to turn her through a large angle without such aids as tugs, hawsers, and anchors, etc.

But a ship does not go down instantaneously, nor is it a simple matter to sink her in an upright position. One end of the ship is likely to sink before the other: most of us have seen photographs of a ship with her bows or stern standing vertically in the water just before the vessel makes her final plunge. Whilst the ship is actually sinking the local current is apt to move her considerably before she is resting on the bottom throughout her whole length. Thus the third difficulty can only be surmounted by a specially fine display of seamanship, and, in such cases as we are reviewing, this display must be rendered under the most trying conditions imaginable.

Now, in the case of the blocking attempt at Santiago the *Merrimac*, Lieutenant Hobson of United States Navy, failed to reach her desired destination after it had been located. The attempt could scarcely have been more gallantly made, but the difficulties, arising from insufficient opportunity to make complete preparations, almost foredoomed the operation to failure.

At Port Arthur, the Japanese made three attempts to block the exit against the egress of the Russian Fleet. No less than eighteen blockships were used. In spite of great determination and splendid self-sacrifice on the part of all concerned no blockship managed to sink herself in the correct position.

During the late war the difficulty of sinking the ship satisfactorily, after reaching the desired position, was made manifest both in the River Tigris and in the Cameroon River. In each case our enemies, the Turks and Germans respectively, *endeavoured to block their own channels before we even arrived on the scene.* In the absence of all opposition from an enemy, in broad daylight, and at their own leisure, they sunk their ships and *failed to block the channels*—two clear illustrations of seamanship difficulties.

All the searchings into past history failed to discover one single occasion in which a blocking enterprise of any real similarity to that desired had succeeded. That fact, taken into conjunction with the difficulties brought to light by a detailed consideration of the problem, was neither productive of encouragement nor conducive to optimism.

The reader will probably admit, at this stage, that the difficulties of blocking the highly fortified canal entrances at Zeebrugge and Ostende appeared almost insuperable.

But where there's a will there's often a way. A way had to be found. *A way was found.*

The factors which combined to make "the game worth the candle" were as follows: firstly, the use of smoke screens; secondly, the element of surprise and the use of diversionary measures; thirdly, detailed preparation and determination combined with efficiency.

The use of smoke screens provided a factor which had been absent in previous attempts in history.

Mention has already been made of the great deterrent afforded by the presence of hostile batteries and of the varying degrees of efficiency of gun-fire as a defence against attacks from the sea. If smoke could be utilised in such a manner as to hide the attacking force from the batteries without completely blinding the former, and if at the same time the attack could be made under cover of darkness so as to prevent aircraft from assisting those batteries, a set of conditions less unfavourable to the attackers would then be forthcoming. Obviously, this necessitated the smoke drifting shorewards ahead of the approaching vessels; *i.e.,* the assistance of a wind blowing more or less directly towards the shore.

It is well here to caution the reader against a commonly erroneous idea in this connection. It is often supposed that the use of smoke was a sort of *panacea* for all evils, that it provided a counter to all obstacles. This was very far from being the case, as will now be explained. Firstly, let us consider the navigational difficulties. Smoke could not possibly assist the ships to avoid shoals when approaching the coast. Smoke could not prevent the vessels from being seen and reported by surface patrol craft, submarines, or aircraft during the trip across the sea. The danger from mines could not be avoided by the use of smoke. It has already been pointed out that it is quite difficult enough to locate one's destination on a dark night when the lighthouses have been extinguished and other navigational aids withdrawn. Even a landsman will realise that if, as an addition to such inconvenient conditions, one places an artificial fog between the approaching vessels and their destination the problem is not going to become any more easy to solve. The utmost that one could gain from the use of smoke was some measure of protection from the shore batteries, but, as just shown, such use provided a further obstacle to be surmounted. Then again there is nothing so fickle in the life of a sailor as the wind. If the wind died away or changed to an off-shore direction, smoke might be practically useless for covering one's approach.

I have sometimes been asked why we made no use of poison gas clouds. There were two main reasons. The last thing we desired was to risk killing those downtrodden Belgians who were still allowed to reside in their unhappy country. In addition to that, the fickleness of the wind might waft the poison gas in the direction of our own vessels.

With regard to the element of surprise and the use of diversionary measures, one of the principles laid down by Stonewall Jackson is, "Always mystify, mislead, and surprise the enemy." The meaning of surprise is apt to be misconstrued. In an operation of this kind one could not arrange for the blockships to arrive suddenly "as a bolt from the blue" at a moment when the enemy have no suspicions whatever that any trouble is brewing. Thus, surprise and mystification had to go hand in hand. The only practical method in such cases, whether in trench warfare or in sea fighting, is to give the enemy as much to think about as one possibly can, to make him wonder what on earth is going to happen next, to mislead him into believing the eventuality is very different from that intended, and, then, as the late war expression so aptly puts it, "when the enemy has the wind up," surprise him by carrying out your main object in view.

Diversionary measures in this particular case were not difficult to evolve. Many different reasons obtained for employing our sea forces off the Flanders coast. To mention a few, there were bombardments from the sea, landing operations on the shore, supporting the flank of the military in their land attacks, mining or mine-sweeping operations, laying submarine traps, supporting aerial attacks, and so on. The presence of our vessels might indicate any one of these objects and each would call for a different set of defensive measures.

The full development of defensive measures cannot be attained until one can clearly ascertain the attacker's object. Even when the latter has been discovered, the time required to bring all your powers of defence into action must vary according to how far you have just previously been misled. Our best course, therefore, was to ensure that our object would be discovered so late in the proceedings that it would be attained before full advantage of the discovery could be utilised. Initiative usually pertains to the attacking force. Where the defence is open to several different forms of attack, the defending commander is apt to be so apprehensive beforehand, and so perplexed at the time, that his position will be weakly defended at all points. As the attack develops and he receives an *apparent* indication of its object he will make haste to concentrate all his defence measures at the threatened position, and then, if the attackers have acted wisely, there is considerable likelihood of his being taken by surprise too late to guard efficiently against the real blow. Uneasy lies the head of the commander who is forced to adopt the defensive role in war.

The diversionary measures actually undertaken will be described presently.

Determination and efficiency are not unknown in His Majesty's Navy. But efficiency of a particular description was required, and this would necessitate special training, which, if practicable, must be continued until every officer and every man knew instinctively what to do and how to set about it, no matter what circumstances might arise, and until every piece of machinery and every device, however intricate, had been proved to be satisfactory for the purpose in hand.

What then were the chances of success? Who could say? Clearly enough, there must have been a divergence of opinion on this point. Difficulties loom large. Optimism, on the other hand, is a very pleasant encouragement. I believe, however, that even the most optimistic individual concerned in the enterprise was not entirely free from qualms as the event drew nearer. Complete success seemed at times to be so much to hope for. But Sir David Beatty and Sir Roger Keyes wouldn't hear of failure, and that alone did much to ensure success. They did not set themselves up on pedestals as men who *could not fail—they left no stone unturned to ensure success*. It would be difficult to imagine anything more calculated to bring about failure than any sign of doubt, or hesitation, on the part of the leaders of an enterprise. There *must* be no failure—that was the long and short of it—it was the spirit which governed the actions of the great leaders of the past.

But sentiment alone is insufficient to guarantee success. It is but a foundation stone on which to commence the building. Rotten timber erected on the firmest foundation will not provide adequate protection against the lightest gale. Nobody realised this more fully than Vice-Admiral Keyes, who was determined that every link of the chain should be of maximum strength commensurate with elasticity and general handiness. Many were the hours given to the consideration of the smallest details; without such work an operation becomes a mere gamble.

CHAPTER 5

Planning the Operation

A war operation, such as this, passes through various stages before it can be put into execution. It emanates originally from a suggestion. If the suggestion seems to bear further consideration certain individuals are ordered to appreciate the situation, that is, to thoroughly thrash out all the arguments for and against and to weigh the chances and effects of success and failure. Should the results of such an appreciation be favourable, the investigation leads to the formation of a Plan.

Plans are based, to a considerable extent, on the personnel and material believed to be available. In like manner the calculations as to future requirements of personnel and material are based on the types of operations which are likely to be carried out. But it is conceivable that a projected plan may be found to involve the unforeseen use of material to the detriment of other operations already in view. Thus the feasibility of putting a naval plan into operation cannot be judged unless fairly complete details are given as to the numbers and types of ships, men, and stores involved. The formulated results of such investigation, arising out of the original suggestion may be designated the first edition of the Plan.

The authorities then consider the Plan both from the view of general outlook and from that of detailed requirements. Let us suppose that the Plan is considered to be of value, and that no objections hold good as to the practicability of execution provided the ships and men *are* available. This latter proviso then requires attention. Many questions have to be considered. Can the ships be diverted from their present duties? What special alterations or additions are necessary? Can the dockyard undertake the work? If so, to what extent will other work in hand be interrupted? Will the men require special training? Are the necessary stores ready at hand? How long will the preparations take?

And so on. A hundred and one points must be carefully enquired into. It is only after a great deal of investigation, correspondence with various departments, and conferences for co-ordinating the results of enquiries, that the details can be arranged. A plan served up in the form of a mosaic is of little more use than the works of a chronometer contained in half a dozen different boxes.

In course of time decisions are arrived at and orders are issued for the preparatory work to be taken in hand. But it is unlikely that all the proposals contained in the first edition of the plan have been agreed to. Modifications are almost sure to be necessary. Perhaps the suggested vessels are required for other purposes and substitutes must be forthcoming. The technical experts may decide that different types of material would lead to improvement. Possibly the facilities for special training of the personnel are not available at the moment. The plan must, therefore, be re-drafted on the basis of the personnel and material available, and must take into consideration the dates by which the various phases of the preparatory work can be completed. All this takes time and serves as a reminder, indeed, that patience is a virtue. The second edition of the plan is evolved and the next stage is reached.

But put aside, for a moment, the question of what material and personnel are available. When a plan, conveying a general idea, has come under the critical examination of the Higher Command to the extent of being "passed" for the commencement of detailed preparation, it has then to be *gradually built up* from the operational point of view. Additions will almost always be necessary as the investigation proceeds, and some time will elapse before the plan can be considered as complete in every particular.

A further duty then devolves upon the operational staff. They must produce the orders necessary to give effect to the plan as detailed in its final edition.

This again is no small affair. The writing of orders is a high art in itself. Orders must not be too centralized or too cut-and-dried. Ample allowance must be made for initiative, while realising that mere go-as-you-please methods are likely to lead to disaster. It is usually the unexpected that happens in war. A single set of orders cannot cover every eventuality. And even if it could, nobody would have either the time or inclination to wade through such a voluminous document. This is clearly enough exemplified in legal matters. Laws are framed to cover every possible case, but as often as not they fail to attain such success. Even so, how many ordinary folk can be bothered to wade through a legal document? What with the alternatives, and saving clauses, such publications are dull to a degree. The marriage laws are typical of this. A man may not marry his grandmother. That clause was presumably inserted for the discomfiture of that unique individual who *might* contemplate such a peculiar alliance.

The issue of orders needs careful training and much experience. Orders must be fool-proof—that is the guiding axiom. If an order is misunderstood it is ten chances to one that the fault lies with the man who gives the order.

If I have sorely tried the patience of the reader it is because of my endeavour to emphasise the point that the order "carry on" is not sufficient to put a suggestion into execution in the matter of a few hours. New situations have to be met by fresh dispositions, and this fact has come very much to the fore in these days of strife.

The operations on the Flanders coast were the outcome of some months of hard work—mental as well as manual. A few details of the plan may now be worthy of consideration.

On December 3, 1917, the plan had emanated from an Admiralty Department under the direction of Rear-Admiral Keyes, Director of Plans, to give him his titles at that time. The nature of the operation and the customary procedure, having regard to the locality concerned, would entail its execution coming under the command of the Vice-Admiral at Dover. The latter apparently desired to modify the plan and submitted his proposals on December 18th. He suggested the idea that an attack on the Mole, not previously mentioned in the plan, should accompany the blocking operations. As a diversion (pardon the anticipation) this idea was eventually embodied after exhaustive consideration had shown it to be necessary.

As already stated this particular type of diversion was somewhat similar to that included in a previous scheme, referred to as having been forwarded in May, 1917, which at that time was considered impracticable by the Vice-Admiral at Dover. The actual method proposed on December 18th by the latter for giving effect to his idea of a Mole attack was not followed, for it happened that Rear-Admiral Keyes took over the Dover Command, with the acting rank of Vice-Admiral, after his own plan had been submitted, and nearly four months before it could be carried out. The coincidence—if it was a coincidence—was extremely advantageous. An operation can be so much better worked up by an officer who has handled the plan from its inception. But in the ordinary course of events such an arrangement is impracticable.

An admiral or general in active employment in the face of the enemy, as a general rule, has not sufficient spare time for the formation of plans in every detail, nor has he a superabundance of staff officers for the purpose. No words of mine could ever do justice to Sir Roger Keyes, so I will not make the attempt. Suffice it to record that every soul in the enterprise possessed complete confidence in his leadership; this fact was half the battle won before we even started.

Admiral Keyes was given an absolutely free hand by Their Lordships; all the details, from A to Z, were worked out under his direction. The "paper scheme" rapidly developed into practical shape; I will endeavour to describe the data and arguments from which its final shape was evolved. Before doing so, however, it may be as well to put on record a fact that might escape the notice of the reader. The responsibility of the Officer in Command of an operation must necessarily be great, but the responsibility of the Higher Command, in this case the Board of Admiralty, which has to either sanction or disallow the execution of proposed operations, is by no means small. That they sanctioned it in this case and also chose the right man to carry it out must never be forgotten.

Having reached a decision as to our object and considered the obstacles in the way of attainment, let us now pass on to the manner in which it was proposed to overcome the various difficulties. We will commence with the most important phase of the operation, namely, the actual blocking and the nature, requirements, and duties of the blockships.

Reference to the previous description of the locality and to the principles governing the use of blockships serves to show that a single vessel of the light-cruiser class, or above, would suffice as far as dimensions were concerned. But nothing possesses such a large element of chance as war; for that reason it was considered advisable to provide at least three blockships at Zeebrugge and two at Ostende.

With regard to the requirements of each blockship, they may be briefly stated as follows. Firstly, she must have the ability to proceed under her own steam to her destination. The task of towing a blockship into position in the face of enemy opposition is quite impracticable. Secondly, her draught of water must not be excessive, having due regard to the depth of the channel. Next, she would require a certain degree of defensive power; it would be rather heartrending, after all one's efforts at taking a blockship to within a short distance of her destination, if any small enemy craft could approach without hindrance

THE BLOCKSHIPS FITTING OUT FOR THE ENTERPRISE

H.M.S. VINDICTIVE BEFORE FITTING OUT.

and sink the ship before her destination was actually reached.

The blockships must also be handy vessels, so that they would be manageable up to the last moment, provided they escaped serious damage. It has been stated previously that these ships must be so fitted and sunk that their removal would be extremely difficult. Five old light cruisers which were available, or rather which could be replaced at their present duties, were chosen for the purpose. They were H.M.S. *Thetis, Intrepid, Iphigenia, Brilliant, and Sirius*; the first three being destined for Zeebrugge and the others for Ostende.

A few months previously a couple of steamers had been fitted out for some such operation under another vice-admiral, but it will be seen that, as a result of detailed investigation of all the obstacles and factors affecting the problem, the Plan described herein differed from its predecessors in that respect; in fact the arguments against the use of merchant vessels were considered from the outset to be overwhelming.

The work of surmounting such difficulties as escorting the blockships across the seas and locating their destinations would require the use of other units, and will, therefore, be described later. Speaking generally, the actual tasks of reaching their destinations *when located* and of sinking themselves in position, difficult though they were, could best be left to the pilotage and seamanship of the blockship officers. Here again, the author is anxious to lay special emphasis on the fact that successful results of the blocking operation—such as had never been attained in history—were absolutely dependent upon the good work of the blockship personnel; to them would the credit be due.

At Ostende, the work of the blockships, with regard to reaching their destination, was confined to that of running the gantlet of the shore batteries when once the entrance had been located, but the latter—*i.e.,* the location of the entrance—presented considerable difficulty.

At Zeebrugge, there would be less difficulty in finding the entrance if the Mole extremity, three-quarters of a mile to seaward, could be located. But a serious factor existed here which was absent at Ostende.

Blockships proceeding into Zeebrugge would have to risk the fire of the Mole batteries during the first part of the approach. They would then have to steam in *behind those batteries* and run the gantlet of the batteries ashore. Now this was a pretty big proposition.

In the second chapter it was shown that the three-gun battery situated on the broad portion of the Mole at its northeastern extremity, taken in conjunction with the establishment of the barge boom and entanglement nets, rendered it extremely hazardous for the blockships to round the Mole *en route* to the canal entrance; in fact it was almost a certainty that they would be sunk by the Mole guns.

Nevertheless, the canal entrance was our objective. Somehow, by hook or crook, the blockships were intended to reach it. Thus, one of the first local problems requiring solution was that of removing, temporarily or otherwise, the obstacle afforded by the three-gun Mole battery. Similarly, though perhaps in a lesser degree, we had also to take into account the battery of six smaller guns on the lighthouse extension of the Mole.

Considered in a general manner, there were three lines of enquiry from which a solution of the problem might be forthcoming. Firstly, that concerning the destruction of the guns or their crews, or both, or diverting their fire, by means of action from a distance. Secondly, that of attaining a similar result by action on the spot. Thirdly, that of rendering the blockships invisible during their passage. These may be dealt with briefly. The first method entailed the use of either gun-fire or poison gas. The outcome of a gun-fire duel between a ship and a battery has already been described sufficiently to show that the chances of destroying the battery guns are exceedingly small. The use of poison gas has been shown to be inadvisable. The third method—that of rendering the blockships invisible to the battery—would have entailed the use of a smoke screen. If such a screen could have the effect mentioned it is obvious to the meanest intellect that it would also have the effect of hiding their destination from the blockships just at the critical period when it would be absolutely essential to see exactly where they were going.

And so no method would suffice, except the second mentioned above, namely, destroying the guns or their crews, or both, or diverting their fire, by means of action *on the spot*. This entailed an attack on the Mole itself, carried out by vessels actually berthed alongside. The author, although well aware of the unpardonable fault of repetition, desires at this stage to lay great emphasis on the fact that an attack on the Mole itself could only be designed as a diversionary measure calculated to directly assist the blockships past one of the positions of danger. The reader is requested to pardon anticipation. Subsequent to the operation, many of the public appeared to have formed the idea that the attack on the Mole was the main attack, and that the use of the blockships was a sort of afterthought. I shall have more to say

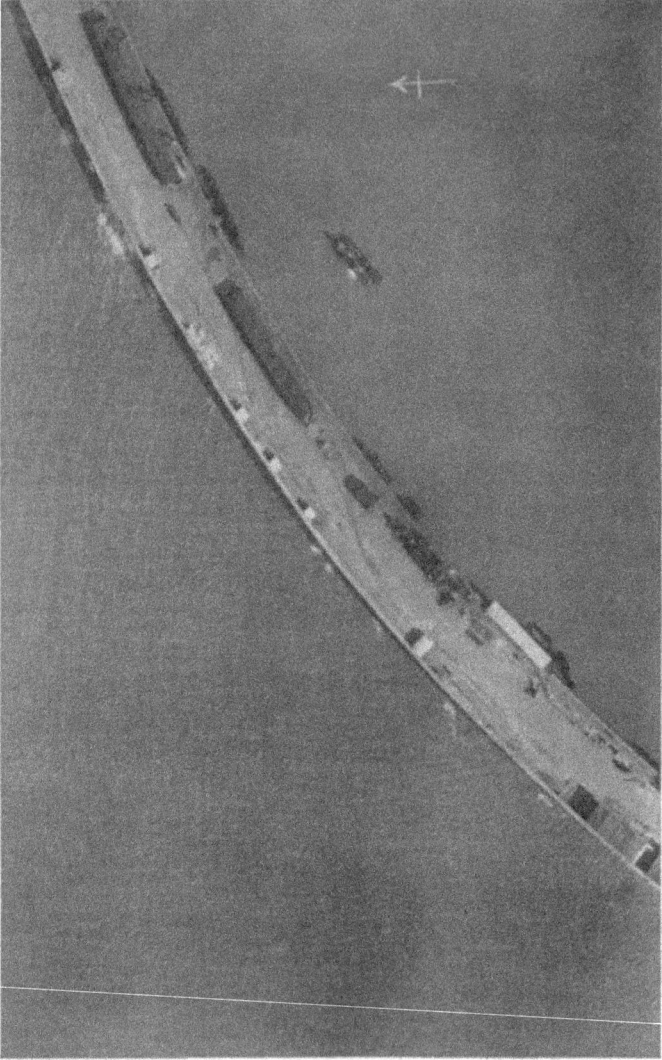

A PORTION OF THE BROAD PART OF THE MOLE.
Note the concrete submarine shelter (white)

about this later.

Just as the three-gun battery provided a serious obstacle to the passage of blockships round the Mole end, so also would it prevent the similar passage of other vessels endeavouring to secure alongside the berthing wharf on the inner side of the Mole preparatory to attacking the Mole batteries. Thus, if the Mole was to be stormed, *the storming parties must land on the outer side of the Mole*, remembering that the three-gun battery could not fire to the northward owing to being twenty feet below the top of the high outer wall. But the outer wall of the Mole was never intended for use as a berthing position for vessels, and probably never had been used by any vessel for such a purpose— hence the complete absence of all berthing facilities as described in an earlier chapter. The development of the argument concerning this projected attack had led us to the point where we needed to consider seriously the practicability of getting any vessel, or vessels, alongside the outer wall, of securing there, and of landing men thence for attacking the Mole batteries.

The depth of water, the construction of the Mole, the rate of the tidal current, and many other matters required careful examination. The depth was a doubtful matter; but, the operation being timed to take place near high tide so that the blockships could enter the canal, there was every likelihood of its being sufficient. Breakwaters when also intended as wharfs are usually built with their inner sides—*i.e.*, the sides protected from bad weather—vertical like the face of an ordinary wall, but with their seaward sides formed of large blocks of material dropped more or less indiscriminately, one above the other, so that the wall will be jagged for the purpose of breaking up the waves in bad weather. In such cases a ship could not possibly secure to the seaward side without being severely damaged, and certainly could not remain there. At Zeebrugge, however, we had reason to believe that the seaward side of the Mole was nearly vertical and that no danger would accrue from jagged blocks of stone or concrete.

At high tide the tidal current on the Belgian coast is flowing at its greatest speed—a phenomenon nearly always found in comparatively narrow waters—and its rate was expected to be about three and a half miles per hour, its direction of flow being to the eastward. So far, then, the matter of reaching a position alongside chiefly concerned the art of seamanship if we leave the enemy's opposition out of account. Next we had to consider the problem of securing alongside and of disembarking the storming parties. The most simple method of berthing

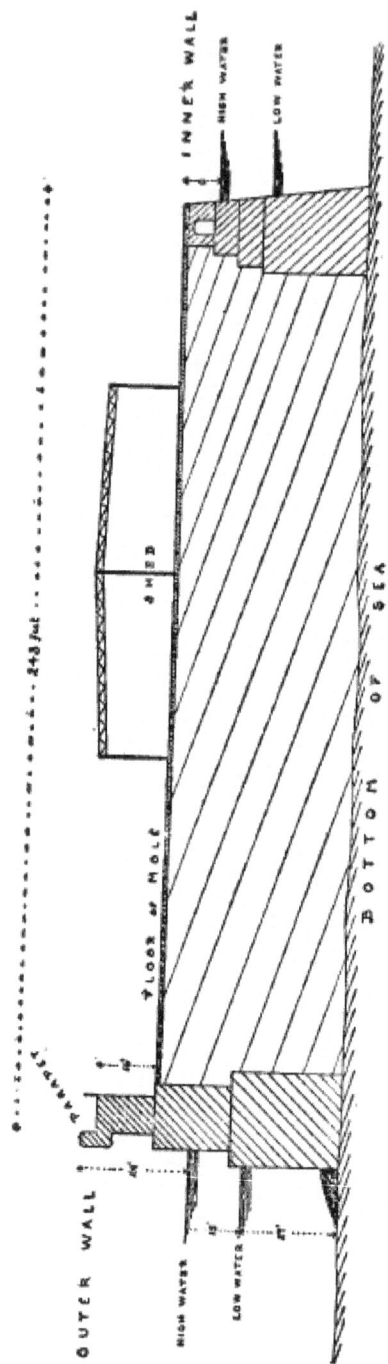

SECTION OF MOLE THROUGH NO. 3 SHED

alongside a wall, in the case of a sizable vessel, is to place the vessel roughly in position and then to use tugs to push her bodily against the wall, afterwards securing the hawsers in the usual manner. This led to the idea of having a second vessel to act as tug and of providing special means to take the place of the ordinary hawser-and-bollard method of securing.

The wall on the outer side, as previously described, rose to a height of twenty-nine feet above the level of high water. This height was far above that of the deck of an average vessel. The fact that the landing would have to be made on a narrow parapet, high above the level of the Mole proper, was also hardly calculated to assist matters. The probable existence of guns on the parapet itself, so placed as to be able to rake the decks of a vessel alongside, and the possible presence of obstructions placed by the Germans on the outer side of the Mole, had to be taken into account. It has also been mentioned above that the use of smoke screens necessitated a wind blowing towards the shore; thus the Mole itself could afford no protection from the wind or sea.

The Austrian military failure on the River Piave, during the late war, afforded a good example of the disabilities resulting from insufficient room to debouch a force which has crossed an obstacle into the enemy's territory. Clearly, it might be very awkward if the storming parties were unable to descend from the parapet rapidly enough to forestall any enemy attempts at concentration near the storming point.

All these considerations led to the choice of H.M.S. *Vindictive* for carrying the main portion of the storming parties.

The attack on the Mole might also provide an opportunity for destroying material thereon. Although this was obviously a secondary consideration it was an opportunity not to be missed. The amount of destructive work which could be done would depend upon the circumstances of the moment, but it was decided to have a special demolition party, provided with the necessary gear, to accompany the primary attacking forces.

Clearly enough, it would be somewhat futile if one only began to consider the work of demolition as soon as the moment arrived for such work to commence. With the object of being prepared in all respects careful consideration, therefore, was given to the different methods of demolition which would be most suitable under varying circumstances. Following such consideration it would be necessary to train one's demolition parties in this technical pursuit and to provide

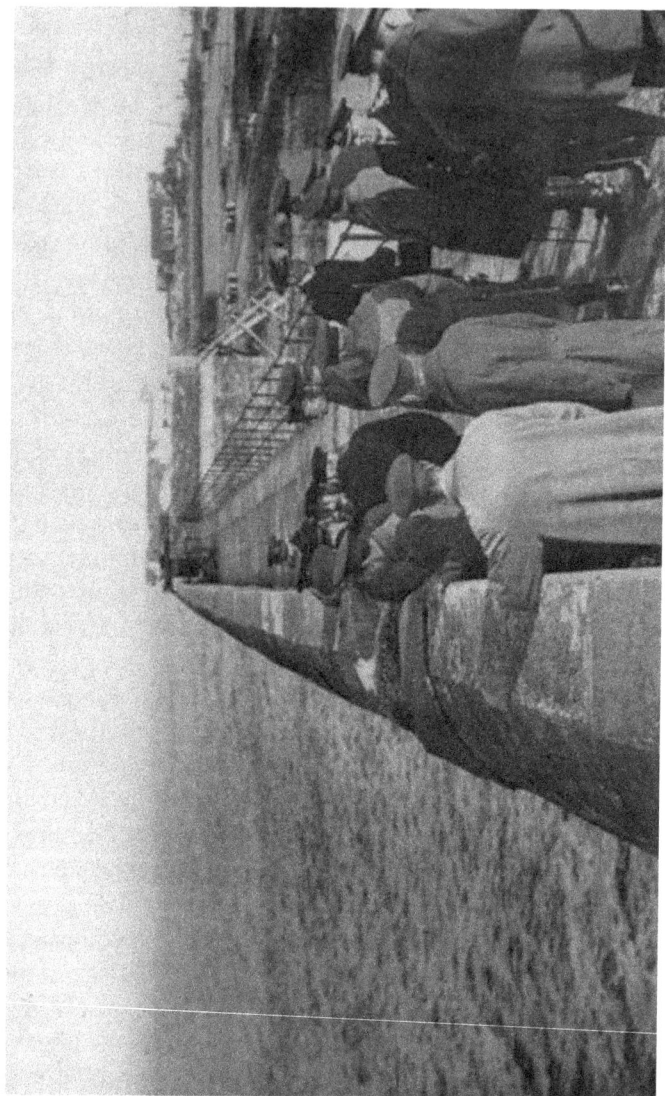

THE OUTER WALL, SHOWING THE PARAPET PATHWAY 16 FEET ABOVE THE FLOOR OF THE MOLE

a sufficiency of suitable destructive material.

When making preparations for an operation of this, or similar type, one is apt to allow secondary objects to loom too large unless great caution is taken to prevent it. In this particular case, however correct it might be to fully prepare, down to the smallest detail, for everything in advance, it was necessary to bear in mind that demolition on the Mole could hardly assist the blockships to seal the canal exit and, even if successful, could not bring us very great benefit. Thus it was clear that demolition should only be prepared for and undertaken provided that it did not hinder the attainment of our main object in the smallest particular.

H.M.S. *Vindictive* had to be fitted with a special deck from which gangways could be extended to bridge the gulf between the ship and the top of the twenty-nine-foot wall. For this purpose she was given a large number of gangways poised at an angle of about forty-five degrees from the ship's side. The idea was that on arriving alongside the Mole, the gangways would be lowered till they rested on the top of the wall. The storming parties, at a prearranged signal, should run out along the gangways and jump down to the parapet pathway four feet below the wall top. They should then get across the pathway, over the iron handrails on its inner side, down to the floor level of the Mole, sixteen feet below, and then start the work. Now, one cannot expect men carrying all their accoutrements and paraphernalia, such as rifles, machine-guns, flame-throwers, bombs and grenades, rifle and gun ammunition, and such-like to jump down a drop of sixteen feet on to a stone surface. So it was arranged that the advanced storming parties should carry long storming ladders to place against the wall on its inner side and thus facilitate access to the floor level. Seamen were to land first, both for the purpose just stated and for securing the ship to the Mole after the *Vindictive* had been pushed alongside the Mole by another vessel.

Owing to the absence of bollards for securing hawsers, special grappling irons, fitted with double pronged hooks, with hawsers attached to them and the ship, were designed for the purpose of hooking on top of the wall. In reality we proposed using the methods of the good old days when vessels grappled each other and indulged in hand-to-hand fighting between their respective storming parties. The weight of these grappling irons necessitated the use of special davits for suspending them in a similar manner to that used for the gangways. Special weapons, such as bomb-mortars and flame-throwers, to

H.M.S. VINDICTIVE'S SPECIALLY CONSTRUCTED GANGWAYS.

Two of the parapet anchors for grappling the Mole can be seen at the end of the bridge in the background

be worked from the ship, were provided for clearing the Mole immediately abreast the ship prior to sending the storming parties over the top. The *Vindictive* also carried most of her original gun armament for engaging enemy vessels *en route*, for shelling the six-gun battery on the lighthouse extension of the Mole, and for defending herself against attacks, when at the Mole, from enemy vessels in a seaward direction. Special howitzers were carried for engaging the shore batteries after the ship was secured, and rapid-firing guns were placed in the fighting-top of the foremast for engaging the batteries on the Mole. The wall being at least twenty-nine feet above the water, no gun at a less height could fire over it in a downward direction. Much other special material—peculiar to the operation in hand—was required, but space does not admit of describing it all in detail.

The reader will already have realised that the *Vindictive* was to be a weird craft indeed—something very different from the usual run of warships even in these days.

Now, as regards the storming of the Mole, it would have been a dangerous policy to put all "*our eggs in one basket.*" There was no small chance of the *Vindictive* being mined *en route*, owing to her heavy draught, or of being sunk by gun-fire, owing to the large target which she would present, before reaching the Mole. It was, therefore, decided to use two other vessels in addition to the *Vindictive*.

The ferry steamers *Iris* and *Daffodil* were chosen for carrying a portion of the storming parties to the attack. There was considerable difficulty in finding two vessels suitable to our purpose; time did not permit of constructing special craft before the projected date of the operation. It must be remembered that we could not write round to all the naval and mercantile ports explaining our requirements. An officer, sent on a tour for the purpose, unostentatiously visited the likely places until he found these two vessels. I often wonder what imaginary yarns he conjured up for the purpose of stifling curiosity.

The *Iris* and *Daffodil* were both well known to Liverpool folk, being used for conveying passengers across the River Mersey many times daily. They were extremely handy craft, could each carry fifteen hundred men if required, and drew very little water, but they possessed two serious disadvantages. Firstly, their decks were so low as to necessitate the use of long storming ladders for reaching the parapet. Secondly, their steaming qualities were comparatively poor, judged from the point of view of the operation for which they were required. Just picture their ordinary daily employment for a moment.

Waiting alongside one of the piers at Liverpool till their usual quota of passengers had embarked, they would make the short trip across the river to the Birkenhead shore and then wait once more. During this second period of waiting the steam pressure would be increased in the boilers in readiness for the next short voyage across the river. Compare that employment with a trip of nearly one hundred miles across the open sea. It will then be evident that the task allotted to these two ferry vessels was by no means simple from the engineering point of view alone.

All this, however, was carefully thought out, and it was decided that their advantages outweighed their disadvantages. Both craft, by nature of their work, were designed to stand heavy bumping alongside piers; their draught was small, and, as already stated, they were easy to handle. After minor alterations they proceeded to the port of assembly in charge of their naval crews and adopted the title H.M.S., much to the amusement of those of us who made their acquaintance for the first time. It is rumoured that one of these two vessels arrived at her destination *with her anti-submarine escort in tow*, which thus early showed that proud spirit to which she so justly proved her right on St. George's Day, 1918.

The first duty of the *Daffodil* on arrival at the Mole was to be that of pushing the *Vindictive* bodily alongside. The former vessel was to place herself at right angles to the latter, bows against the latter's side, and to continue pushing until *Vindictive*, which would previously have anchored, was secured by means of the grapnels. *Daffodil* was then to drop alongside *Vindictive* and her parties were to climb over the latter and up to the Mole. The *Iris* was to go alongside the Mole ahead of *Vindictive*, to anchor, to grapnel the parapet, and to land her storming parties by means of ladders against the wall, her decks being too low to allow the use of large gangways as carried in *Vindictive*.

In the event of *Vindictive* being sunk, *Iris* and *Daffodil* were to storm the Mole as best they could and do everything possible to knock out the three-gun battery or divert its fire from the blockships.

It was believed that the Mole garrison consisted of about one thousand men. But what of re-enforcements arriving from the shore? Access to the Mole would entail the crossing of the viaduct by such re-enforcements. Therefore the viaduct must be destroyed. Consideration on this point led to a decision to utilise one or more submarines filled with explosives and to blow them up under the viaduct, so as to cut the latter in twain.

This particular phase of the operation had not been included in the original Plan evolved at the Admiralty. As previously stated the first edition could not be expected to cover every single investigation of every point in the problem. The attack on the viaduct, after a large amount of experimental work ordered by Vice-Admiral Keyes, took the following shape.

Two submarines, each carrying several tons of high explosive, were to accompany the expedition. They were each to carry a crew of two officers and four men, who, after securing their craft underneath the viaduct, were to light the time fuses and then to take to the boats. Each submarine carried a small motor-driven dinghy for this latter purpose.

So much, then, for the blockships, storming vessels, and submarines at present.

CHAPTER 6

The Vessels Involved: Their Duties

In addition to the special vessels mentioned in the preceding chapter, many other vessels and craft were required to assist in the operation. One can imagine the amateur reckoning up the probable number as follows. Three blockships at Zeebrugge and two at Ostende, three storming ships and two submarines at the former place. That makes ten vessels of sorts. Allow a few more for other purposes—say, fifteen altogether. As a matter of fact, there were one hundred and sixty-two. Let us see why so many were required.

Take the requirements necessitated by the use of smoke screens. It has already been stated that the section of coast on which the Germans had established heavy gun batteries was twenty-one miles in length. Smoke screens were required to mask those guns so that the approach of the blockships and storming vessels should remain undiscovered until the latest possible moment. This meant that a large number of craft were necessary for smoke screening alone. Again, if the smoke screens were to be efficient the smoke would have to be emitted within a short distance of the coast; *i.e.,* in comparatively shallow water. Thus shallow-draught vessels were necessary. Shallow draught goes hand-in-hand with small dimensions. The carrying capacity of small craft is very limited; this constituted an additional reason for employing large numbers.

Further craft were required for assisting to locate the destination, for dealing with enemy vessels putting to sea during the attack, for defending our ships against other enemy vessels already at sea, for assisting to tow some of the smaller units across the seas, for rescuing the crews of the blockships, and for various diversionary measures. The latter included long-range bombardments from the sea and subsidiary attacks on the Mole, the units required being monitors and their at-

ONE OF THE MONITORS.

H.M. SHIPS IRIS (RIGHT) AND DAFFODIL

tendant craft and fast motor boats. Other diversionary measures, not requiring naval vessels for their accomplishment, were bombing attacks by aircraft and bombardments from our shore guns.

The aircraft were intended to attract the attention of those on duty in an overhead direction, whilst encouraging the remainder to keep under cover. The long-range bombardments would tend to keep the enemy's larger batteries occupied in expending ammunition in their endeavour to locate and silence our guns. Subsidiary attacks, carried out by fast motor craft against the Mole, and against German vessels berthed at its inner side, were calculated to confuse the situation as far as the enemy were concerned. It was arranged that the R.M.A. siege guns on the northern flank of the Allied army should bombard for the purpose of simulating a prelude to a land attack.

The reason for the employment of one hundred and sixty-two vessels, not including aircraft, will now be somewhat more clear. The various classes comprised cruisers, submarines, ferry-boats, monitors, destroyers, motor launches, small motor boats of a fast type, and one ordinary ship's steamboat; the latter was to be used in connection with rescuing the crews of the submarines.

With the exception of the blockships, storming vessels, and submarines, the majority of the craft were drawn from the forces attached to the Dover Command; these latter, being in full commission already, did not require new officers and men to be specially appointed for our purposes. Seven French torpedo craft and four French motor launches were included in the operation. The aircraft were drawn from the 61st and 65th Wings of the Royal Air Force.

Space does not admit of describing the work of all these units in detail, but it may be of interest to mention one or two.

Whenever an operation of this description is afoot, it is extremely advisable that the personnel destined to take part in the more hectic part of the fighting should not only be trained to the last ounce, but quite fresh on arrival. The individual cannot give of his best when fatigued—a truism exemplified again and again during the late war. But ships do not cross the ocean without any effort on the part of their personnel. It is not a case of merely turning on a tap, saying, "hey presto," and going to bed. Far from it. Engines do not revolve merely for the asking. Large vessels carry large engineering complements, but always require about half on duty at a time when at sea. Small craft may have small engines, but their complements are also small. So, whether the vessel be large or small, the work below calls for strenuous duties from the engineering personnel—only those who have undertaken such duties can realise the immense effort and the accompanying fatigue which falls to their lot. Then again the ship cannot navigate herself. The steering and the lookout duties both call for great concentration of attention, especially at night when steaming without lights in the close company of other vessels, in the vicinity of shoals, and in enemy waters. Guns' crews must stand by the guns so as to be ready at a moment's notice.

Now, this expedition would have to steam many miles across the seas. How then could the crews be fresh on arrival? This particular problem was solved as follows. Arrangements were made to provide each blockship with a number of men, over and above the minimum required at the climax of the operation, for the purpose of handling the vessel and its engines during the passage overseas whilst those men required for the "final run" would be resting. Extra officers could not be spared for this purpose.

The *Vindictive*, *Iris*, and *Daffodil* were differently situated in this respect. It was intended—as I shall explain presently—to bring these three vessels back on completion of the operation; the total number of personnel on board need not be kept down to the barest minimum. In fact, they were each to carry two complete sets of personnel, namely, those remaining in the ship throughout and those landing on the Mole.

The submarines, motor launches, and fast motor boats, owing to lack of accommodation, could not be given extra personnel for the trip across; it was, therefore, decided to tow all such craft throughout the greater portion of the passage across the seas. Even that decision did not relieve the crews of all duty, but gave them some respite, and, what was equally important, helped to ensure their arrival in the vicinity of their place of duty.

The rescue work required much thought. Bearing in mind the main object which had to be attained, it will be understood that all such questions as rescue work and retirement, however important from the point of view of humanity, must be relegated to a comparatively secondary consideration.

One cannot wage war without "breaking eggs." He who attempts to do so will seldom accomplish anything worth while. The lives of men are, indeed, a precious responsibility on the shoulders of their leader, but his primary duty in action is to obtain the utmost value from his men rather than to adopt the negative attitude of merely preventing their lives from being lost. This does not signify that lives should be thrown away without a thought. Not one life should be sacrificed in the execution of superior order unless the order is absolutely essential to the success of the work in hand, or, putting it in another way, unless the life is given so that others may live. The leader, therefore, has a difficult problem to solve. How far is he justified in risking failure through the natural desire to preserve life? The armchair critic, who has never been faced with such responsibility, who can have no conception of the different situations which arise in war, may sneer at the leader who places too great a store on the lives of his subordinates, or may hurl accusations of callous indifference at the superior whose successful operation is accompanied by a long casualty list. But we can leave any such critic to his sneers and accusations, knowing, as we do, that he is least dangerous to the community in war-time if he remains in his chair.

Each blockship, as already stated, was to carry the minimum number of personnel which could bring success. But the minimum number was large.

During the "final run" to their destinations they would require the engineering and stokehold parties, lookouts, guns' crews for self-defence, the navigation party conning and steering the ship, and complete spare navigation parties for taking over command in an emergency. These with a few others, such as signalmen, brought the total in each ship up to no less than fifty-three.

In the case of the *Merrimac* at Santiago, during the Spanish-American war, Lieutenant Hobson was accompanied by only about half a dozen men. At Port Arthur the Japanese blockships, at each of their attempts, also carried very small crews. But it must not be forgotten that all those attempts failed.

Now, it was decided to give each blockship a large lifeboat and some life-saving rafts, and also to arrange for other craft to proceed to the rescue. The chances of recovering any of the personnel certainly appeared to be very remote, especially when one realised that the rescue would have to be effected practically underneath the enemy's guns, and even behind their trench defence system on the coast-line.

The chances of rescue must bear some relation to the numbers to be rescued. For this reason it was decided to disembark the oversea passage crews from each blockship before arriving within the danger zone.

When the question arose as to which of the motor launches should be used for effecting the rescue of the crews from the blockships, volunteers were asked for. In spite of the almost incredible difficulties and tremendous risk involved the number of applications for this dangerous task was most embarrassing. Eventually lots were drawn and the winners were greatly envied by their less fortunate *confrères*.

The organisation necessary to ensure efficient co-operation, and co-ordination of effort, was no small matter. Every vessel, however small, had important duties to fulfil. At any moment during the operation success might depend on the action of a single unit: it would be difficult to conceive any circumstances where the value of initiative would be more pronounced. Nothing could be left to chance—any suggestion of possible failure was unthinkable.

CHAPTER 7

Matters Affecting the Passage

Safe passage across the seas, especially from the navigational point of view, provided much food for thought. The liability of new shoals to form and of old shoals to move their position, the consequent lack of dependence on the charts, and the absence of the usual navigational aids have already been mentioned.

These navigational difficulties, increased by the low visibility which obtains at night, combined to form the first of the three main obstacles to be encountered in blocking operations of this nature, namely, the difficulty of locating the destination.

Considerable amusement was caused in naval circles, subsequent to the operation, when a certain individual, from another country, published a special piece of "inside information," to wit, that the method whereby *Vindictive* reached Zeebrugge Mole was a great secret, known only to Captain Carpenter and one other, involving intricate calculations in connection with astronomical phenomena. I was extremely interested in this suggestion for it was the first that I had heard of it. As a matter of fact the safe navigation was largely the outcome of a very fine piece of work by two officers specially lent from the Hydrographic Department of the Admiralty, (Captain H. P. Douglas and Lieutenant-Commander F. E. B. Haselfoot).

The major portion of the area through which the various forces were to pass was surveyed under great difficulties.

The surveying vessels were often forced to remain within the danger zone of the German batteries, and, owing to shortness of time, had to utilise every possible opportunity for fixing positions of buoys, taking soundings, examining areas where new shoals were suspected, marking the limits of old shoals, laying down special marks to assist the passage of the expedition, and to enable the bombarding vessels to take up their positions with accuracy. Old obstructions had to be removed and wrecks had to be correctly charted. The vagaries of the weather rendered the task all the more difficult, and interference from the enemy was experienced on more than one occasion. Incidentally both these officers were on board H.M.S. *Botha* when she rammed and sank the German torpedo-boat A-19, which was out with a few others on one of their very infrequent tip-and-run escapades off Dunkirk; this was a pleasant interlude for these hard-worked officers. No country in the world can boast of such an efficient Hydrographic Department as our own. Their work in the war passed almost unrecorded, but none the less appreciated by those of us "who went down to the sea in ships." No praise could be too great for the work of the surveyors employed on our behalf.

It will be readily understood that little reliance could be placed on large conspicuous buoys laid by us near the enemy's coast. On discovering such navigational marks the enemy would presumably either move them a mile or so, for the purpose of interfering with our navigation, or else remove them altogether. Buoys, to be of any practical use, must be conspicuous, hence the likelihood of their being seen by the enemy unless placed in position at the last possible moment. This alternative was actually followed; it does not require much imagination to realise the difficulties and dangers in placing them in readiness for the operation and in removing them again on each occasion when the operation was postponed.

The strong tidal stream in the southern portion of the North Sea renders navigation rather anxious work in misty weather, or in darkness, especially as the normal rate of the current is much influenced by weather. Naturally, there is less danger of hitting a shoal which one is endeavouring to avoid, if the ship is steaming either directly with or against the current; the error in such cases is confined to the time at which any particular position will be reached. But when steaming *across* the current a small eccentricity on the part of the latter may make all the difference between reaching the desired position and missing it altogether. The current running parallel to the Belgian coast attains a speed of about three knots under normal conditions. Should a three-knot allowance be made when steaming across the tide there would be a serious error of position at the end of an hour's run if the tidal stream happened to be running at the rate of two and three-quarters or three and one-quarter knots; it must be realised that a ship cannot discover the rate of the tidal stream in a given area until she has completed her passage through it; i.e., until she has already suffered from its eccentricities.

For the purposes of the particular case under review it was necessary for the expedition to arrive at an *exact* position, thus tidal calculations and navigational aids assumed great importance. But they alone were insufficient to ensure accurate navigation. Compasses must be correct, or their errors known, and the speed of the ship due to its own engines requires to be carefully gauged. For a given speed of engine the speed of a ship varies according to her draught and the state of the ship's hull under water. All these considerations will serve to show the extreme necessity for working out courses, speeds, and times beforehand with the utmost accuracy, for repeatedly checking them to ensure the absence of clerical error, for reconsidering allowances for the vagaries of the elements, and for correcting the results from day to day according to the tidal differences due to the ever-changing phases of the moon. The careful navigator always follows a similar procedure, but, in ordinary cases, he knows that a fault in position can probably be remedied in time to avoid untoward incident. In our movements, however, there would be small chance of remedy if the blockships failed to find the canal entrance, or if the submarines were unable to locate the viaduct, or if the storming vessels missed the Mole.

Preparation for the passage across the seas involved yet another matter of considerable importance. Vast numbers of mines had been laid, both by ourselves and by the enemy, during the previous three and a half years, in the areas through which the expedition must pass before reaching the permanent German defence mine-fields near the Flanders coast. Doubtless other mines had dragged with the tide across our desired route. Special mine-sweeping work was, therefore, necessary to render the major portion of the passage even tolerably safe from mines. The reader can probably appreciate the difficult nature of that task with its attendant risks and necessity for thoroughness.

In addition to the one hundred and sixty-two vessels whose duties have been mentioned, other supporting squadrons were necessary far out at sea. The possibility of our intentions having become known to the enemy had to be borne in mind. In such an event the enemy would, of course, adopt special measures to ensure giving the expedition a warm reception on arrival, but a most important eventuality for us to guard against was that of meeting a superior concentrated enemy force already at sea waiting to intercept us *en route*. Scouting craft, both aerial and naval, were therefore required; it was also advisable that our fighting fleet should be conveniently situated in case the chance arose of defeating any such counter to our expedition.

Whenever we employed our small craft to operate in enemy waters we had to bear in mind a certain possibility. The enemy on becoming aware of our movements, or intentions, and perhaps feeling unusually courageous, *might* say, "Here are a number of small enemy vessels close to our harbours, let us engage them with the whole strength of our fleet and thereby achieve a great victory for the Fatherland." And so, in case the German Fleet left their harbours, unlikely though it might be, our Grand Fleet was always "in the offing" at such times ready to meet the so-called High Seas Fleet and send them down to the place where they ought to go.

The man-in-the-street must have wondered what the Grand Fleet was doing at sea so often in view of the fact that the enemy hid themselves almost throughout the war. The difficulty lay in the fact that we could not be perfectly certain that the constitution of German naval valour would continue to include ninety-nine per cent of discretion. Time after time the Grand Fleet hoped against hope that they might meet the enemy. The operations off the Belgian coast seemed to hold out yet another slender hope; this, pardon the anticipation, proved to be as forlorn as usual. The history of the High Seas Fleet, with respect to their oft-repeated desire to try conclusions with the Grand Fleet, can be briefly narrated. In the four and a quarter years following the outbreak of war the High Seas Fleet came out once, and once only, with the express intention of meeting the Grand Fleet—and that was to surrender! On the one other occasion when they met our fleet, incidentally by accident, they concentrated all their efforts at escape and then claimed the victory. The German Navy never had any traditions—now they have one less!

The reader may well ask what connection these remarks have with the subject of the blocking operation. A very close connection indeed.

Napoleon—perhaps the greatest student of war and certainly one of the greatest generals that the world has seen—remarked, and repeated again and again, that in war "the moral is to the physical as three is to one." Every great leader understands the value of morale and every man who has served his country in war has at least a subconscious realisation of the moral factor.

Just consider the moral effect of the German inactivity. In our men the uppermost feelings towards the enemy were those of contempt.

There is small need to consider the morale of the High Seas Fleet, for is it not recorded by their own Admiral, von Scheer, that the men mutinied at the last because they believed they were being sent out to fight our fleet? Take the case of our Dover Patrol force. They knew that the enemy could choose their own time for dashing out of the Belgian ports to attack our cross-channel communications. They knew that the chances of intercepting such enemy under adverse conditions, such as during darkness or fog, were very small. Yet month after month passed by and the enemy surface craft did next to nothing. Sometimes our advanced patrols came into touch with enemy patrols. On each occasion, I believe almost without exception, the enemy craft turned and ran at utmost speed for home. In the case of our small motor boats there had been meetings with those of the enemy within a mile or two of the latter's bases: here again, there is no recorded instance of one, or even two, of their craft standing up to one of ours.

The reader will understand the resultant moral effect. Some day perhaps we shall hear the romantic story of these adventurous small craft working from the Dover area—how one of them coolly steamed in underneath Ostende Pier one night to repair her engine whilst the German sentries paraded up and down just overhead, how another ran in behind Zeebrugge Mole in broad daylight and fired her torpedoes at German vessels berthed alongside, and so on. Is it difficult to imagine the feeling of superiority and confidence possessed by our personnel?

The morale of the German naval forces in Flanders concerned us much more closely than that of the High Seas Fleet. Under ordinary circumstances we should have been exceedingly apprehensive of any German torpedo craft at Zeebrugge or in the vicinity, especially those at Blankenberghe, but experience had served to show that they were none too ready to further the *"über"* portion of *"Deutschland über Alles."* Thus we were all the more ready to take risks which may have seemed to be uncommonly close to the border-line between "justifiable" and the reverse.

In recounting the preparations which followed naturally upon the main considerations connected with the problem in hand there has been a certain amount of unavoidable anticipation.

It has already been explained that the conduct of the operation fell to the vice-admiral commanding the Dover Patrol, and that a very large number of vessels of various classes and many specially trained personnel were required. Thus the fitting out of the vessels, the preparation of material, and the training of the personnel also came under the direction of the vice-admiral.

It must not be forgotten that the ordinary work of the Dover Patrol could not be interrupted even for one day at this period. The lines of communication across the Channel, important as they had already been throughout the war, were now of such vital importance that the Allied situation on the main battle front depended on the work of the Dover Patrol more than ever before. During February and March, 1918, when the preparations for our enterprise were in full swing, and especially during the latter month, the Germans were concentrating every possible effort to break down the Allied resistance. Their final great "push" was in full swing and the Allied troops were being hard pressed almost to the point of giving way. British, Colonial, and American re-enforcements were being poured into France by every available route; guns, ammunition, and stores were passing across the Channel in an endless stream of shipping. The situation was critical to a degree. If the Dover Patrol force had failed at such a time the war might have had a very different ending. And in the midst of this terribly anxious period we were forced to request great additional effort for the purposes which the author is endeavouring to describe.

One may be pardoned for thinking that the blocking operation, with all its complicated requirements, should have received undivided attention, but such a thing was impossible. Those were busy days at Dover. Special material, such as artificial fog apparatus, had to be constructed and fitted in the craft concerned. The use of the apparatus had to be practised with a view to discovering the conditions under which the best results could be obtained. Neighbouring commands, such as at Portsmouth and The Nore, were exceedingly helpful in this latter respect. The use of howitzers, flame projectors, bomb-mortars, grappling irons, scaling ladders, and many other fighting appliances not usually found in men-o'-war had to be investigated.

A special factory was established at Dover under Wing-Commander Brock—of whom I shall have much to tell—mainly in connection with the developments and use of artificial fog, but also to further the design and production of other material. Sixty men worked at this factory. Their output, both in quality and quantity, was most satisfactory in spite of the many handicaps with which such innovations have to contend. The difficulty of obtaining special material, when the output of every large firm in the country was already earmarked for other purposes, was not lessened by the fact that our urgent demands could seldom be supported, owing to the necessity for secrecy, by explanations as to the purposes in view.

The use of artificial fog in war was by no means an entirely new idea. The device had already been utilised by our naval forces off the Belgian coast, and a quantity of data on the subject was available as a result of its use in fighting on land. But all forms of fog screens—and there were many—had hitherto possessed disadvantages which would militate against satisfactory results in an enterprise such as we contemplated. The main difficulty attached to the smoke apparatus at Dover was that a very visible flame was emitted; this would have completely given our presence away as the smoke was intended to *hide our presence* and cover our advance. Some attempts had been made to surmount this difficulty, but experiments proved the apparatus to be hopelessly unsuited to our requirements. The reader, however, will not desire to be introduced to a highly technical treatise on this subject. Suffice it to say that, as a result of prolonged experimental work, a new type of fog was evolved which satisfied all requirements. The trials were not altogether devoid of humour. It is rumoured that on one occasion a fog produced in the Dover Straits refused to dissipate itself for three days, with the result that mercantile captains said some very hard things about the clerk of the weather.

The blockships and *Vindictive* were fitted out at Chatham. That dockyard was already being taxed to its utmost. The situation demanded that every man should strive to exceed his previous utmost efforts—one of the few points on which our enemies may congratulate themselves. Secrecy was, of course, essential. Yet in the case of the ships fitting out at Chatham the number of men who played an indirect part in the operation ran into four figures. The same thing applied at Portsmouth where the *Iris*, the *Daffodil*, and the submarines destined to attack the railway viaduct at Zeebrugge were fitted out.

The director of Naval Construction, Sir Tennyson D'Eyncourt, and the Director of Dockyards, Rear-Admiral L. E. Power, brought all their valuable knowledge, and that of their respective staffs, to bear on the problem. Much of the usual formality governing inter-departmental procedure was waived. Paper work was reduced to a minimum. The real nature of the operation was made known to few at that period. The war had taught men not to ask questions unless the information was an absolute necessity. Nevertheless many must have wondered what was afoot; special steps had to be taken, therefore, to prevent leakage of information, of which more *anon*.

CHAPTER 8

The Personnel

No naval or military training is necessary to realise that the success of any war operation is mainly dependent upon the personnel. In these days of machinery and munitions, however, we are apt to become ultra-materialistic in our imagination. We read of so many million rounds of ammunition, so many thousand tons of merchant shipping, such and such new-fangled weapons. But the necessity for efficient personnel is, after all, the crux of the whole matter. What use a ship without a crew, or an aeroplane without a pilot? Truly the question of personnel is paramount. No belligerent state ever suffered from a surplus of fighting men in the midst of a war. How strange it seemed to us in those critical days that we had ever been content to rely on an overseas expeditionary force of only 150,000 men.

The ordinary use of warships against the enemy involves no special requirements of personnel beyond those which can be foreseen when the ships are originally designed. Design naturally results from projected employment whether the design be constructional or instructional. But for the purposes of this unusual kind of operation special types of officers and men were required and special training had to be arranged for. The operation itself—in official parlance—was considered to be *hazardous*. Success would depend upon the work of the personnel to an unusual degree. This fact was early recognised.

It is difficult to define the type of men required. They should be volunteers as far as that was practicable. They must be "all out for business." In view of the hazardous nature of their enterprise it was advisable that they should be unmarried.

In the Grand Fleet alone there were many thousands of men spoiling for a fight. Nor was this surprising. During nearly four years of waiting, tuned up to the last note of efficiency, there had been only one action in which the major portion of the main fleet was engaged, and only a few smaller actions in which opportunities were available for the crews of our large ships to show their worth. But how many of the public realised the vastness of its work?—the incessant patrolling, the continual sweeps up and down and across the North Sea, with only a glimpse of an enemy vessel on the rarest occasions, and that but a momentary vision of her stern disappearing at the utmost speed as the vessel fled to her nearest port of refuge. As a blue-jacket was heard to remark, "It's always tip and run with devilish little of the tip."

The everlasting practices, manoeuvring, and drills, designed towards the attainment and upkeep of efficiency, may have been novel enough for the first few months, but the novelty soon wore off. Not that the men ever showed any sign of weariness. It was more a case of hope deferred.

I was in that fleet for three years and three months and can speak from experience. One marvelled at the spirit of the men. They were always ready for "the day"—hungry for it, praying for it. Even the theatrical entertainments, which they organised in their spare time, were brimful of topical allusions to the absent enemy.

The personnel of the Grand Fleet—I especially allude to those who had served in the Fleet from the outbreak of war—were, indeed, spoiling for a fight. They had read from time to time of the splendid actions fought by their contemporaries in other theatres of the war; it was only human that they should feel extremely envious of these others.

It must not be forgotten that the efficiency of our main fleet at the outbreak of war was mainly due to the untiring efforts of its personnel. The work of the fleet in the years immediately preceding the war had been exceedingly strenuous; very different from the sea life of a decade earlier. The days of "hurrah" cruises, when gunnery practices took second place to festivities, had long since passed. Manoeuvres, firing exercises with guns and torpedoes, night attacks and steam trials at sea were alternated with "rests" in harbour, where evolutions, drills, and instructions of all sorts, conferences and war games had kept us pretty well occupied. Admittedly, then, service in the main fleet required a high state of efficiency; an individual who fell short of this requirement was not wanted. Thus, speaking generally, the personnel of the main fleet at the outbreak of war were only there because they were considered to be deserving of a place on the efficiency roll. Yet many of these very officers and men had not seen an enemy ship since the outbreak of war. It is not difficult, therefore, to imagine their envy of those others to whom opportunities had been vouchsafed to prove their worth in action.

The choice of the personnel for our particular enterprise had to be governed, to a certain extent, by those most readily available. The question thus arose as to whether the Commander-in-Chief of the Grand Fleet, Sir David Beatty, would consent to lend any of his officers and men for the operation. The Vice-Admiral was anxious that the Grand Fleet should be given a share in this affair. The Commanders-in-Chief of the three southern dockyard ports and the Commandants of the Royal Marine Artillery and Light Infantry were also consulted; many personnel at these latter establishments would be awaiting draft in the ordinary course of events and might, therefore, be more easily spared than those from the Grand Fleet.

If the German High Seas Fleet had shown any activity it is a doubtful matter whether Sir David Beatty would have allowed his officers and men to leave the fleet. It must be understood that it was not merely a case of borrowing these men for a day or two, but for a period of several weeks, so that they could be specially trained for their somewhat unusual duties. Sir David Beatty, however, considered that the risk of rendering his ships temporarily short-handed was justified in view of the importance of our expedition. His chief difficulty lay in the matter of selection. Owing to the necessity of secrecy he could not issue an ordinary memorandum to all and sundry stating our object and asking for volunteers. So each flag officer was requested to produce a certain number of officers and men from his own particular squadron. Likely individuals were to be asked if they were prepared to undertake something "hazardous"; no further intimation as to the nature of the enterprise was to be promulgated. Similar methods of selection were adopted at the naval and marine depots. It is not difficult to imagine the buzz of excitement which passed through each ship when rumour suggested that there was something afoot.

If the nature of the operation had been divulged and volunteers requested, there would have been twenty thousand names sent in. That was the commander-in-chief's own opinion. But the secret must be safeguarded. So the selection was made by the officers—so many men from each ship, seamen, stokers, and marines. At that stage the selected men knew nothing except that they were required for something "hazardous."

Life in the fleet was not altogether free from hazard in the ordinary course of events. With one's living space surrounded by the most destructive of high explosives in close proximity, perhaps a matter of inches, with the seas either mine-strewn or, in the absence of mines, containing lurking submarines, with the ever-present danger of collision between vessels steaming at high speed without lights on the darkest night, it cannot be said that naval life in war-time carries an insignificant insurance premium.

But the coming operation was something different. It was declared to be "hazardous." If the usual life at sea as described above carried no such descriptive title, the word "hazardous" meant much.

Though little enough was known as to the business ahead, it was sufficient to raise the envy of the great majority of men who were not fortunate enough to be selected. One could well imagine the little knots of men who gathered together in the evening and discoursed on the injustice of being left behind. The intense interest with which the special training of the chosen few was watched could almost be felt. For boat-pulling, physical drill, and route marching, commenced immediately, were the order of the day, just to prepare the men for the more intensive training to follow.

A good deal of consideration had to be given to the choice of officers. The question of seniority of the blockship commanders gave food for thought. Each of these vessels would also require at least three executive officers. The chance of the captain being bowled over early in the proceedings was none too small. So the conning and steering arrangements and the whole system of command in each ship was to be triplicated. Thus each officer must be ready to take over the responsibility of command at a moment's notice. Similar considerations affected the choice of officers for the storming vessels. Still further executive officers were required for charge of the storming parties. Engineer officers must be forthcoming for these special vessels. At first all these officers, just as in the case of the men, knew nothing of the circumstances under which they were required, except that it was for a hazardous business.

The majority of the officers and men for the blockships and storming vessels were drawn from the Grand Fleet; most of the remainder were obtained from the naval depots.

When visiting the United States of America at the end of 1918 I was often asked to explain why American naval personnel were not included in the enterprise. On more than one occasion there were strong evidences of disagreeable insinuations having been circulated through pro-German influences. It was suggested that relations between the British and American squadrons in the Grand Fleet left much to be desired, and that feelings of jealousy had caused us to decline American assistance for the purposes of our enterprise. Nothing could be further from the truth. The American battle squadron was never referred to as such. They formed the "sixth" battle squadron of the Grand Fleet. Their ships and ours constituted *one* fleet, working for a single end and guided by common sentiment. For the furtherance of successful co-operation the Americans had literally "thrown overboard" everything that could weaken the combination. Their signalling arrangements, tactical manoeuvring, and special gunnery methods had all been brought into line with ours. The unselfishness and sacrifice involved can only be fully appreciated by members of our own sea service.

From the day of their arrival the Americans had been actuated with but one purpose, namely, that of leaving no stone unturned to enhance their value as a re-enforcement. Admiral Rodman, who commanded the Sixth Battle Squadron, was ever in close touch with Admiral Beatty. The genuine friendship between his squadron and the rest of the fleet will never be forgotten in our service. There was but one fleet. But the question of utilising their personnel for our immediate affair was governed by something more than cordiality and co-operation. Secrecy had to be maintained. If we had transferred a few score American officers and men to Chatham, where there were no American ships, for special training with our own, curiosity would have been aroused at once, comment would have followed and, in a very short while, the secret might have been public property.

Admiral Beatty and Admiral Rodman had discussed the whole subject and decided that American assistance was inadvisable for the reason given. I was also asked if it was true that an American officer had come over to Zeebrugge in *Vindictive* as a stowaway. It was not true.

Admiral Rodman had previously held an important post in connection with the Panama Canal, and he let us have the benefit of his experiences with regard to questions of salvage. Nearly a year later he was kind enough to attend a large meeting with the author in New York, where, in no uncertain language, he nailed the pro-German insinuations to the board.

Amongst the first officers to leave the Grand Fleet were those destined to command the blockships; the fitting out of the latter had

105

already commenced. The usual custom concerning seniority for command of light cruisers was waived, these officers, whose ranks varied from a Commander to a Lieutenant of less than three years' standing, being selected from those available mainly by virtue of their character and capability. Those selected to command *Iris* and *Daffodil* were also sent south as early as practicable. On arrival at Dover they were told the "secret." It was probably self-control combined with the somewhat artificial reserve arising from good discipline which enabled them to refrain from giving vent to their feelings of elation.

One of them told me that he had the sensation of being released from prison; the opportunity of being able to show his worth had come at last. Each officer read through the "plan" so as to make himself acquainted with the broad outlines of the whole enterprise. One of the blockship commanders expressed the opinion that the blocking of Ostende would be "easy meat" compared to the undertaking at Zeebrugge, and he earnestly requested that he might command a blockship destined for the latter place. This request was granted. Incidentally his opinion was wrong. Subsequently, thanks to his own splendid efforts, he caused his comparison between the two places to appear all the more erroneous by assisting to make the blocking of Zeebrugge seem relatively simple.

The main ideas governing the preparatory work, as already stated, had been evolved under the direction of Admiral Keyes. Many questions, however, of a more local description remained to be decided on the spot. The blockship officers, therefore, thoroughly investigated every detail which bore on their duties and devised many local improvements, especially in connection with the handling of the vessels.

They left nothing undone to ensure a successful issue of their efforts. No other subject held any interest for them in those days. Just how to take their ships to their allotted positions—that was their one consideration. The question of being rescued after their work was completed held a very secondary place. Perhaps the rescue vessels might be able to do something towards it. Perhaps not. Anyway, that mattered nothing in comparison with the crucial point. And so they schemed and discussed and organised and tested. And what a grand reward they obtained for their labours!

I should like to mention in passing that the first blockship officer to come south was Lieutenant Ivor B. Franks, in whose hands much of the early work connected with fitting out the blockships was placed, with splendid results which reflected great credit on him.

He commanded *Iphigenia* during the first two attempts made against Zeebrugge, but, most unluckily for him, he developed appendicitis just before the final attempt. It was largely due to his earnest entreaties that Admiral Keyes gave the command to the previous second-in-command, who was a Lieutenant of only one year standing. Once again Lieutenant Franks, for whom we all felt the greatest sympathy, had shown the value of his judgment.

During this period the constructive work on the ships proceeded apace.

The *Vindictive* rapidly changed her appearance. Every unessential fitting that could be removed in the time at our disposal was wafted away. The foremast was cut off just above the fighting-top. The mainmast was removed altogether and a large portion of it was fitted horizontally across the deck, extending several feet over the port side of the ship, as a bumpkin designed to prevent the port propeller from bumping against the Mole at Zeebrugge.

Special fenders were fitted on the ship's side to prevent damage to the latter when secured to the Mole, and a fender of colossal proportions was added to the port side of the forecastle for the express purpose of bumping the Mole on arrival.

Other alterations and additions have been described in Chapter 5.

H.M.S. *Hindustan*, Captain A. P. Davidson, D.S.O., was lent as a depot vessel for our officers and men who had been concentrated at Chatham. There was then no living accommodation on board *Vindictive* or in the blockships.

The vice-admiral took an early opportunity of assembling all the officers and making the whole plan known to them collectively. The secret was to be kept from the men until later, in accordance with the principle of never divulging a secret to anybody except those to whom the information is indispensable.

The personnel specially required for storming the Mole at Zeebrugge were divided into three main parties, viz., Seamen storming parties under the command of Captain Henry C. Halahan, D.S.O., R.N., Marine storming parties (drawn from the 4th Battalion) under the command of Lieutenant-Colonel Bertram N. Elliot, D.S.O., R.M.L.I., and a demolition party consisting of both Seamen and Marines under the command of Lieutenant-Commander Cecil C. Dickinson, R.N.

The Marine Infantrymen were put through intensive training at one of the southern depots; this training was arranged and personally supervised by Lieutenant-Colonel Elliot, whose powers of imagination and organisation were of a high order and whose optimism was very encouraging. He was tremendously enthusiastic from the first moment when he was let into the secret. As second-in-command of the Naval Forces in Servia he had previously rendered splendid service and had been awarded the D.S.O. After the fall of Belgrade I believe that he had traversed the entire country on foot in his endeavour to help his force to safety. I remember a lady telling me that she and her friends had been much interested on recent nights in watching a large party of Marines indulging in peculiar antics on a hill opposite her house; also that the hill was partly covered with strips of canvas in a seemingly aimless fashion. I expressed my astonishment at the strange proceeding. Incidentally the canvas strips were laid out to represent different portions of Zeebrugge Mole, though, at that period, the men believed they represented some enemy position elsewhere.

The Marine Artillerymen, destined to man the howitzers and some other guns in *Vindictive*, were trained at another depot.

The seamen were largely trained at Chatham under military supervision and advice; the excellence of this training received a well-deserved tribute in the official despatch. The demolition parties were also trained at Chatham.

Training in night fighting was the main idea. Instruction in bombing, bayonet fighting, and all types of trench raiding was given. The men believed that they were required for some special service in France; their enthusiasm was unbounded.

Taking everything into consideration and looking at the operation of attacking the Mole from a general point of view, it was not dissimilar to a trench raid on a large scale. The preparatory bombardment, the rush "over the top," the probability of encountering barbed wire, the descent to the main level of the Mole, the hand-to-hand fighting in the dark, and finally the clearing of dug-outs, all combined to liken that phase of the operation to one of the many night raids with which the military were so well acquainted on the western front. The senior officers of the Seamen and Marine storming parties had both gained much experience of such fighting ashore. It was to be a raid of the first water, a super-raid. The military officers were most enthusiastic about our men. They declared that these men could carry any position. For they were all picked men; and even so some of them were weeded out as not quite reaching high-water mark at the game. It was generally conceded that the Hun, wherever he was to come to close quarters

LIEUT.-COL. BERTRAM N.
ELLIOT, D.S.O., R.M.L.I.

LIEUT.-COM. ARTHUR L.
HARRISON, R.N.

WING-COM. FRANK A.
BROCK, R.N.A.S.

CAPTAIN HENRY C.
HALAHAN, D.S.O., R.N.

with such antagonists, would have an uncomfortable evening.

It has been mentioned above that special personnel were not required for the large majority of vessels which were already in full commission and employed on active duty in the Dover Command. The personnel required for the blockships and storming vessels and for other special purposes amounted to eighty-six officers and sixteen hundred and ninety-eight men; of these, seven hundred and fifty, in the aggregate, were drawn from the Royal Marines.

Having been working in the Plans Department of the Admiralty when the operation was originally thought out under Admiral Keyes, my further services had been lent to him, after he took over the Command at Dover, in connection with the operational staff work. Very much to my delight I had then been offered the billet of navigator of the expedition, and my duties were to include those of placing *Vindictive* alongside the Mole. The vice-admiral originally proposed to direct the operation from on board *Vindictive*, but was forced to the conclusion that he could do so more satisfactorily from a destroyer, thus avoiding the possibility of being confined to any single position in the area of the attack. In the vice-admiral's absence Captain Halahan, appointed in command of the seamen storming parties, became the Senior Executive Officer in the ship. It was pointed out that that fact would result in the unusual case of the Senior Officer on board not being responsible for the handling of the ship.

Captain Halahan would not even listen to any suggestion of difficulty arising from such a situation, and, I am anxious to record this fact, he proposed that his acting rank of Captain should be transferred from himself to me, so that the officer responsible for handling the vessel should also be the Senior Executive Officer on board in accordance with the usual service custom; in other words that he should be made junior to myself. This proposal was typical of Halahan, who, in my opinion, was one of the finest fellows that our Service ever knew. His death brought an irreparable loss to the navy. Throughout the greater part of the war he had been in command of the naval guns on the northern front and within field-gun range of the enemy for no less than three years.

He had fought in most of the great battles on that part of the Allied lines. A more efficient, earnest, upright, and altogether large-minded officer never fought for his country or paid the supreme sacrifice more readily. The days which we spent together working at the details of the enterprise, his wonderful enthusiasm, and his certainty of success are unforgettable. I feel that I could not continue this story without recording my unqualified admiration for this splendid officer.

Needless to say, it was unnecessary to carry his proposal into effect, for his unselfishness had served to guarantee that all questions of rank were immaterial where the only thing that really mattered was the attainment of our object.

I regret that my lack of literary ability prevents my doing justice to such men.

It would be difficult for anybody to speak too highly of Wing-Commander Frank A. Brock. He was a rare personality. An inventive genius, than whom the country had no better, it was his brain that differentiated this blocking enterprise from all previous attempts in history in one most important particular. The difficulty of reaching the destination in the face of a strenuous opposition had hitherto brought failure, but he provided an antidote in the form of a satisfactory artificial fog designed to protect the blockships from the enemy's guns during the critical period of approach. That in itself was a wonderful achievement, but his inventive mind was not satisfied therewith. To him we owed the special flares intended for turning darkness into light.

A special buoy was wanted—one that would automatically provide its own light on being thrown into the water. Brock made so little of the problem that he produced such a buoy, designed, constructed, and ready for use in less than twenty-four hours. Special signal lights were required. Brock produced them. Flame projectors, far exceeding anything hitherto known, were mooted. Brock produced them also. No matter what our requirements were Brock was undefeated. With a highly scientific brain he possessed extraordinary knowledge of almost any subject. He had travelled much and could tell you all that was worth knowing of any country from Patagonia to Spitzbergen. He was no mean authority on old prints and books, was also a keen philatelist, and was blessed with a remarkable memory. Wherever he went he carried with him a pocket edition of the New Testament, which was his favourite possession; his knowledge of the contents was quite unique.

And with it all he was a great shot and an all-round sportsman. His fine physique was well remembered by many a Rugby footballer from the days when he played in the pack of one of the leading club fifteens. His geniality and humour were hard to beat. But of all his qualities, optimism perhaps held first place. At times we, who were far from being pessimistic, thought his optimism excessive, but it was justified absolutely with regard to the success of the enterprise.

Sad to relate, the only occasion on which I can remember his optimism failing to carry him through was connected with his own personal safety. He had telephoned up to Halahan in our office and mentioned having broken a looking-glass. "That means seven years bad luck," said Halahan, in a jocular spirit. "Never mind," came the instant reply, "it shows that I'm going to live for another seven years, anyway."

Both Brock and Halahan had done so much to ensure our success, it was indeed sad that they did not survive long enough to see the results.

My readers will excuse me, I feel sure, for bringing such personalities to their notice. It is very difficult to continue the story without writing of many others to whom we owed so much in the preparatory work. But there will be a chance of mentioning some of them later on, when we come to the actual description of the fight.

CHAPTER 9

The Waiting Period

At last all constructive preparations were completed; the various ships and small craft were commissioned and concentrated at their respective starting-points. The blockships and *Vindictive* steamed out to the loneliest of anchorages in the Swin Deep, situated about eight miles south of Clacton, Essex. It was a curious looking squadron that steamed down the Medway that day, the blockships with their funnels looming extra large in the absence of masts and the *Vindictive* with her gangways protruding into mid-air like almonds in the side of a tipsy cake. The *Hindustan* looked respectable enough. She was mother to us all and her captain was a very tolerant and helpful father.

The *Iris* and *Daffodil* joined us almost immediately. The Marines embarked a few days later. They had been sent to a southern port on the understanding that they were off to France; the officers alone knew the truth. They duly boarded the waiting transport with stores, ammunition, and baggage, the latter labelled to a French port. They must have wondered where they would sleep that night. The transport duly left harbour and headed for the French coast, but presently altered course in a most unusual manner. Word was passed round that the course was peculiar; all crowded on deck in their endeavour to solve the problem. It was a misty day with the rain coming down in torrents; the land was soon obscured. The officers chuckled at the general bewilderment, but held their peace. At last the transport eased down and finally stopped engines. Out of the mist loomed the *Iris* and *Daffodil*, into which vessels the Marines were transferred.

A second voyage was then commenced, but it was not of long duration. Other ships presently hove in sight, and strange craft they appeared. Cruisers without masts and another looking like a home for lost coal-tips. These were the blockships and *Vindictive*. Then appeared a recognisable vessel—th *Hindustan*. Some of the Marines went to the latter, the remainder to *Vindictive*. I can well remember the astonished look on their faces as these men boarded my ship. Even the heavy downpour of rain seemed to be unnoticed. One man remarked as he came on board, "Well, it's darned good to be aboard a blessed something, but I'm blowed if I know what she is."

That day and the next were spent in settling down. On the evening of the second day the men were told the secret. In *Vindictive* they all mustered on the quarter-deck and after bridge. Sunset had long since been heralded by the time-honoured bugle call. The evening twilight was fading rapidly. There was a stillness in the air which seemed to be reflected from the tense attitude of the assembled men. One could have heard the proverbial pin drop. It was my duty to take them into our confidence. After the nature of the enterprise had been outlined a few sentences were sufficient to illustrate the task allotted to the *Vindictive*. It seemed advisable to point out that many other operations of a hectic nature, besides those of the blockships and storming vessels, were to be attempted. I emphasised this by mentioning that if, during our visit to Zeebrugge Mole, they heard a thunderous explosion they could say to themselves, "That's one of them." These words came back to me afterwards, as I shall relate in due course.

As soon as the business in hand had been promulgated it was considered advisable to exert a very rigid censorship on outgoing mails. Correspondence was permitted, but strictly on the understanding that the letters would be retained at one of the mail offices until the operation had been completed. This regulation was modified later owing to the waiting period being unexpectedly prolonged. Field post-cards were then issued and could be posted in the ordinary manner. There were the usual sentences, such as "I am quite well," "I am not quite well," "I have received your letter," "I have not received your letter," etc., in the style of the French exercise books of one's youth. Such postcards were familiar enough amongst the military, but were a novelty to most of us; they caused a good deal of amusement, especially when the sender omitted to delete the sentences which misrepresented his feelings towards the intended recipient.

All shore leave was stopped; even cases of serious illness or accident would have to go to *Hindustan*, and remain there, instead of to a shore hospital.

Secrecy was absolutely essential, but not always easy to ensure. At our anchorage it was comparatively simple, but elsewhere we had to depend more upon trust in our fellow men than rigid regulation. The secret was well kept, and fortunately so. Surprise is mainly dependent upon secrecy. For if information of an impending attack becomes known there can be no hope of taking the enemy unawares.

I wonder how many people realise the necessity for keeping rumours to themselves during war. Rumours must be either true or untrue. If untrue they are not worth passing on. If true, then untold harm may result from repetition. Suppose for a moment that the impending operation at Zeebrugge had become a topic of general conversation. In due course the information would have reached our enemies and the expedition would almost certainly have met with complete disaster. The lives of many picked officers and men would have been lost, and the whole affair would have gone down to history as a fiasco. Under such circumstances each person who had repeated the rumour on its way to the enemy would have been morally guilty of manslaughter—surely that is not an exaggerated deduction.

Alas, human nature is often weak. There is some modicum of satisfaction in showing superior knowledge to one's neighbour.

The Japanese, in their war with Russia, set the world a wonderful example of silence. After losing a high percentage of their battleship strength not a word was spoken and the world remained in ignorance for many months.

A writer—I think it was Chesterton—once suggested that memorials should be erected in recognition of negative qualities. If that idea were adopted I wonder how many tablets would be found to state that *"Here Mr. So-and-so heard a rumour and did not repeat it to his friends."*

When dealing, in Chapter 8, with the question of the type of personnel required for an enterprise of this description, I mentioned that they should be volunteers as far as that was practicable. The reader may perhaps consider that the meaning of the word "volunteer" was being unduly "stretched" if the men were to be unaware of the real nature of the operation until they were already trained and actually standing by to go across. Nevertheless, the men were volunteers in the true meaning of the word. Let me explain. It was of great importance that no officer or man should take part in the enterprise unless he was "for it," heart and soul.

So, as soon as the secret had been made known and the men were thoroughly aware of all the difficulties and risks involved, it was given out that any officers or men who wished to withdraw could do so. It was fully recognised that they might have private reasons for wishing to avoid risks of an unusually high degree. We were not concerned with the nature of such private reasons and we wished to make certain that no pressure was brought to bear for the sake of influencing their decision. They were, therefore, informed that any individual who desired to withdraw should merely give in his name and remain behind. They were further told that no reasons would be asked and, to make doubly certain, that no reasons or explanations of any description would be allowed under any circumstances whatever. That was fair enough. Not a single officer or man withdrew.

In *Vindictive* there were several men, of non-combatant rating, who, in the ordinary course of events, were destined to be left behind when the expedition started. They comprised cooks, stewards, canteen-servers, and the like. Some of them were not even naval men, but merely there as representatives of, or workers for, the firm which provided the canteen. They naturally knew the secret and they openly expressed their desire to remain in the ship so as not to miss the fun. We decided to consider such requests. Extra men would come in handy for dealing with the wounded as well as for assisting with the commissariat. Eventually it was decreed that those who volunteered to come over with us should give in their names.

As far as I can remember every one of them volunteered. It must be realised that these were not fighting men; their sole training had been that of the camp follower. Small chance of meeting the enemy in hand-to-hand combat would come their way. The work of tending wounded between decks—we already had our full quota of stretcher bearers for working in more exposed positions—and that of providing the necessary sustenance carries little glory or excitement. Nevertheless, these men volunteered and they afterwards rendered splendid service.

Take another case. When the *Vindictive* was fitting out at Chatham there was an officer on board, remaining from the previous commission, for temporary duty. He knew nothing definite of the coming operation, but evidently thought a good deal. His method of volunteering was to remark: "I don't know, sir, what the old ship is going to do, but it looks like dirty work and I should like to be there." It was vulgar, but expressive. That officer remained with us, and afterwards covered himself with glory.

In the blockships there were also incidents which served to illustrate this thirst for dangerous employment.

Owing to the difficulties of rescue work, as has already been explained, it was decided to send each blockship to her final destination with the smallest possible number of crew; the number in each case amounted to fifty-three. Thirty-four extra men, however, were required for getting each ship to the edge of the danger zone, whilst the fifty-three on whom the final run depended were resting. That meant that in each ship thirty-four men, who knew all about the coming event, who had experienced much hard work and considerable discomfort, were to be disembarked just when the fight was about to begin. One can imagine their feelings, but questions of individual disappointment could not be allowed to affect the plan of action. The disembarkation of these "surplus" crews was to be carried out with the aid of small craft specially detailed for the purpose. In the *Intrepid* one day there was a minor edition of a mutiny. Several men demanded to see their captain. The latter ordered them to state their business. "Well, sir," said the spokesman, "me and my mates understands as how some of the crew have got to leave the ship on the way across to Zeebruggy. The 'jaunty,' (master-at-arms), says it's us lot and we ain't a-goin' to leave."

Their captain explained the situation. He pointed out that there would be too many for one rescue boat and that overloading might lead to the loss of everybody. But the men were inclined to be adamant. Finally their captain decided to take a spare gun's crew and ordered the "mutineers" to draw lots for the honour. The sequel is worth recording even if it necessitates anticipating the main story. When this particular blockship stopped during the oversea voyage, the craft detailed to take off her surplus crew failed to appear alongside—she had broken down. So the whole crew went to Zeebrugge and, extraordinary to relate, every soul of them was rescued.

This voluntary spirit was very heartening to all concerned. I have only mentioned a few specific cases, but there were many others of a similar description. It is no exaggeration to say that once the men knew the secret they were more than mere volunteers—they were *determined* to come across with us.

It must not be assumed that all was in readiness as soon as the ships, having been duly fitted out, had assembled at the Swin and embarked their personnel. Much remained to be done. Steam trials, gunnery practices, adjustment of compasses, and tests of all the special material were indulged in. Handling the ships from both the main and auxiliary conning positions, testing communications, manipulating the grappling irons and Mole gangways, drilling the guns' crews and am-

117

munition parties, training the stretcher parties, and giving instruction in first-aid also helped to keep us fully occupied.

Of course it was impossible to practise sinking blockships or taking storming vessels alongside breakwaters. Breakwaters are only to be found in such public places as Dover, Portland, etc.; it would have been inadvisable to publish our intentions in such a manner. Thus, as far as these special vessels were concerned, the seamanship difficulties could not be lessened by proper realistic practice. The suggestion that we might use *Hindustan* as the Mole did not appeal to us much, especially as the *Vindictive* was originally built for ramming and consequently had a very large ram; we had no desire to start badly by sinking one of our own battleships.

The life on board *Vindictive*, uncomfortable as it was owing to our numbers greatly exceeding the normal complement, was not altogether devoid of humour. As one walked round the ship there would be a bloodcurdling yell and a party of men with fixed bayonets would charge round a corner and hurl themselves upon an imaginary foe. The steel helmets, gas masks, and respirators gave these men a weird appearance, such as one is unaccustomed to see on board ship. Some carried *knobkerries*—loaded ash sticks; others grenades, flame projectors, or machine-guns. There was no half-heartedness about the men. Clearly enough they meant business; we had no misgivings about the result. Those days were busy indeed. When work had finished for the day opportunities for sports arose, and there were occasional concerts in the evenings. The tugs-of-war evoked much friendly rivalry between the various sea regiments—the seamen, stokers, Marine Light Infantry, and Marine Artillery. One afternoon a boxing tournament took place and the fighting augured well for the near future.

One day, two officers from a blockship paid a call on the *Vindictive*. Visiting cards were not required; we were obviously At Home. But we were quite mystified when one of the officers produced a small chunk of iron and remarked that he had brought it on board in case we ran short of ammunition. He then explained that, during the passage from his vessel, some description of explosive missile had burst within a few yards of his dinghy, and the piece produced had fallen into the boat. Incidentally he accused *Vindictive* of firing the missile, but we pleaded not guilty or alternatively, as the lawyers say, asserted that he had no right to cross the firing line! Apparently it was a portion of a bomb of sorts fired from one of the ships, fortunately without any other result than to cause considerable merriment to the occupants of the dinghy.

Such an incident in the ordinary course of events would have led to very pertinent enquiries, but we were too much preoccupied with the business in hand to worry about such trifles.

The thoughts uppermost in our minds concerned the chances of favourable weather conditions. The barometers came in for an amount of tapping which was not calculated to improve the instruments. We all became weather prophets those days. Many and varied were the daily forecasts.

One night we rolled unpleasantly in a heavy gale and soon after midnight a small vessel was seen firing distress signals. This provided an excellent opportunity for testing our illuminating rockets, by the aid of which we observed a tug struggling to grapple a lighter which was dragging its anchors. The worst aspect of heavy weather was the consequent expenditure of fuel which we could ill spare. Thanks to the captain of *Hindustan* our period of waiting was made as comfortable as we could have hoped. He was indefatigable in arranging diversions for our amusement and in keeping us informed of the latest war news. Each day brought more serious reports from the battle front in France and made us all the more anxious to give the enemy a nasty shock whilst cheering up our own troops. During the late evenings most of us sought for quiet corners where we could write letters. I think we all found those letters were very difficult, but one's feelings at such a time are of too private a nature to bear analysis.

Captain Halahan used to discuss every point of the coming enterprise with me; his insight and keenness were most marked. We often talked far into the night and always came to the conclusion that however difficult the operation might be for our forces we would not be in the German's shoes for anything. We had a plasticine model of the Mole chiefly constructed from the data obtainable from aerial photographs. Colonel Elliot, commanding the Marine storming parties, and his officers often joined us. We all realised the difficulty of berthing the storming vessels at exactly the desired position alongside the Mole and endeavoured to make the storming plan as elastic as possible. The primary consideration—as far as that phase of the operation was concerned—appeared to be that the ships should secure to the Mole *somewhere*.

The mere presence of the ships, combined with all the attendant noise and fireworks, would create a diversion of no mean order. The actual landing on the Mole and the occurrences that followed would increase the diversion which had already commenced. With regard to *Vindictive* we originally aimed at securing her alongside the Mole, heading to the westward, with her stern seventy yards westward of the three-gun battery. It was realised that there might be considerable difficulty in recognising one's exact position alongside the outer wall relative to objects on the Mole itself. Eventually, as will be described later, the ship secured to the westward of the designed position, but, though the actual fighting on the Mole was affected, the main object of the diversion was attained.

The blockship officers paid us many visits and we were all very cheery. No less than four old shipmates had come down from my late ship in the Grand Fleet—H.M.S. *Emperor of India*. It was a curious fact that all five of us were in the thick of the affair and all survived. One commanded the *Intrepid* with another as one of his officers. One commanded the *Daffodil*. One was on board *Iris*. Their services will be mentioned later.

One night we had an *Emperor of India* dinner on board the *Intrepid*. A storeroom of sorts did duty for a mess and I think the sub-lieutenant cooked the dinner. There was no serious talk that evening and I don't think we forgot to drink confusion to the enemy. When we broke up the party we little knew that we should be conveying that confusion within twenty-four hours.

I have described our life at the Swin in some detail, but what of the other one hundred and fifty-four craft which were not with us? They were busily preparing too, but, for the most part, were actively engaged in their ordinary Dover Patrol duties at the same time. Little peace can have come their way. The aircraft, too, were very actively employed. Day after day they brought us back photographs of Ostende and Zeebrugge, taken at great risk with a fine contempt for danger. If we wanted the details of any portion of the Mole it was forthcoming, in the shape of an aerial photograph, in a few hours. This work was carried out by the 61st Wing of the Royal Air Force. Special cameras were used for this purpose; I believe that they had been designed by the previous Vice-Admiral at Dover. We studied those photographs with the aid of stereoscopes and magnifying glasses by the hour.

But photography was not the only thing required of the aircraft. They had to prepare for the bombing attacks which would provide further diversions; preparation required much observational work both by day and by night. The aircraft detailed for the bombing attacks were drawn from the 65th Wing of the Royal Air Force. These flyers were fine fellows and no less determined to make the affair successful than the rest of us.

Many of the smaller craft were commanded by officers of the Royal Naval Reserve and Royal Naval Volunteer Reserve. I have mentioned elsewhere that the whole success of the operation might, at a critical period, depend upon the action of a single unit. Instructions leaving a high degree of initiative to the recipient were, therefore, necessary. Clear appreciations followed by rapid decisions were required. The vice-admiral emphasised that point most strongly. He trusted his men, whether Reserve or Volunteer or otherwise. His trust was not misplaced; all these officers commanding the small craft behaved most admirably, exactly as was expected by those who knew their worth.

CHAPTER 10

Meteorological and Tidal Conditions

The periods during which the conditions would be favourable for our enterprise depended upon various factors. The extent to which we could make use of any particular date during one of those periods depended, in turn, upon meteorological conditions.

It has been shown elsewhere that, for the purpose of utilising the artificial fog, we required a wind blowing more or less toward the Belgian coast from seaward. It was also necessary for the wind to be light so that the small craft would not be hampered by rough seas. Light winds are often accompanied by fog, especially in the North Sea, and fog would be a serious obstacle. Rain would be detrimental to the use of aircraft.

The depths in the entrances to the canals at Zeebrugge and Ostende were such that the blockships could only navigate during the period around high water. It was, therefore, necessary for the vessels to arrive at about that state of the tide.

Again, it was essential to carry out the operation during the night for reasons already mentioned. In this respect, however, the word operation must not be used too loosely; the periods of approach to the objectives and of retirement therefrom must both be included in that term. The approach had to be undiscovered till the latest possible moment. That necessitated darkness throughout the approach, which latter may be considered as comprising the passage during the last twenty miles of the oversea voyage. Obviously the greater part of the whole passage conducted during darkness the less would be the chance of losing the element of surprise.

Likewise the retirement must be made before daylight if the concentration of the shore batteries was to be avoided. I have already stated that the German guns could make things very uncomfortable

Specimen Diagram for ascertaining
Available Period

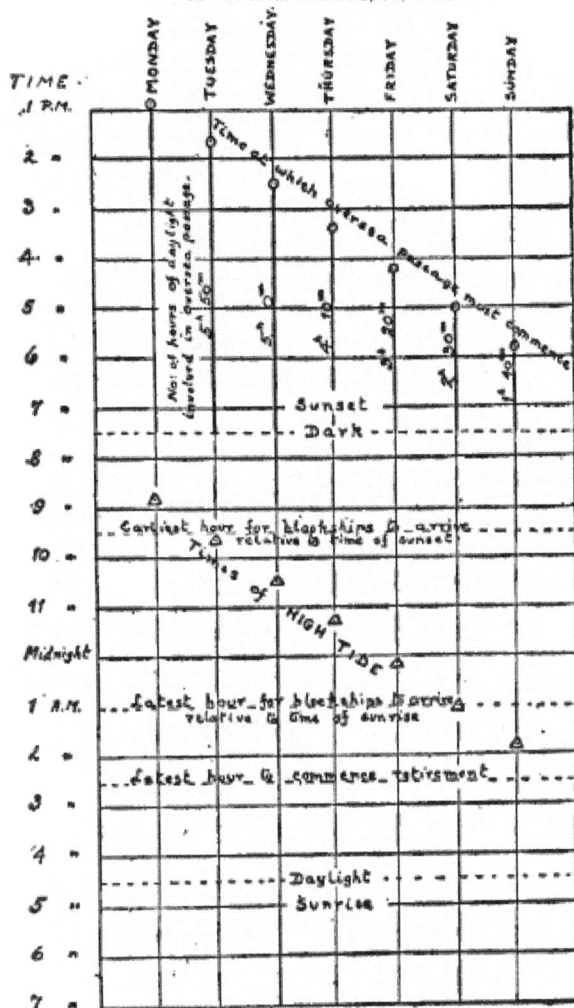

TIME P.M. — MONDAY, TUESDAY, WEDNESDAY, THURSDAY, FRIDAY, SATURDAY, SUNDAY

Time at which oversea passage must commence

No. of hours of daylight involved in oversea passage. 5.50

Sunset
Dark

Earliest hour for blockships to arrive relative to time of sunset

Time of HIGH TIDE

Latest hour for blockships to arrive relative to time of sunrise

Latest hour to commence retirement

Daylight
Sunrise

Explanation of Diagram.

Data on which Diagram is based

Sunset · 7 p.m.	Daylight · 4.30 a.m.
Dark · 7.30 "	Sunrise · 5.0 a.m.

Duration of Oversea Passage · 6 hours
" " Approach · 2 "
" " Attack · 1½ "
" " Retirement · 2 "

Time of High Tide indicated by △
Note · Blockships to arrive at or near High Tide.

Conclusions

The Period Available is
Tuesday to Saturday (both incl)
On Monday High Tide is too early
On Sunday High Tide is too late

Notes.

On Tuesday nearly 6 hours of the oversea passage must be made in daylight. On Saturday there is no time to spare incase of late arrival.

for ships up to a maximum distance of fifteen to twenty miles, provided that the ships could be seen. The retiring forces should, therefore, be outside that range before there was sufficient daylight to see so far; the latter state of visibility would obtain at least half an hour before sunrise. Allowing a speed of about ten knots for retirement, this meant that the ships must leave the coast about two and a half hours before sunrise after completing the operation. The attack itself was expected to continue for about one and a half hours. The reader does not require to be an advanced mathematician to realise that the attack must commence not later than about four hours before sunrise, that is, during the middle portion of the night. Of course, the attack was the all-important matter; any question of safe retirement must be a secondary consideration. Nevertheless, the question of retirement, similarly to that of rescuing the blockships' crews, had to be taken into account.

From the foregoing it will be seen that the attack should be preceded and followed by a considerable period of darkness, and should more or less coincide with the time of high tide. The latter only occurs about every twelve hours and takes place roughly fifty minutes later each day. The number of consecutive days on which high tide would occur in the middle portion of the night was, therefore, very limited.

With regard to visibility, as far as naval operations are concerned, strong moonlight is almost as disadvantageous as daylight. Half the nights per month may be termed moonlight nights in that respect. The state of the moon on any particular night is known beforehand, the state of the clouds affecting moonlight may change from hour to hour.

Just one more calculation. In mid-April the period sunset to sunrise is about eleven hours in length. Allowing two hours for the approach-passage through the danger zone, one and a half hours for the attack, and two hours for the retirement (to be completed half an hour before sunrise), it follows that the maximum number of after-sunset hours available for the open sea passage would amount to five. That was the best possible condition for us, but could only be utilised if high water occurred about four hours before sunrise. If high tide occurred any later our time of arrival would necessarily be later and our retirement could not be completed before daylight. If high tide occurred any earlier our time of arrival must be earlier, in which case there would be less dark hours available for our open sea passage on the way across.

The length of the open sea passage would be approximately six hours. Thus even on the most favourable date, some of the open sea passage would have to be made in broad daylight. Six days before that (the tide being five hours earlier) the whole of the open sea passage would have to be made in daylight, only the approach-passage, *i.e.*, the last two hours of the whole trip, taking place after sunset.

A rather complicated set of conditions, astronomical, tidal, and meteorological, was thus required.

It was almost too much to expect that everything would be favourable during the possible period; it is practically certain that a commander who refused to move until all conditions were exactly as desired would never accomplish anything. Nevertheless we sincerely hoped that fortune would be kind to us.

The men were kept informed of the chances as forecast from the current weather conditions; their eagerness for favourable predictions was manifest. There is much advantage to be gained by a commander taking his men into his confidence. In this particular case the men realised that leakage of information would entail disaster; that was sufficient to ensure that the confidence would be respected; the rigorous censorship was there to make doubly certain. It is always more irksome for those who wait in ignorance than for those who know the reasons for delay. So after prayers each morning the latest forecast was divulged, other items of interest were made known, and the keenness of the men was maintained.

CHAPTER 11

The Orders and Instructions

The work of drafting, reproducing, and distributing the necessary orders and instructions to the large number of craft concerned was not so simple as it may sound. The amount of instructions required in an operation of this sort can only be appreciated by those who have had experience of staff work during war. The command to "carry on" is only applicable when the means have been provided and the manner of its use has been made known.

To mention a few of the items: Separate orders for the oversea voyage were required for each squadron destined to make the passage independently of the remainder. Others were needed for the voyage of the main force, others to cover the aerial attacks and the long-range bombardments. The supporting squadrons must have their instructions. Still further orders were designed to deal with the period of "approach." Then there were those for the main attack on the Mole, for the demolition work, for the destruction of the railway viaduct, and for the proceedings of the artificial-fog craft; also those for the blockships and the rescue work. The retirement required its own share. Even now we have not mentioned those designed to meet possible eventualities, such as encountering enemy vessels *en route*, or returning to harbour if postponement of the enterprise was necessary.

Having decided *where* and *how* things should be done, the remaining question was *when* they should take place. The operation with its various phases and diversions could not be carried out on the go-as-you-please principle. Every item needed to be carefully fitted in to suit the remainder. The timing of each event was of paramount importance. A long-range bombardment or an aerial attack, if delayed, might destroy our own vessels. The blowing up of the viaduct was calculated to render *hors de combat* all human beings within a certain

126

distance—our own men on the Mole must not be endangered by it. It would be useless for the blockships to arrive before the fire of the Mole batteries had been suitably diverted. Aerial bombers flying at a hundred miles per hour could not accompany the ships steaming at about one-tenth of that speed. The line of fire from the bombarding vessels could not very well coincide with our approach course, hence the necessity for the monitors to take up independent positions. And so on. How could a satisfactory synchronisation of events be arranged?—that was the problem.

There were only two methods to consider: firstly, that of centralised command by signal; secondly, that of working in accordance with a prearranged time table.

The former method was obviously impracticable. Signals passed by either the wireless or visual method, during the approach, would make our presence known to the enemy and thus preclude all chance of taking the latter by surprise. After the attack had commenced signals would be impracticable for obvious reasons, chief amongst them being the deafening noise and the presence of artificial fog. So direction by signal could be ruled out.

Recourse was had to the time-table method. A table was made out showing the exact times (by clock) that the main force was to pass through various positions and to arrive at the several destinations. All other movements were to synchronise according to plan. The time table naturally varied for each day according to the projected time of arrival of the blockships, this, in turn, depending on the time of high tide. But that was not all. It was necessary to guard against unexpected delays due to accident, and against vagaries of the tidal stream. Every unit should know, at a late stage of the oversea trip, if the blockships were likely to be late or early, and the probable difference between actual and projected time involved.

We would not be satisfied with the degree of punctuality usually associated with certain railways. A few minutes out, one way or the other, might be serious; an error of half an hour would probably be disastrous. But the oversea passage involved a journey of approximately a hundred miles for the blockships and storming vessels, though rather less for the Dover contingents. That fact, combined with the usual unwieldiness of a fleet comprising over one hundred and fifty vessels, was not likely to render punctuality very easy of attainment. The disadvantages of daylight made it inadvisable to leave our bases extra early for the sake of having plenty of time to spare. Careful calculations were necessary and the resulting time table was circulated to all concerned.

Before leaving this consideration of the timing question it may be of interest to mention that the storming vessels were to be twenty minutes ahead of the Zeebrugge blockships on arrival in the vicinity of the Mole. In that twenty minutes we were to get alongside and land the storming parties; the latter were to take the necessary steps to put the batteries out of action as far as the safety of the blockships was concerned. At the expiration of the twenty minutes the blockships were to pass round the end of the Mole and make their dash for the canal entrance. The reader may wonder why twenty minutes was the chosen interval. Too long a time might allow the German defences to recover from the initial surprise; too short a time might not enable the storming vessels to complete their work before the blockships were seen by the enemy. Twenty minutes, short though it was, was chosen as a compromise.

All this operational staff work was carried out at Dover under the direction of the vice-admiral, who, as previously stated, was already overloaded with duties and responsibilities arising from the work of the Dover Patrol.

The office accommodation was hardly palatial; the building might certainly have been satisfactory as a small apartment house in pre-war days, but, as the admiral's office of our busiest naval command outside the Grand Fleet, it was not quite up to standard. The small staff were pretty busy for a few weeks. Meals were either bolted down or missed. The night hours did not bring over-much sleep.

Visits to the Grand Fleet were also necessary; one grudged the hours spent in the train. Conferences and discussions, visits to the ships fitting out at the dockyards, inspection of special material, trials of the artificial fog, and the above-mentioned expenditure of stationery helped to keep one occupied. Occasional aerial trips assisted to clear away the cobwebs from one's brain; they constituted a first-class tonic.

We had no printing-press. All orders had to be typed and reproduced by a duplicating machine. Secrecy was as essential in this work as elsewhere; information had to be confined to the minimum number of persons. The ordinary office staff had all the Dover Patrol work to attend to; that was as heavy as it was unceasing. It was a new experience to turn the handle of the duplicator, and, in shirt-sleeve garb, to clip up the pages. We obtained the assistance of a civilian clerk from the Admiralty, and I vow that individual discovered the real meaning of "overtime"; incidentally he was a very rapid and accurate worker and helped us enormously.

At last the office work was more or less completed. Improvements were thought out from time to time and had to be embodied, even up to the eleventh hour. That was natural enough, seeing that we had very little previous experience to guide us in the detailed planning of the Mole attack and blockship work. It was a great relief when the paper work was finished; those of us who had other business in hand could then turn our attention to preparations of a more material nature, much of which has already been described.

CHAPTER 12

The First Attempt

The first period, during which the tidal and astronomical conditions would be favourable, approached. The period was limited to about half a dozen days for the reasons stated in a previous chapter. The weather looked ominous; none of us were very hopeful of an early start. Those last few days of waiting were rather trying. So many things might happen to prevent the operation from taking place. Some of us were inclined to be apprehensive, not of the result if we once came to grips with the enemy, but of the operation being cancelled, or of its being indefinitely postponed, which generally means the same thing. Another great attack on the Belgian coast had previously been planned and prepared, but had never come off. I hesitate to think of the effect on the general morale of the personnel if our enterprise had suffered the same fate. Disappointment is hard enough to bear at any time, but on such an occasion as this it would have just about broken one's heart.

On the eve of the first day of the first period our anxiety about the weather was tremendous. The wind blew hard that night. The morning had nearly dawned before some of us could make ourselves realise that looking at the weather would not do any good. We endeavoured not to offend it by saying unkind words. We touched wood many times when we gave vent to our hopes bred of optimism. Patience is a virtue indeed. But the first day was obviously unfavourable, so we commenced to wait for the second.

At last there was a decided improvement. A state of readiness was ordered. The wind had fallen very light and we were as hopeful as we were anxious to be "up and doing." The order to raise steam was next received and followed shortly after by the order to "carry on" as previously laid down in the time table. All was bustle then. Unnecessary baggage was transhipped to a harbour vessel against the day when some of us might require it. In due course the final arrangements were made and we shortened in our cables. Then we weighed anchors and started off. The officers and men of *Hindustan* cheered us vigorously; answering cheers were given as we steamed close past her. *Vindictive* and the blockships all cheered each other, enthusiasm was in the air. Thank goodness we were off at last. Thank goodness, also, that nothing had occurred to prevent our showing what we could do. Those were the thoughts uppermost in our minds.

Iris and *Daffodil* were sent on ahead so that *Vindictive* could take them in tow when we were clear of the shoals. It will be remembered that *Iris* and *Daffodil* did not possess a high degree of steaming power, either in the way of speed or reliability.

It had, therefore, been decided that *Vindictive* should tow both these vessels across the sea until in the near vicinity of Zeebrugge Mole; that would help to ensure their arrival. I read afterwards in one account of this affair that *Iris* and *Daffodil* towed *Vindictive* into action!

The squadron formed into "line ahead" in the order *Vindictive, Thetis, Intrepid, Iphigenia, Brilliant,* and *Sirius.* The wind was blowing rather weakly, but from a favourable direction. The sea was very calm and, altogether, conditions appeared to be most promising. There were no glum faces in our little community just then. As soon as we had cleared the shoals we all stopped for a few minutes while *Vindictive* took *Iris* and *Daffodil* in tow; that accomplished, we set course for Rendezvous A, where we had to meet the vice-admiral and the remaining vessels from Dover. During our passage through the various channels between sandbanks we passed a large number of homeward-bound merchant ships. The contrast between them and our vessels was not merely confined to the matter of appearance.

Each of these merchant ships was just completing a successful operation, namely, that of bringing necessities of life to this country after running the gantlet of the enemy submarines and mines. On the other hand, we were just setting out for the purpose of reducing such risks in the future. One could not help realising the fact that these mercantile mariners had risked their lives over and over again without ostentation, with small hope of glory, with practically no reward. Fine fellows indeed! What a debt of gratitude we all owed them! Some of them, doubtless, had been torpedoed three and four times, losing all their effects each time, but here they were again with yet another voyage to their credit. We overtook a few vessels outward bound with their troubles to come. Some of these ships were neutrals. We wondered what they thought of us and how they would describe us when they arrived at their destinations. We could reckon on the enemy having agents at all the neutral ports with their "ears well trimmed to the wind" when in the presence of neutral mariners from British ports. We also wondered if these neutrals could fail to recognise the difference between British and German treatment of merchantmen at sea, and whether such recognition would not make them chary of talking too much.

Presently we sighted a large number of small craft. They seemed to be dashing up from every direction, at first in an apparently aimless fashion, but presently one recognised the method in their madness. At schedule time we stopped, heading towards our goal. The crowd soon sorted themselves out.

The vice-admiral with his flag flying in the destroyer *Warwick* took up a position of advantage. Destroyers and blockships took small motor craft in tow. Other vessels acted as tugs for the submarines. Motor launches, puffing for all the world as if they lacked training, thus acting an untruth, assembled according to their ultimate duties. Somebody remarked that we resembled a sea-circus, there were so many turns taking place simultaneously. One hardly knew which to admire most. The destroyers throbbing with latent energy, some of them shouting through their safety valves that they were in a hurry to get to business. The motor launches, pretending the sea was rough and often rolling heavily in their pretence, producing a similar impression to that of a certain famous automobile which, though cheap, always "gets there" even if some parts are missing at the end of the journey. The C.M.B.'s (which, being interpreted, signifies Coastal Motor Boats, though the word "coastal" hardly seems appropriate) were tearing through the water and almost leaping into the other element as if to emulate the flying-fish. Perhaps the word "crowd" was most suited to the appearance of this heterogeneous collection of craft, but they were very different from a crowd in their behaviour.

Punctually at the scheduled hour the signal was hoisted to proceed. The expedition, making its debut as such, set course for the eastward. Enthusiasm was at its highest pitch. Final preparations were then the order of the day. In *Vindictive* emergency rations and field dressings were distributed. Small arms were inspected, ammunition was stowed ready for use. Demolition charges were placed in a handy position for rapid removal to the Mole, gangways were triced up, bombs were fused, howitzers and flame-throwers were prepared. Hoses were flaked down for fire brigade uses, fire extinguishers were provided in specially dangerous corners, duplicate charts were placed in the conning tower. To guard against the eventuality of all the navigating personnel being rendered *hors de combat* during the fight or the charts being destroyed, the retirement courses were painted up on the armour inside the conning tower. A year later I found this painting untouched, although the ship had been in the Germans' hands (after being sunk by us at Ostende in May, 1918) for many months—I wondered if they understood its signification. All the other craft in company were equally busy.

We passed through further rendezvous, B and C and D, etc., carefully checking our progress at each so as to ensure working to the time table.

The bombarding and supporting squadrons had proceeded independently. We were accompanied by aircraft during the daylight hours of our passage; their special duty was that of scouting for German aircraft and preventing those that might have seen us from giving any warning of our approach.

The wind gradually became very fitful and made us rather apprehensive of its changing to an unsuitable direction. Surely we were not to be robbed of our long-awaited opportunity at the eleventh hour. Daylight faded into twilight and the latter gave way to darkness. It was a clear night, but as black as india ink. Presently a distant flash of light was seen away to starboard. Then another and another. A compass bearing laid from our charted position gave evidence of something happening at Ostende. Then searchlight beams were seen searching the heavens in an uneasy manner. What could it mean? A hurried glance at the time table explained everything.

Our aircraft had opened the ball. The booming of guns was heard quite plainly and the glare of the flashes was distinctly visible. Zeebrugge then joined in the game. In a little while we could make out the trail of the "flaming onions," rushing heavenwards, hanging stationary for a few seconds, and then slowly falling in their curiously serpentine manner, for all the world like colossal snakes writhing in their death agony. The firing became more intense and we were more anxious than ever to get to work. It was obvious enough that our aircraft—the 65th Wing of the Royal Air Force from Dunkerque—were setting about the enemy in determined fashion. Our turn was to come shortly, according to plan. Alas, "the best laid schemes of mice and men gang aft agley." We had stopped to disembark the surplus blockship crews—*if they could be found*, and to slip the small craft from their towing hawsers in readiness to penetrate the danger zone. The wind seemed to have died away for a moment and then commenced to blow from a *southerly* direction.

Seldom has an admiral been faced with such a difficult situation. A decision had to be given, and quickly. The nature of the operation admitted of no delay. The wind at the moment was hopelessly unfavourable for our use of artificial fog. The latter was essential. It would mean sheer slaughter if there were no cover from the shore batteries during the approach. On the other hand, the wind might change again. Here was the whole expedition within a short distance of our objectives. The major part of the passage had been completed in spite of all the difficulties and practically without incident. The aerial attack had commenced. The monitors were shortly to send their messages of destruction hurtling on their way to the enemy. We had been seen by all sorts of neutral vessels. Most of the conditions were favourable—the wind alone was seriously against us. Another chance might never come. He who risks nothing attains nothing. Discretion is the better part of valour. What was it to be?

In all the pages of naval history I cannot remember having come across any occasion where a more difficult decision had to be made. After Teneriffe Nelson had realised his mistake of allowing impetuosity to influence sound reasoning to the extent of attacking when the conditions were unfavourable. Not only was that first attack a failure, but it had foredoomed the second attempt to failure also. The vice-admiral avoided the same mistake—he ordered the operation to be cancelled for that night. Much has been written of the attack which eventually took place. References to the Nelson touch have not been unknown. But this latter comparison, as I have shown, was curiously inapt if intended to cover the whole direction of the enterprise.

There was no time for feelings of disappointment. We had to return at utmost speed so as to be ready to start again next day if the conditions allowed. Our bases lay many miles to the westward, but we were heading in an easterly direction. "Course West" was signalled immediately. *Vindictive* held the honoured post of "Guide of the Fleet." Complete instructions had been laid down for turning round at night. It must be remembered that we had seventy-seven craft in close, very close, company. We duly turned round, hoping that all craft had received the signal. Our hopes were not entirely realised. In a few moments the close company became too close for comfort. Small craft shaved across our bows so narrowly that they left the impression of having gone through us. Shouts were heard, mingled with the puffing and spluttering of internal-combustion engines. We wondered which particular vessel we should sink first. But out of chaos came some semblance of order and presently we were homeward bound without any very serious casualties.

Away in the distance there were occasional gun and searchlight flashes, but the monitors had received the cancellation news in time to preserve their silence. During the turn to the westward one of the small craft, in imminent danger of collision, had momentarily switched on her navigation lights. Others followed suit until our force resembled Brighton Esplanade indulging in a Venetian fete as viewed from the sea. "Out Lights" was immediately ordered and passed from one craft to another by megaphone or flash-lamp; darkness reigned once more as we sped homeward. Although we had shown a blaze of lights, the enemy patrols, we heard afterwards, failed to see us; this was scarcely a token of their efficiency.

So it was a case of *"if at first you don't succeed, try, try again."* This abortive attempt was by no means without value. We had rehearsed the concentration and the oversea passage of the main force; the other vessels had practised reaching their various destinations; the aircraft had carried out their attack; the routes and navigational aids had been severely tested. Naturally enough much valuable experience had been gained and, after all, no harm had resulted provided that the enemy remained ignorant of our efforts and intentions. But certain incidents had occurred to increase our reliance on the small craft. During the turn to the westward disentanglement without serious accident was only achieved as a result of fine seamanship and initiative on the part of those in command; these qualities had thus been evidenced under most realistic and difficult conditions. We felt that, if they could deal successfully with such a situation as *that*, they could be relied upon to tackle any situation, however difficult or unexpected.

A couple of incidents that occurred may illustrate the point. During the turning manoeuvre one of the coastal motor boats received a heavy blow in the bows from another craft. A hole resulted and the water commenced to pour through it. She would probably have sunk in a minute or two but for the resource of her commanding officer. He ordered one of the men to sit in the hole. This reduced the inflow of water, but can hardly have been a comfortable proceeding for the individual concerned. The boat was then worked up to high speed. The reader probably knows that the bow of one of these fast motor boats gradually raises itself as speed is increased until the fore part of the boat is completely clear of the water. In this case the hole was above the sea when twenty-seven knots had been attained. The man who had found a new use for his anatomy then withdrew himself. Whether the commanding officer of the boat desired to remain with the guide of the fleet out of sheer friendship or whether he was uncertain of his geographical position, I know not. But he evidently decided to remain in company. *Vindictive* was steaming at a modest ten knots or so; the motor boat could not afford to proceed at less than twenty-seven knots; so he steamed round and round the remaining seventy-six vessels until daylight, when he was detached to his base.

Another coastal motor boat, soon after leaving Dover on the outward trip, developed some defect which put the engines out of action. The young officer in command obtained the services of a trawler to tow him back to Dover, where, on arrival, he had the matter put right. All that took time. He started off again about five hours late. Now, the occupants of this boat had no intention of missing the affair for which they had prepared so long. They decided to get to Zeebrugge as soon as possible—at full speed they might yet be in time. So at full speed they went, straight as a die for their goal, right across nets, mines, and shoals. The sixty miles were covered in less than two hours. The aerial attack was in full swing. Searchlight beams were passing dangerously near them, the heavens were filled with bursting shell and flaming onions. Suddenly out of the darkness loomed some black shapes—"Houses ahead!" shouted somebody. "Hard-a-starboard and stop her!" As she turned round to seaward they made out the town of Blankenberghe; they had escaped running ashore by the narrowest of margins.

On they went again for Zeebrugge Mole. Things were quieter now. That was strange in itself. What had happened to the long-range bombardment? Where were the smoke screens and why was nothing happening at the Mole? Our ships must be much overdue. Whatever could it mean? Presently some strange craft were seen and a moment later the motor boat was under fire. So she sheered off and the commanding officer did some hard thinking. There was only one possible explanation—the operation must have been postponed. So the next item on her programme was to return to Dover. It wouldn't do to be late getting back, so away they went—hell for leather—straight across everything once more. And they arrived back at Dover, after having completed the whole voyage both ways, before their *confrères* who were with the main force!

At dawn we had completed most of the open-sea passage on the return journey. The force split up—the various units deconcentrated.

Vindictive and her old friends returned to her home of the last few weeks. The *Hindustan's* enthusiasm of the day before gave place to curiosity. The former positions in the anchorage were reoccupied. Coaling was then the order of the day; not a moment was to be wasted; with luck we might start again before nightfall.

But it was not to be. The conditions were hopeless and perhaps that was all for the best. We needed some rest. As soon as everything was in readiness for the second attempt, we piped down and then, for the first time, we had a chance to talk things over.

It would be untrue to say that we were not disappointed. The fear of indefinite postponement was now much stronger. But everybody realised to the full that the chances of success under adverse conditions were practically nil. Discussion paved the way to many suggestions of improvement—at any rate, we intended to derive what benefit we could from the abortive attempt.

CHAPTER 13

The Second Attempt and Return

I will not weary the reader with a repetition of our life at the
Swin—the second edition differed little from the first. There were
still chances of a new start during the present period. The weather,
however, was most unkind. We summoned up all the patience that we
could muster. The news from the battle front in France was becoming
increasingly serious. We felt that somehow or other, we didn't quite
know how, a successful operation on our part might help to stem the
German advance. If only we could get started!

At last our second chance came. The wind had changed back to
a northerly direction. The "stand-by" order was received. "Carry on"
followed. Once again we started off, as enthusiastic as ever; if our
previous determination had not increased it was because no increase
was possible.

Hindustan cheered us out again, and, in our inmost thoughts, we
thanked them. Soon after we had cleared the Swin anchorage a destroyer hove in sight and signalled that she had a letter for *Vindictive*.
We ordered her to stop a couple of miles ahead of us and transfer
the letter by boat. Commander Brock came on board with it; we
had thought he had been prevented from joining us. "We must push
in tonight," that was the tenor of the letter. The message was passed
round the ship and down the line of blockships. It reflected our own
feelings—"We must push in tonight." Once again we passed many
merchant vessels with their crews crowded on deck to view the unusual spectacle which we made. The wind had gradually increased
in strength, an uncomfortable sea was rising. The prospects appeared
none too rosy for the small craft. Some twenty miles had been covered
when the almost inevitable became a certainty—the operation was
once more postponed.

The open sea had become so rough as to render the use of small craft quite impracticable. There was nothing for it, back we had to go once more.

Little enough was said on the subject this time; we were learning to hide disappointment. The reaction from all our hopeful optimism caused us to wonder if any other chance would be offered us. Surely this enterprise was not to be stillborn after all the signs of life that it had shown. It is advisable, perhaps, not to analyse our thoughts too fully, but they tended to breed fatalism. We tried to look upon the turn of events as a "rub of the green"; we endeavoured to appear unruffled.

The men were wonderful; their behaviour was beyond praise. If there was any discontent it was carefully hidden. The vice-admiral visited us at the earliest opportunity and explained the situation to the officers and men. That gracious act was enormously appreciated; we all felt, more than ever, that if *he* could not bring off this operation nobody would ever do so.

The first period of favourable tides was over. The next period would not commence yet awhile. Drills and practices were restarted. A second battleship was sent to the Swin to relieve the congestion in the *Hindustan*. *Vindictive, Iris,* and *Daffodil* had no accommodation for the Marine storming parties, which had to be transferred to the *Hindustan* and her sister depot. The waiting period was not wasted.

Opportunity now offered for embodying in the instructions the various suggestions for improvements. Each was fully discussed and considered from all points of view. Even further experiments with the artificial fog were carried out. It was then decided to rewrite all the previous instructions which required modification as a result of the experience gained during the two attempts. This was a welcome change from the confined life on board. The Admiralty clerk reappeared at the admiral's office.

A most important discussion was held concerning the chances of the secret having leaked out. At first sight one might have thought that the operation ought to be cancelled altogether, for had we not been seen, and almost certainly reported, by a large number of neutral vessels? Such an eventuality was by no means outside the pale of probability, and we also had to reckon with the chances of having been seen by German aircraft and submarines. Nevertheless, this obstacle to our future success was imaginary rather than real. To begin with, what value would have been placed on such reports? It would naturally depend upon the source of the information.

Submarines or aircraft might have been mistaken; anyhow, their reports could hardly provide conclusive evidence of our intentions. Information received by the Germans from neutral sources might have been specially intended to mislead. The probable effect of such latter "intelligence" depends to a certain extent on the psychology of the recipient. The Germans were past-masters at chicanery; the first inclination of such individuals is to disbelieve others; a prevaricator always labours under that disadvantage.

There could, therefore, be no *certainty* that our two abortive attempts had given birth to a new obstacle. History relates many failures resulting from the imagination of difficulties which had no real existence in fact. One of the best examples, curiously enough, was connected with the Walcheren expedition, where the imaginary difficulties had loomed large, only a few miles to the eastward of Zeebrugge. It is no exaggeration to state that if we had allowed our imagination to create half the obstacles which might have existed we should never have decided upon the enterprise at all.

The drafting, typing, duplication, and distribution of the new editions of instructions were completed in two or three days. The dates of the next period were worked out and a new time table issued.

It has already been shown that the chances of being discovered *en route* largely depended upon the number of daylight hours which would be involved in the passage of the expedition. Daylight, in itself, does not necessarily imply a high degree of visibility. If the weather were sufficiently misty to reduce visibility, without militating against safe navigation, daylight would not be so disadvantageous. In making out the period, therefore, we included an extra day at its commencement for use if misty weather obtained; should that day be clear it would be inadvisable to attempt the enterprise. That decision was strictly in accordance with the principles on which the enterprise was based. But principles are intended as guides; it is a false idea that they may never be departed from. In an operation of this description, depending upon a rather delicate combination of circumstances and conditions, it was necessary to consider just how far we should be justified in ignoring one unsuitable condition if all others were favourable.

Once more we summoned up all the patience that we could muster.

The First Lord of the Admiralty, Sir Eric Geddes, accompanied by

Sir Rosslyn Wemyss, who had relieved Lord Jellicoe as First Sea Lord, paid a visit to *Vindictive* and some of the blockships; it is probable that they were exceedingly struck at the optimism of all concerned.

An incident, illustrating the spirit of the men, may be worth recording. It came to my ears that certain of the engine-room personnel did not propose to remain below whilst the ship was alongside the Mole; as they put it "they intended to land on the Mole for a run round." Of course, that would never do, so the ship's company were informed that, however much their spirits might actuate their intentions, any man who left his post during the action would be summarily dealt with. They knew what that meant. Shortly afterwards some stokers requested to interview their officer. The interview was somewhat as follows:

"Me and my mates, sir, understand that we ain't allowed to leave the stokehold and have a go at the Hun," said their spokesman.

"Of course not," interposed the officer; "you would be deserting your post in action."

"Well, sir," continued the stoker, "we wants to know if we may *guard the prisoners* in the stokehold."

The request was not granted; it spelt too much discomfort for the prisoners.

Soon the first possible date drew near.

In view of the eventual results it may be of interest to recall the fact that on April 19th (three days before we actually started) Admiral von Capelle, Secretary for the German Navy, made a speech in which he said: "Even the greatest pessimist must say that the position of our opponents is deteriorating rapidly, and that any doubt regarding the final success of the U-boat war is unjustified."

I wonder if von Capelle remained an optimist much longer.

Another German of high culture and position had previously said, "Questions of right or wrong, justification or no justification, do not concern us. The chief thing is that we are the stronger, and that if anyone questions this fact we should smite him on the mouth till he grows wiser."

Well, we *did* question the fact, and not only questioned it, but we put it to the test.

PART 2

One crowded hour of glorious life
is worth an age without a name

Foreword

A brief introduction to Part 2 of this book may assist the reader. The previous chapters have dealt with the general idea of the operation, the more important details of the plan, and the preparatory work involved.

We are now approaching the actual events which occurred during the operation itself as carried out at the third attempt.

For reasons stated in Part 1, Chapter 3, I do not propose to deal further with the enterprise at Ostende; the preparatory work for the blocking of that place has been fairly well covered in the foregoing pages. As a matter of historical interest a list of all vessels employed in the simultaneous operations at Zeebrugge and Ostende is given in the Appendix. Doubtless the Ostende story will be told in due course by one of those who took part in the operations at that place.

Unless the reader's mind has clearly grasped our intentions as portrayed in the Zeebrugge plan it may be difficult to understand the connection between the actual events which occurred. The more important details of the plan have already been described, but chiefly under the consideration of each separate phase of the enterprise, or of the duties of each class of vessel, rather than as related items of one complete operation. It may be advisable, therefore, to describe briefly the various phases, in their proper sequence, showing the relation between them, even if this involves some repetition; thus the way will be paved to a detailed narrative of the several events which occurred, and the reader, whilst following any particular item, will be enabled to keep the whole picture in view.

Briefly, then, the main points of the plan for the blocking of Zeebrugge were as follows:

The expedition was to cross the seas during the afternoon and evening, stopping for a few minutes about twenty miles from its destination for the purpose of disembarking the surplus crews of the blockships. At about this time the first of the diversions, in the form of aerial attacks, were to commence, to be shortly followed by the opening of the long-range bombardments. Meanwhile the expedition, working to a prearranged time table, was to approach the coast.

At given intervals during the approach small craft were to be detached to carry out the duties of smoke screening, of diversionary attacks, of locating the destination, and of dealing with enemy vessels which might emerge from their harbours or which were already at sea.

Immediately following the long-range bombardment, the storming vessels, having located the Mole, were to proceed alongside the high outer wall and land their storming parties over it to attack the Mole batteries—this constituting the main diversion of the enterprise. A few minutes later, the submarines, having steamed into place beneath the railway viaduct, were to blow up the railway. Twenty minutes after the storming vessels were due to arrive alongside, the blockships were to pass round the end of the Mole and were to make their dash for the canal entrance, running the gantlet of the shore batteries, whilst the Mole attack was in full swing. On arriving in the canal the blockers were to turn and sink their ships across the navigable channel. Rescue craft were to follow the blockships for the purpose of rescuing the crews of the latter. Meanwhile, the various diversions, the smoke screening, and the work of the inshore supports, were to be continued sufficiently long to enhance the chances of the rescue. After an hour or so from the commencement of the attack on the Mole all forces were to withdraw.

The foregoing brief summary serves to indicate that at any given moment after the approach had once commenced there would be many different events taking place simultaneously.

For instance, early in the proceedings there would be a combined aerial attack and long-range bombardment whilst the main expedition, under cover of darkness, was silently approaching over the mine-fields, momentarily expectant of discovery by the enemy's patrol vessels.

Later—say, ten minutes after the storming vessels had arrived at the Mole—the storming parties from *Vindictive, Iris,* and *Daffodil* would be attacking the northeastern end of the Mole; *Vindictive's* howitzers would be bombarding the shore batteries; small craft would be bombing the central part of the Mole; submarines would be blowing up the railway viaduct; the submarine's crews would be pulling away for dear

143

life; other small craft would be laying their smoke screens close off the enemy's batteries and attacking German vessels on the inner side of the Mole; the blockships would be nearing the Mole in preparation for their final dash; patrol vessels, in support, would be guarding the attackers from enemy craft; star shell and search-lights would be illuminating the darkness; the booming of heavy guns, the yapping of quick-firers, and the crashing of shell would provide a fitting accompaniment.

The enterprise was to be decidedly intensive. If all went well the defence should certainly be mystified and not a little worried by the time the blockships arrived in the picture.

Thus, and thus only, should we be following out the maxim of Stonewall Jackson, "Always mystify, mislead, and surprise the enemy."

The enterprise divides itself naturally into three main phases, namely, the Approach, the Attack, and the Retirement; as far as practicable Part II will describe each of these phases in turn, whilst dealing more or less separately with the work of each class of vessel.

CHAPTER 1

The Start

The break of dawn on April 22, 1918, the first of the seven days of our tabulated period, found many anxious individuals on deck discussing the chances. There was an almost entire absence of wind; the sea was consequently as smooth as the proverbial mill-pond. The general feeling amongst us was that of straining-at-the-leash. We had suffered two major disappointments during the previous period, but we instinctively felt that we had now arrived at a period of maximum anxiety—we knew that the coming week would settle the matter once and for all. Presently light airs from the northward began to catspaw the glassy surface and to increase in frequency and strength until they settled down to a real northerly breeze. Our hopes ran high, but the matter of visibility still claimed our attention. There was the usual early morning mist; this was quickly dispelled when the sun rose above the horizon. It soon became evident that our hopes for misty weather were to be denied us. By 8 a.m. the visibility was extreme, as they say in meteorological circles; one's horizontal range of vision from shipboard was only limited by one's height of eye above the level of the sea. This condition, to say the least of it, was disconcerting.

It would be high tide at Zeebrugge and Ostende soon after midnight. Arrival at such an hour would entail making much of the over-sea passage in broad daylight, and this, as previously mentioned, would in turn lead to grave risk of being seen by the German patrols, whether the latter were in the air, on the sea surface, or submerged keeping periscope watch. Although this disadvantage might even lose us the element of surprise on which we had concentrated so much effort, any postponement of our departure until the morrow would entail a reduction of our available period by one-seventh. The armchair critic who knows nought of such matters cannot easily conceive either the difficulty of arriving at such decisions, or the weight of responsibility which lies on the shoulders of the man by whom the decision must be given.

Early in the forenoon it was evident that all conditions except visibility were in favour of starting our third attempt. Our hopes ran high in spite of the fact that previous experience had shown us how fickle the weather could be. Somehow we felt that our chance had come at last.

We were in telephonic communication with Dover *via* a lighthouse in the vicinity of our anchorage. Perhaps the word "communication" rather exaggerates the actual facts of the case. The line apparently passed through a certain holiday resort whose telephone exchange was below par and whose operative, in the kindness of her heart, generally managed to connect at least four persons simultaneously on our particular line. The resulting cross talk, further confused by the eternal argument between the tidal stream and the telephone cable, and our impatience at any and every interruption, with its resultant increase of knowledge of the vernacular to the lighthouse crew, were hardly conducive to easy conversation on important matters. "Harold" was particularly exasperating that morning. Having fixed "Mabel" for lunch in a couple of hours, he apparently thought it necessary to 'phone her details of his past.

To the Vice-Admiral at Dover fell the responsibility of deciding whether we should start or not. After a discussion on the telephone the die was cast—we were ordered to "proceed in execution of previous orders." The order was passed to the ships and the requisite preparations were put in hand immediately. We raised steam without delay. Baggage, final letters, and all unnecessary paraphernalia were disembarked. Once again determination and expectancy had expanded into enthusiasm. The time for "action" had arrived.

I do not think we had any feelings of anxiety now except with regard to the weather. Surely nothing would prevent the culmination of all our hopes at this eleventh hour. No suggestion of failure ever occurred to us. Our confidence in the face of the many obstacles, when considered in cold blood months afterwards, may have seemed to be almost an impertinence. Everybody knew exactly what was expected of him. There was no actual excitement except that inseparable from intense enthusiasm. Last-minute orders or signals were not required, everything worked just as smoothly as if we had been merely starting off on a picnic.

Engines were reported "ready" shortly after lunch. Just before weighing anchor I had gone below to don my sea-boots and other appropriate "togs"; on reappearing on deck I found several officers grouped for a final snapshot and was requested to join them. Alas, that was indeed the last photograph for several of them. The cheering which had taken place on both the previous attempts was indulged in once again as the ships proceeded to sea and was only eclipsed by the cheers which welcomed the survivors to Dover on the following day.

Of the earlier part of the oversea trip little need be written. *Vindictive* took *Iris* and *Daffodil* in tow and was closely followed by the blockships. In due course the Dover forces were sighted; the combined force, accompanied by aeroplanes, formed on *Vindictive*, which was "Guide of the Fleet."

The fast motor boats and the two submarines were taken in tow, and the vice-admiral, with his flag flying in the destroyer *Warwick*, directed the whole movements and gave the signal to proceed as soon as all were formed up. The visibility had already decreased and sufficient clouds were massing overhead to revive our anxieties about the weather. Light squadrons which had preceded us for the various duties of "supporting" or "bombarding," etc., had not reported any enemy patrol craft.

On board each ship eleventh-hour preparations were being made— such as rigging stations for attending the wounded, distributing first-aid packages, passing hoses along in case of fire, fusing bombs and shell, testing electric circuits, providing candle lamps in case of electrical failures, grouping ammunition round the guns, donning clean underclothing as a guard against septic wounds, darkening ship to prevent any warning of our approach, placing spare charts in alternative positions, testing smoke-screen apparatus and flame-throwers, and many other such things.

Before darkness set in a signal was received from the vice-admiral reading "St. George for England." It was reported to me as being a personal signal to myself, but I subsequently ascertained that it was intended as a general signal to be passed down the line of ships. It was made in the semaphore code from *Warwick* and has often been misquoted as a signal hoisted with alphabetical flags.

One garbled version described the signal as having been "flashed to all ships just before reaching the Mole." This story of a flash-light having been used just when the ships were endeavouring to take the enemy by surprise under cover of darkness is really too fantastic to

VICE-ADMIRAL SIR ROGER J. B. KEYES K.C.B., K.C.V.O.,
D.S.O., R.N.

pass uncontradicted. Believing it to be a private signal, a reply was determined upon. The reply, (May we give the Dragon's tail a damned good twist), to the admiral's signal, judged by the ordinary standards, was somewhat impertinent, but impertinence was in the air that afternoon. Incidentally my signalman substituted the word "darned" for "damned" and, when corrected, spelt the word "dammed" as a compromise.

Our prearranged timetable had laid down the exact minute at which we were to pass through certain lettered positions, the latter being marked by buoys placed by the surveying officers mentioned previously. Position G was to be the parting of the ways, namely the position at which the forces destined for the inshore attacks on Zeebrugge and Ostende should separate *en route* for their respective destinations. That position was so chosen that the forces should arrive at their destinations simultaneously, making due allowance for direction and strength of the tidal stream and for actual ship-speed through the water.

This idea of simultaneous operations at the two places was not the only important factor for consideration; it was also necessary that all other phases of the attack, such as long-range bombardments and aerial attacks, should synchronise with the movements of the blockships. It was, therefore, necessary to either work exactly to schedule as laid down in the time table or else inform all units of any change in the zero time, the latter being the minute at which *Vindictive* should pass through position G. This in turn necessitated forecasting the zero time as a result of the observed times of passing the previous positions. We had left position A a few minutes ahead of time and passed through position D with barely a minute in hand. "No alteration of zero time" was therefore communicated to all units.

After passing position D the whole assembly of vessels stopped for a few minutes for the triple purpose of disembarking surplus blockship crews, ascertaining the exact direction of wind (this information being required for the use of the smoke screens), and reforming into "approach order" after casting off the tow of the submarines and small craft. It was then pitch dark, the moon being entirely obscured by clouds. It has been stated elsewhere that the *Intrepid* did not disembark any of her surplus crews. The small vessel detailed to take these men failed to appear owing to a breakdown; this must have pleased the *Intrepid's* surplus crew who, it will be remembered, had shown a strong disinclination to leave their ship. To some extent *Thetis* and

Iphigenia were similarly placed; history relates that when the small vessels arrived alongside many members of the surplus crews could not be found, so anxious were they to complete the operation which they had begun so well.

No time was lost in reforming the squadron and we started off again for position G. At about this time all conditions of wind and sea were still favourable, but slight rain had begun to fall and to reduce the already very limited visibility. The rain thus provided the first of the incidents which could not be foreseen.

The result of the rain was twofold. Firstly, it somewhat delayed the commencement of the long-range bombardment on Zeebrugge owing to the reduction in visibility rendering the monitor's position doubtful. Secondly, and far more important, it acted very adversely against the use of aircraft. The difficulty and danger of flying in wet weather is too well known to need enlargement here, but the difficulty of locating the positions which were to be bombed was enormously increased. As related elsewhere our aerial bombers had made a magnificent attack on the occasion of our first attempt and they had become none the less determined to render a good account of themselves when the operation finally took place. Imagine their intense disappointment. It was not difficult for those who knew the splendid work of our Air Force to realise that they would stop at nothing to achieve their object. In spite of all the difficulties it is impossible to conceive of greater determination than was shown, but the rain rendered the attack impossible. The losses amongst these very gallant airmen amounted to a high percentage of those who started on their errand.

At position G the Ostende blockships parted company; inwardly we wished them the best of luck.

The main portion of the oversea passage having been completed, the "Approach" now commenced.

CHAPTER 2

The Approach

After zero time the remaining units kept in close company until such times as each, according to their respective instructions, was deputed to proceed independently to carry out its particular duty.

The force was preceded by the vice-admiral in *Warwick* with some half a dozen other craft in company ready to fall upon and destroy any enemy patrol vessels which might be encountered. We were now steaming through the German mined areas and were hoping against hope that no mines would be touched to the main detriment of the element of surprise. If any mine had exploded the enemy could not have failed to have their suspicions aroused. The rain gradually increased and the wind became more fitful. Hot soup was distributed to the men in *Vindictive* at about 10.30 p.m. and a "tot" of rum was served out about an hour later to those who desired it.

About fifty minutes before midnight the hawser with which *Vindictive* was towing *Iris* and *Daffodil* suddenly parted. It was then too late to retake these vessels in tow and, indeed, it would have been a difficult and dangerous task in the rain and inky darkness with so many vessels in close company, to say nothing of the loss of time and the obstacle to accurate navigation. Speed had to be somewhat eased temporarily to allow *Vindictive* to drop back to her original position relative to the other vessels. In accordance with the plan the blockships eased speed for the purpose of arriving at the Mole some twenty minutes after *Vindictive*.

We were momentarily expecting to meet the German patrol vessels and to be discovered from the shore. Suddenly a light-buoy was seen. A hurried bearing laid down on the chart agreed exactly with the reported position of a buoy off Blankenberghe. Incidentally a captured prisoner had recently stated that this buoy had been withdrawn or moved elsewhere, but we had promulgated its original position to all concerned because we suspected that this particular individual was a disciple of Ananias. This agreement between our position by "dead-reckoning" and that of the buoy was decidedly heartening, for we had obtained no "fix" for several miles and were running through a cross tidal stream of doubtful strength.

The difficulties attached to forecasting the movements of tidal streams were borne out in the case of the bombarding monitors, H.M.S. *Erebus* and *Terror*. In addition to being somewhat hampered by the low visibility resulting from the rain, these vessels, on arrival at their firing positions, discovered that the tidal stream was flowing in exactly the opposite direction to that anticipated; this, in turn, caused some delay in opening fire, but, as events subsequently showed, the delay was of no great consequence. The bombardment was carried out without any further hitch. The Germans do not appear to have been able to locate the monitors until the firing was nearly completed. The few German shell which burst in the vicinity of the firing ships were doubtless directed by some means of sound-ranging and direction-finding. On finishing the bombardment the monitors took up their positions for covering the subsequent retirement of the attacking forces.

It may be stated here that, barring the impossibility of aerial attack, the delay in commencing the long-range bombardment, and the parting of the towing hawser, there was no hitch of any kind sufficient to alter the general idea of the enterprise. Everything was carried out to schedule time.

Soon after passing the Blankenberghe light-buoy the enemy appeared to suspect that something more than a bombardment was afoot. Star shell were fired to seaward and searchlights were switched on. That was exactly what we had hoped for. If only they would continue to illuminate the atmosphere our navigational difficulties would be enormously reduced. The star shell were extraordinary. They burst with a loud report just overhead and lit up our surroundings to the maximum of the then visibility. Much to our surprise no enemy vessels were encountered or even seen; presumably the enemy set the greater dependence on their mines.

To the southward, that is, between us and the shore, our smoke-screeners had laid down a "pea-soup" fog. Nothing was to be seen in that direction except the glare of searchlights and of gun flashes, the latter being presumably directed against the fast motor boats which had run into the anchorage behind the Mole for the purpose of torpedoing vessels secured alongside. At this stage the wind died away completely and the rain was heavier than ever.

In *Vindictive* we took up our action stations. Our battery guns had been instructed not to open fire until it was certain that our individual presence had been discovered. The guns in the fighting-top on our foremast were in readiness to engage. Rocket men had been stationed to fire illuminating flares for the purpose of locating the Mole. The storming parties were under cover awaiting the order to storm the Mole. The cable party were in the forecastle standing by to drop anchor at the foot of the high wall. Other parties with wire hawsers were stationed to assist the *Daffodil* in her important task of pushing *Vindictive* bodily alongside. Crews were standing by the bomb-mortars and flame-throwers for clearing the Mole before sending the stormers over the wall. The Engineering and Stokehold personnel were at their stations below for giving immediate response to all requirements from the conning positions. The first lieutenant—Lieutenant-Commander R. R. Rosoman, R.N.—was in the conning tower, from where the ship was being steered by the quartermaster, in readiness to take over the handling of the ship immediately I was rendered *hors de combat*. It was a decidedly tense period, but there were others to follow.

At a given moment by watch-time *Vindictive* altered course towards the Mole—or rather towards the position where it was hoped to find the Mole. Almost immediately we ran into the smoke screen. *The wind had now changed to an off-shore direction*, diametrically opposite to that on which the screening plans had been based. I thought at the time that this smoke screen was the thickest on record—that opinion was changed later.

The visibility at this time can hardly have amounted to a yard—the forecastle was invisible from the bridge. The firing of star shells and guns, and the flashing of searchlights became more frequent. *Vindictive* was being conned from the flame-thrower hut on the port end of the conning-tower platform. This position was especially suitable in that it plumbed over the ship's side and thus provided a very good outlook for berthing at the Mole. There was a curious absence of excitement. Even the continued repetition of the question, "Are you all right, sir?" from my first lieutenant—a prearranged idea to ensure a quick change over of command—became monotonous. Nothing had yet been seen of the Mole from *Vindictive*. This comparatively quiet period was not of long duration.

CHAPTER 3

The Commencement of the Attack

A few seconds before the schedule time for the last alteration of course—designed to take us alongside the outer wall—the smoke screen, which had been drifting northwards before the new wind, suddenly cleared. Barely three hundred yards distant, dead ahead of us, appeared a long low dark object which was immediately recognised as the Mole itself with the lighthouse at its extremity. We had turned up heading direct for the six-gun battery exactly as arranged in the plan. Those who know aught of navigation will realise how far this was a fluke—probably the various errors in compass direction, allowance for tide, etc., had exactly cancelled one another. Course was altered immediately to the southwestward and speed was increased to the utmost.

The Mole battery opened fire at once; our own guns, under the direction of Commander E. O. B. S. Osborne, replied with the utmost promptitude. The estimated distance at which we passed the Mole battery was two hundred and fifty yards off the eastern gun, gradually lessening to fifty yards off the western gun. It was truly a wonderful sight. The noise was terrific and the flashes of the Mole guns seemed to be within arm's length. Of course it was, to all intents and purposes, impossible for the Mole guns to miss their target. They literally poured projectiles into us. In about five minutes we had reached the Mole, but not before the ship had suffered a great amount of damage to both *materiel* and personnel.

Looked at from the view of a naval officer it was little short of criminal, on the part of the Mole battery, that the ship was allowed to reach her destination. Everything was in favour of the defence as soon as we had been sighted. Owing to the change of wind our special arrangements for covering the battery with smoke had failed in spite of

Drawn by Charles De Lacy from details supplied by the Author

DIAGRAMMATIC SKETCH OF THE ATTACK

A—H.M.S. Vindictive
B—H.M.S. Daffodil
C—H.M.S. Iris
D—Coastal Motor Boats
E—Steam pinnace
F—Motor dinghey

G—Submarine C 3
H—S.S. Brussels
I—German destroyers
J—To Blankenberghe
K—Motor launches
L—Entanglement net boom
M—H.M.S. Phœbe

N—H.M.S. North Star
O—Position of approach channel
P—Rescue craft
Q—Rescue craft
R—H.M.S. Iphigenia
S—H.M.S. Intrepid
T—H.M.S. Thetis

U—Trenches on Mole
V—Trenches ashore
W—H.M.S. Warwick
X—The barge boom
Y—The Canal
Z—German batteries

the magnificent work of our small smoke vessels which, unsupported and regardless of risk, had laid the screen close to the foot of the wall, that is to say, right under the muzzles of the guns. From the moment when we were first sighted until arriving alongside the Mole the battery guns had a clear target, illuminated by star shell, of a size equal to half the length of the lighthouse extension itself.

To my mind the chief reasons for our successful running of the gantlet were twofold, firstly, the fact that we were so close, and secondly, the splendid manner in which our guns' crews stuck to their work. With regard to the former, a longer range would have entailed more deliberate firing, and this in turn would have given time for more deliberate choice of point of aim. A few projectiles penetrating the engine or boiler rooms, or holing us at the water-line, would have settled the matter. The range being so short one can conjecture that the German gunners, realising that they could not miss, pumped ammunition into us at the utmost speed of which their guns were capable without regard to the particular damage which they were likely to cause. Their loss of serenity, due in the first place to the novel circumstances of the case, must have been considerably augmented by the fact that our own projectiles were hitting the wall near the gun muzzles—it was too much to hope that we should actually obtain any hits on the guns themselves.

The petty officer at one of our six-inch guns, when asked afterwards what ranges he fired at, said that he reckoned he opened fire at about two hundred yards and he continued till close to the Mole.

"How close?" he was asked.

"Reckoning from the gun muzzle," he replied, "I should say it was about three feet!"

One can picture the situation as seen from the Mole itself. A hostile vessel suddenly looming out of the fog at point-blank range, the intense excitement which resulted, the commencement of fire, the bursting of shell on the wall, the ardent desire to hit something as rapidly and as often as possible, the natural inclination to fire at the nearest object, namely, that part of the vessel on their own level, and the realisation that in a few moments the guns would no longer bear on the target. One can imagine the thoughts that were uppermost in their minds, "Hit her, smash her, pump it in, curse those guns of hers, don't lose a second of time, blow her to bits!" One cannot blame those gunners. To use a war-time expression, "They had the wind up." We had counted on that, we had concentrated all our efforts at "putting the wind up." Yet if anybody had seriously suggested that a ship could steam close past a shore battery in these modern days of gunnery he would have been laughed to scorn. Yet it was easy. The reason is not far to seek.

Those who worship *materiel* have followed a false god. The crux of all fighting lies with the personnel—a fact borne out again and again on this particular night just as throughout past history. If the German gunners had been superhuman this tale would not have been told, but human nature, reckoned with by the attackers, was on our side; the initiative was ours.

The material damage was very great, but, though it may sound paradoxical, of not much importance. The upper works and upper deck of the ship received the brunt of it. The most serious matter was the damage to our gangways. Several were shot away and many others damaged beyond further usefulness and, so far as could be observed at the time, only four were left us for the work in hand. Two heavy shell penetrated the ship's side below the upper deck. One passed in just beneath the foremost flame-thrower hut and burst on impact. The other came through within a few feet of the first and wrecked everything in its vicinity. Two other heavy shell came through the screen door to the forecastle and placed one of the howitzer guns out of action. The funnels, ventilators, bridges, chart-house, and all such were riddled through and through.

The damage to the personnel was exceedingly serious. Orders had been given that the storming parties should remain below, under cover, until the ship arrived alongside. The number of personnel in exposed positions was to be limited mainly to those manning the guns, rocket apparatus, and flame-throwers. The senior officers of the storming parties, however, stationed themselves in the most handy position for leading and directing the assault, with the result that they were exposed to the full blast of the hurricane fire from the Mole battery. Military officers had always acted in a similar manner whatever their instructions might be. One cannot help feeling that in any fighting service, where discipline is based on leadership rather than on mere driving force, officers will do the same thing.

Captain Halahan, commanding the naval storming forces, who had repeatedly told me this was to be his last fight, was shot down and killed at the outset. Commander Edwards, standing near him on the gangway deck, was also shot down and completely incapacitated. Colonel Elliot, commanding the Marine storming forces, and his second-in-command, Major Cordner, were killed on the bridge, where they had taken up a commanding position in full view of the gangway deck. Many others were killed or wounded. The death of so many brave men was a terrible blow. Nobody knew better than they the tremendous risk attached to their actions—the pity of it was that they should not have lived to see the success for which they were so largely responsible.

At one minute past midnight the ship actually arrived alongside the Mole, one minute late on schedule time, having steamed alongside at sixteen knots speed. The engines were immediately reversed at full speed and the ship bumped the Mole very gently on the specially constructed fender fitted on the port bow.

The conning position in the flame-thrower hut was well chosen, our heads being about five feet above the top of the Mole wall. We had previously devoted many hours to studying photographs of the Mole with the idea of recognising objects thereon. Our aerial *confrères* had photographed every portion of the Mole from almost every conceivable angle with both ordinary and stereoscopic cameras. We had also had picture postcards and other illustrations at our disposal. Though none of us had ever actually seen the Mole itself we felt pretty sure of being able to recognise any portion of it immediately. In that we were over-confident. The smoke, the intermittent glare and flashes, the alternating darkness and the unceasing rain, added to the disturbance of one's attention caused by the noise and the explosion of shell, rendered observation somewhat difficult.

As far as we could see we were to the westward of our desired position. The engines were, therefore, kept at full speed astern and the ship, aided by the three-knot tide running to the eastward, rapidly drifted in that direction. When sufficient sternway had been gathered the engines were put to full speed ahead to check her. A low building was then observed on the Mole abreast the ship, but it was not recognised immediately as the northeastern shed (No. 3), which we had expected to appear much larger. The distance in the uncertain light was also very deceptive, the building in question appearing to be situated within a few feet of the outer wall, whereas it must have been at least forty-five yards away.

But time was pressing. Our main diversion had certainly commenced, but at all costs we must have it fully developed before the blockships arrived at twenty minutes past midnight. The order was therefore given to let go the starboard anchor. A voice tube, for this purpose, led from the flame-thrower hut to the cable deck. The order was certainly not given *sotto voce*. But the noise at this time was terrific. I could not be certain whether the order was received as no answer was heard in reply. Certainly the anchor was not let go. Meanwhile the engines were ordered at full speed astern and full speed ahead alternately to keep the ship in position; the manner in which these orders were carried out by the engine-room staff, under the command of Engineer Lieutenant-Commander Bury, was admirable. No reply being forthcoming to questions as to the delay in anchoring, Rosoman left the conning tower and went below to investigate. The din had now reached a crescendo. Every gun that would bear appeared to be focused on our upper works, which were being hit every few seconds. Our guns in the fighting-top were pouring out a continuous hail of fire in reply. One could aptly say that we could hardly hear ourselves think.

At last I had news from the cable deck—this was a great relief as I feared that the two heavy shell which burst between decks had killed all the anchoring party. The starboard anchor had jammed somewhere. It had been previously lowered to the water's edge and nothing was holding the cable, but it refused to budge. The port anchor was, therefore, dropped at the foot of the wall and the ship allowed to drop astern until a hundred yards of cable had been veered. The cable was then secured.

The ship immediately swung bodily out from the Mole. With the helm to starboard she swung in again, but with her bows so tight against the Mole, and her stern so far out, that the foremost gangways just failed to reach the top of the wall. With the helm amidships the ship lay parallel to the wall, but no gangways would reach. With the helm to port the ship again swung away from the Mole. This was an exceedingly trying situation. Everything now depended upon the *Daffodil* (Lieutenant H. G. Campbell).

It will be remembered that, as a result of the towing hawser having parted, and in consequence of our increase of speed when running alongside, the *Iris* and *Daffodil* had been left behind. We knew that whatever happened we could absolutely depend on Gibbs, (Commander Valentine F. Gibbs), and Campbell making short work of any surmountable difficulty, and our trust was not misplaced. They must have cut off a considerable corner to have arrived as early as they did. The *Iris* steamed past us at her utmost speed, which was very slow, and went alongside the Mole about a hundred yards ahead of *Vindictive* exactly as laid down in the Plan. Of her more *anon*.

After we had been struggling against our difficulties alongside for about five minutes *Daffodil* suddenly appeared steaming straight for our foremast in a direction perpendicular to the Mole. Campbell pushed her nose against us, hawsers were passed to his vessel, and he shoved us bodily alongside the Mole, exactly in accordance with the Plan. Really he might have been an old stager at tug-master's work, pursuing his vocation in one of our own harbours, judging by the cool manner in which he carried out his instructions to the letter.

Immediately the two foremost gangways reached the wall they were lowered until they rested on it. No other gangways were then available. The order was at once passed to "Storm the Mole."

Owing to the light wind of the preceding day we had not expected to find any swell against the wall. The scend of the sea, however, was so heavy and so confused, as each wave rebounded, that the ship was rolling considerably. Every time she rolled over to port there was a heavy jarring bump which was probably caused by the bilge on the port side of the ship crashing down on the step of the Mole some few feet below the surface. The whole ship was shaking violently at each bump and rolling so heavily that we were greatly apprehensive of sustaining vital damage below the water-line.

The Stokes gun batteries had already been bombing the Mole abreast the ship. The flame-throwers should also have helped to clear the way for our storming parties. The order had been given to switch on the foremost flame-thrower. Unfortunately the pipe leading from the containers to the hut had been severed somewhere below by a shell explosion. This was not noticed before the order was obeyed, with the result that many gallons of highly inflammable oil were squirted over the decks. One hesitates to think what would have happened if this oil had become ignited.

Incidentally the actual nozzle of this flame-thrower was shot away just after the order to switch on had been given by the officer in charge, Lieutenant A. L. Eastlake, attached R.E., who held the proud position of being the sole representative of the military on board the attacking vessels. Eastlake was the only other occupant of the hut and I don't think he will easily forget the brief period that we experienced in that decidedly uncomfortable erection. Sparks were flying about inside, but somehow, at the time, one did not connect that pyrotechnic display with the fact that they emanated from the medley of missiles passing through it. Curiously enough neither of us was hit, but our clothing sadly needed repair—an experience which was common enough in shore fighting, but unusual afloat where the missiles are generally rather too large to pass through one's headgear without removing one's head en route.

The other flame-thrower fared no better. Commander Brock was in charge. He lit the ignition apparatus and passed down the order to "switch on." The whole outfit of oil ran its course, but unfortunately at the very commencement the ignition apparatus was shot away, with the result that the instrument was converted into an oil thrower instead of emitting a flame.

Lieutenant-Commander B. F. Adams, leading a party of seamen, stormed the Mole immediately the gangways were placed. The only two gangways which could reach the Mole were, to say the least of it, very unsteady platforms. Their inboard ends were rising and falling several feet as the ship rolled; the outer ends were see-sawing and sliding backwards and forwards on the top of the wall. My own personal impression at the time was that these gangways were alternately lifting off and resting on the wall, but apparently that was not so. The fact remains, however, that the run across these narrow gangways with a thirty-foot drop beneath to certain death was not altogether inviting.

The first act of the advance party, in accordance with the instructions, was to secure the ship to the wall by means of the grappling anchors. A great struggle to do this was undertaken. The foremost grappling anchors only just reached the Mole. Some men sat on the top of the wall and endeavoured to pull the grapnels over the top as they were lowered from the ship. These grapnels, by virtue of the use for which they were designed, were heavy. That fact, combined with the continuous rolling of the ship, made it exceedingly difficult to control them. Rosoman and a party of men on board joined in the struggle, but a heavy lurch of the ship broke up the davit on which the foremost grappling iron was slung and the latter fell between the ship and the wall.

Adams' party were followed out in great style by the remainder of the seamen storming parties led by their surviving officers, and then by the Marines. I propose to tell later of what occurred on the Mole itself in so far as I have been able to gather from the parties concerned.

As soon as it was clear that the grappling anchors had failed us owing to the heavy swell there was no other alternative than to order *Daffodil* to carry on pushing throughout the proceedings.

A curious incident which has never been explained occurred just previously. Some individual in *Vindictive* had hailed *Daffodil* and called to them to shove off, "By whose orders?" came the response shouted by Campbell from *Daffodil's* bridge. "Captain Halahan's orders," was the reply. As a matter of fact poor gallant Halahan had been killed some ten minutes earlier. "I take my orders from Captain Carpenter," shouted Campbell.

"He's dead," was shouted back.

"I don't believe it," responded Campbell, and incidentally he was right, though I have not the faintest idea what he based his belief on. As Mark Twain would have said, "the report of my death was much exaggerated." The incident was certainly curious, but of course (this for the benefit of those who, during the war, saw spies and traitors at every corner) there can only be the explanation that some poor wounded fellow must have been delirious.

Campbell had been shot in the face, but such a trifle as that did not appear to have worried him, and he continued to push the *Vindictive* alongside from the moment of his arrival until the whole hour and five minutes had elapsed before we left the Mole. Originally the *Daffodil* had been detailed to secure alongside *Vindictive* as soon as the latter was secured to the Mole and then to disembark her demolition parties for their work on the Mole. That part of the plan could not be carried out, however, though several of his parties climbed over her bows into *Vindictive* on their way to accomplish it.

The demolition charges had been stowed outside the conning tower ready for use; on the passage across we had come to the conclusion that this was a case of risking the success of the whole landing for the furtherance of a secondary object, and the charges had therefore been removed to a safer position. This change of arrangement was indeed fortunate, for the deck on both sides of the conning tower became a regular shambles during the final approach. Yeoman of Signals John Buckley, who had volunteered to take up a position outside the conning tower in readiness to fire illuminating rockets had remained at his post until killed. We found him there at the foot of his rocket tube in the morning, a splendid fellow who had been as helpful in the work of preparation as he was unflinching in the face of almost certain death. All the signalmen except one had been either killed or completely disabled, and almost every soul on the conning-tower platform had made the supreme sacrifice.

On the order being given to storm the Mole the storming parties had rushed up every available ladder to the gangway deck. At the top of the foremost ladder the men, in their eagerness to get at the enemy, were stumbling over a body. I had bent down to drag it clear when one of the men shouted: "That's Mr. Walker, sir, he's had his arm shot off." Immediately Walker, who was still conscious, heard this he waved his remaining hand to me and wished me the best of luck. This officer, Lieutenant H. T. C. Walker, survived.

The high wall, towering above our upper deck, was now protecting the hull of the ship from gun-fire; no vital damage could be sustained in that way so long as we remained alongside. The chief source of danger from which vital damage might accrue before we had completed our work at the Mole was that of the fast German motor boats stationed at Blankenberghe. The latter harbour was barely five minutes' steaming distance away, and, as the enemy would now be fully cognisant of our position, we might reasonably expect a horde of these craft to come to the attack with torpedo. It does not require much naval knowledge to realise that the difficulty of avoiding torpedo fire under such circumstances would be well-nigh insuperable. Where a torpedo craft of that description can suddenly rush in from the outer darkness a large vessel has to depend upon remaining unseen; but of course such tactics were now impossible, and, still further, a torpedo could not be avoided even if seen coming towards the ship. That we were not attacked in that manner was mainly due to the work of certain of our smaller craft specially detailed to deal with the Blankenberghe force; former experience of the latter also led us to believe that the German personnel in those boats had no stomach for a fight.

Our guns in the fighting-top were directing a murderous fire into their special targets. Chief amongst those were the heavy gun battery at the end of the broad part of the Mole and the lighter battery on the lighthouse extension. In neither case could the enemy's guns bear on the ship, and we had the advantage of taking the former battery from the rear and giving the latter a taste of enfilading fire from its western flank. But there was another target of importance. Immediately abreast the ship a German destroyer was berthed alongside the inner wharf of the Mole only eighty yards distant from the ship. We had an uninterrupted view of the greater part of her between the two northern sheds, her bridges showing well above the ground-level of the Mole. Our guns in the fighting-top, in charge of Lieutenant Charles N. B. Rigby, R.M.A., riddled that destroyer through and through. We could see the projectiles hitting the Mole floor whenever the gun was temporarily depressed, and then shower upon shower of sparks as they tore through the destroyer's upperworks. The vessel appeared to have sunk, as very little of her upper deck could be seen, although we had such an elevated view-point, but now I think it possible that the wall protected her vitals and that she escaped complete destruction from our gun-fire.

There seems little doubt that our fighting-top was now coming in for the attention of most of the enemy guns. Presently a tremendous crash overhead followed by a cessation of our fire indicated that a heavy shell had made havoc with poor Rigby and his crew of eight men. As a matter of fact, that shell had wrecked the whole fighting-top, killed all the personnel except two gunners who were both severely wounded, and dismounted one of the guns. The only survivor who was not completely disabled—Sergeant Finch, R.M.A.—struggled out from the shambles somehow and, without a thought for his own wounds, examined the remaining gun, found it was still intact, and continued the fight single-handed. He continued to serve this gun and again did great execution until a second shell completely destroyed the remains of the top and put Finch completely out of action. The splendid work of Lieutenant Rigby and his guns' crews had been invaluable, and one cannot but attribute the complete success of our diversion very largely to these gallant men. Rigby himself had set a wonderful example; all who knew him had never doubted that he would do so. Finch survived and was afterwards voted the Victoria Cross by the men of the Royal Marines.

As soon as the ship had been securely anchored the howitzer guns manned by the R.M.A., in charge of Captain Reginald Dallas-Brooks, R.M.A., commenced to bombard the targets specially assigned to them. The German batteries on the mainland were shelling our position at the Mole for all they were worth, but their efforts must have been hampered by the continuous fire of our howitzers. The presence of such weapons on board ship was, to say the least of it, most unusual. Vindictive's nature had undergone an unusual change as soon as she was secured to the Mole. Our position was known to within a few yards. Both direction and range of the enemy's batteries had been worked out beforehand for any position alongside the wall. We were, therefore, in the novel situation of being able to drop heavy howitzer shell upon the enemy's batteries less than a mile away, a decided change from ordinary battleship target practice where ranges of ten to fifteen miles were the order of the day.

The 7.5-inch howitzer gun on the forecastle could not be used. A heavy shell had burst amongst the original gun's crew and had killed or disabled them all. A second crew was sent from one of the naval six-inch guns in the battery and was just being detailed to work the howitzer when another shell killed, or disabled, all but two men. Soon after opening fire the midship 7.5-inch howitzer was damaged by another shell which killed some of the crew, but the remainder repaired the gun under great difficulty and managed to resume the firing later on. The eleven-inch howitzer on the quarter-deck was extremely well handled. This gun fired at a steady rate throughout the proceedings in spite of the darkness, the fumes, the difficulty of manhandling such large projectiles in a cramped-up space and the battering that the ship was receiving around them. The behaviour of the R.M.A. throughout was fine; they worked with a will which may have been equalled elsewhere, but which has certainly never been surpassed; the example set by Captain Brooks was altogether splendid.

Mention must be made of the pyrotechnic party, as we called them. Having located and reached the Mole ourselves, an early duty was that of indicating its extremity to the approaching blockships. For this purpose a rocket station was rigged up in my cabin below. The rocket apparatus protruded through a port in the stern of the ship and had been placed at an angle calculated to carry the rocket behind the lighthouse before bursting, so that the lighthouse would show clearly against an illuminated background. One of the party was told off for this position, instructed as to the object to be attained, and ordered to carry on according to his own judgment. I believe this man had never previously served afloat and had never been in action, but, like the rest of them, he did his bit without the slightest hesitation and, judging by results, with one hundred *per cent* efficiency. Others of the pyrotechnic brigade landed with the storming parties and worked the portable flame-throwers, special flares, etc., before finally attending the smoke-making apparatus and assisting with the wounded. Lieutenant Graham S. Hewett, R.N.V.R., was in command of the pyrotechnic party.

A few minutes after the storming of the Mole had commenced a terrific explosion was seen away to the westward, and we guessed that the submarine party had attacked the viaduct. A seaman was standing near me at the time and brought back to me an old remark of mine, referred to earlier, when he asked, "Was that it, sir?" The explosion presented a wonderful spectacle. The flames shot up to a great height—one mentally considered it at least a mile. Curiously enough the noise of the explosion could not be distinguished. The experiences of the submarines will be related presently.

At about 12.15 a.m. the blockships were expected to be close to the Mole, and a momentary glimpse of them was obtained as they passed close to the lighthouse on their way to the canal entrance. So far so good. We saw nothing more of the blockships and received no further news of them until the operation had been completed. Nevertheless, no news was good news under the circumstances and we felt quite confident that the blockships had not been seriously hampered by the German Mole defences. Our primary object was, therefore, attained; the diversion had been of sufficient magnitude.

Our further tasks were firstly that of continuing the diversion until the crews of the blockships had had a reasonable chance of being rescued subsequent to sinking their vessels in the canal, secondly of re-embarking our storming parties and withdrawing to seaward, and thirdly of carrying out demolition work on the Mole during our stay alongside. It will be noticed that these three tasks are not mentioned in their proper sequence of event but in their order of importance. It is obviously true that demolition work might be of assistance from the point of view of diversion, but not to a great extent when one realises that the enemy were already so animated with a desire to destroy our ship that they would hardly care one way or the other what our particular action on the Mole might be. The presence of the ship was the main diversion and so, at all costs, the ship must be kept alongside until the diversion was no longer required and until our storming parties had returned.

At about half an hour after midnight the full force of the diversion had been developed. Although the ship was still being hit continuously and the inferno showed no signs of abatement one can say that the conditions had become stabilised. As far as we could gather we could not augment our efforts, but could only carry on for the time being. So we carried on.

Being somewhat anxious as to the state of things between decks I took the opportunity of a hurried visit below. On my way down from the bridge I met Lieutenant E. Hilton-Young, R.N.V.R., our parliamentary representative. He was attired in his shirtsleeves and minus any head-gear. His right arm was bandaged. I remember that he was breaking all the accepted rules of the drill-book by smoking a large cigar as he performed his prearranged duties of supervising the foremost six-inch guns and his self-appointed duty of cheering everybody

H.M.S. Vindictive's Bridge and Flame-Thrower Hut (Right).

The fighting top is shown above, and from behind, the bridge.
The conning tower is below the bridge. A large shell passed through the hole to the
right of the man in white uniform.

up. On enquiry he informed me that he had "got one in the arm." I heard afterwards that even when he had collapsed, he refused to, have his wound attended to, and had to be taken below by force. Eventually his right arm had to be amputated, but with his unfailing resource he did not let many hours pass by before commencing to educate himself in the art of left-handed writing.

Every available space on the mess deck was occupied by casualties. Those who could do so were sitting on the mess stools awaiting their turn for medical attention. Many were stretched at full length on the deck, the majority being severely wounded. Some had already collapsed and were in a state of coma; I fear that many had already passed away. It was a sad spectacle indeed. Somehow, amidst all the crashing and smashing on deck, one had not realised the sacrifice that was taking place.

During a fight at sea the personnel below know little or nothing of how things are going. This especially applies to the stokehold and engine-room personnel, who are, indeed, in an unenviable position. It applies, also, to the wounded who have been carried below. It is not difficult to imagine their feelings, especially when one considers how rapidly a vessel may sink after sustaining a vital injury. One does not need to be an advanced psychologist to understand the importance of keeping those stationed between decks supplied with information as to what is occurring on deck. So I shouted out something about everything going splendidly, the Mole being stormed, the viaduct being blown up and the blockships having passed in. The cheer that went up will live long in my memory. Those who could stand crowded round and forgot their wounds. Some of those on the deck endeavoured to sit up to ascertain the news. I did not then know that I had been reported as killed. The crowd almost barred my way in their excitement, and the question which caught my ear more than any other was, "Have we won, sir? Have we won?" just as if the whole affair had been a football match.

The medical officers and their assistants, under the direction of Staff-Surgeon McCutcheon, were working at the highest pressure. The wounded were literally pouring down every available ladder in a constant stream. Dressing stations had been improvised at intervals along the deck. The ward-room and the sick bay being the two main stations. Everything humanly possible was being done to render first-aid and to alleviate suffering. There was no lack of ready helpers. All those of the latter who could do so were bringing the wounded down. Many of the less severely wounded were attending to those others who were badly hit. A marine with his own head bandaged up was supporting in his arms an officer who was unconscious with a terrible wound in the head, and only relaxed his hold when the officer died. The work of McCutcheon and his *confrères* was beyond all praise; untiring energy, consummate care, and withal real brotherly bearing characterised their actions.

The news of the blockships spread quickly, and one heard every now and then renewed outbursts of cheering. The news had reached the stokehold and did much to relieve the tension amongst the personnel in that part of the ship. A few pieces of shell had fallen into the engine room, but no damage had been done.

A return to the lower bridge showed little apparent change in the situation. Shell were still hitting us every few seconds and many casualties were being caused by flying splinters. Large pieces of the funnels and ventilators were being torn out and hurled in all directions—one wondered how much more of this battering the ship could stand. The exact nature of the various missiles and the direction from whence they came were of course unknown to us. It was afterwards suggested that the shore guns to the westward of Blankenberghe were doing much of the mischief. Certainly our position, tangential to the Mole, brought such a thing into the realm of possibility, but it would seem doubtful whether those German batteries, from which we were probably invisible, would risk hitting their own guns on the Mole from that flanking direction. However, all our guns which could fire at the enemy were fully occupied in accordance with the prearranged plan, so there was no particular object in ascertaining the position of new targets.

Our chief anxiety at this period was the safety of *Daffodil*, which seemed to bear a charmed life. *Vindictive's* hull was amply protected by the wall itself, but *Daffodil* was far more exposed. As already mentioned the loss of *Daffodil* would almost certainly have entailed the loss of the whole of the storming parties on the Mole.

CHAPTER 4

The Fight on the Mole

As soon as the two foremost gangways reached the wall a party of seamen led by Lieutenant-Commander Adams had commenced the storming of the Mole. Lieutenant-Commander A. L. Harrison, the senior officer of the seamen storming parties, had been wounded in the head and was too dazed to land on the Mole until later. Commander Brock, having completed his duties in the aft flamethrower hut, also stormed the Mole.

Adams and a handful of men made their way along the parapet to the left and found an observation hut situated on it close by. This was bombed, but no occupants were found inside. Brock is believed to have gone inside this hut for the purpose of examining its interior; there is no authentic evidence that he was ever seen again. Adams stationed some of his men to guard a ladder leading from the parapet to the floor of the Mole and then returned to find us struggling with the grappling anchors as already described. Adams then reconnoitred again to the eastward and located a German machine-gun firing at the parapet from the trench system on the floor of the Mole. Barbed wire surrounded this trench, which interposed between *Vindictive* and the three-gun battery at the end of the broad part of the Mole. The seamen were then detailed to bomb the trench position, but in doing so they suffered many casualties from machine-gun fire. The position on the parapet was almost entirely exposed to gun-fire from the Mole itself, the lookout station affording the only cover. The German vessels berthed at the inner side of the Mole had also joined in the fight.

The terrific noise, the darkness, the bursting of shell, and the hail of machine-gun bullets rendered it exceedingly difficult for any one individual to make such observations as would lead to a connected account of the fighting on the Mole itself.

Just before arriving alongside the Mole, Lieutenant-Commander Harrison, in supreme command of the seamen storming parties after Commander Halahan's death, was struck on the head by a fragment of a shell; he was knocked senseless and sustained a broken jaw. On recovering consciousness he proceeded over one of the gangways to the parapet, where he took over command of the party detailed to attack the Mole batteries to the eastward, Lieutenant-Commander Adams going back to obtain re-enforcements. Gathering together a handful of his men, Harrison led a charge along the parapet itself in the face of heavy machine-gun fire. He was killed at the head of his men, all but two of whom were also killed, these two being wounded.

Harrison's charge down that narrow gangway of death was a worthy finale to the large number of charges which, as a forward of the first rank, he had led down many a Rugby football ground. He had "played the game" to the end. To quote the final words in the official notification of his posthumous award of the Victoria Cross—

> Lieutenant-Commander Harrison, although already severely wounded and undoubtedly in great pain, displayed indomitable resolution and courage of the highest order in pressing his attack, knowing as he did that any delay in silencing the guns might jeopardise the main object of the expedition, *i.e.*, the blocking of the Zeebrugge-Bruges Canal.

With Harrison's death the navy lost an officer who was as popular and as keen as he had been invaluable to the success of this particular operation, especially in the preparatory work.

Able-Seaman McKenzie, one of the survivors of Harrison's party, finding himself alone, did good execution with his Lewis gun in spite of being wounded in several places; he eventually returned to *Vindictive* after accounting for a number of the enemy.

The marines, now commanded by Major B. G. Weller, R.M.L.I., had followed the seamen over the gangways.

The prearranged details of the operations on the Mole had to be somewhat modified owing to the fact that *Vindictive* was further to the westward than originally intended. The reason for the latter has already been given, but a further word may not be out of place. The responsibility for the actual position of the ship was entirely my own; the error in position was, therefore, my own also. When the attack was originally planned the intention had been to endeavour to place the ship with her stern seventy yards from the western gun of the battery

171

on the lighthouse extension. Actually *Vindictive's* gangways rested on the Mole nearly three hundred yards to the westward. One can only conjecture what would have happened, under the circumstances of the failure of the smoke screen owing to the change of wind, if the ship had proceeded past the six-gun battery at a speed sufficiently slow for berthing so close to the battery itself. Whether the ship would ever have reached the Mole, or whether there would have been any storming parties left on arrival alongside, can only be guessed. It certainly looks as if our mistake in position was as providential as it was unintentional.

Lieutenant F. T. V. Cooke, who afterwards greatly distinguished himself, led out the first party of Marines and silenced a party of Germans who were observed firing at the parapet from a position near No. 2 shed. Another party under Lieutenant Lamplough then established a strong point near No. 3 shed for the purpose of dealing with any enemy approaching from the westward. His party also attacked and bombed a German destroyer berthed at the inner side of the Mole.

Another party was ordered to the eastward to re-enforce the seamen. As soon as the position was more clear the main party of the Marine force, under Captain E. Bamford, commenced an assault on the German positions covering the Mole battery.

It is not possible to say how many of the storming parties reached the Mole—the loss of officers and men and the resulting temporary disorganisation naturally prevented the collection of definite information. Suffice it to say that a large number stormed the Mole in furtherance of our diversion, and that the latter was undoubtedly successful in that we attained our primary object of assisting the blockships to pass an all-important obstacle in the Mole batteries.

Before passing on to other phases of the operation a general idea of the difficulties faced by the storming parties may be of interest, together with a brief account of the manner in which these difficulties were surmounted.

From the time of our arrival the Mole abreast the ship was subjected to extremely heavy fire. Presumably the shore guns, including the Kaiser Wilhelm battery with its twelve-inch guns and the Goeben battery (9.4-inch guns) situated almost within point-blank range, were shelling the Mole for all they were worth, regardless of damage to their own property or of danger to their own personnel. That, of course, would be a correct action, the repulse of the enemy always being of first importance.

The parapet on the high wall was almost entirely destitute of cover. The difficulty of placing the scaling ladders from the parapet to the floor-level of the Mole and of descending them whilst carrying such paraphernalia as rifles, bombs, flame-throwers, Lewis guns, etc., can easily be imagined. The difficulty would certainly not be lessened by the fact that the men would have their backs to any enemy who might be awaiting them on the Mole itself. The fighting amidst entirely strange surroundings in the face of properly organised strong points held by the enemy would not be easy. Add to that the certain losses and consequent disorganisation entailed during the assault, the difficulty of recognising friend from foe at night, and the blinding glare of star shell or searchlights alternating with momentary periods of inky darkness.

Undoubtedly the assault would be difficult enough. But what of the retirement? The bodies of any men who were killed or disabled on the Mole could only be re-embarked by way of the vertical ladders against the wall. It would be bad enough to descend them in the first place, but a herculean task to carry a body twenty feet up a vertical ladder under incessant shell and machine-gun fire. Yet—and I think this fact sums up the splendid gallantry of these men—of the large number of men who stormed the Mole, many of whom were killed or completely disabled, the total number left on the Mole after the retirement, including both dead and wounded, amounted to little more than a *dozen*.

Daffodil, as already described, was prevented from landing her demolition parties in the prearranged manner, but some of them, led by Sub-Lieutenant F. E. Chevallier, had climbed into *Vindictive* and made their way to the Mole. Lieutenant C. C. Dickinson, commanding the demolition parties, and a party of his men on board *Vindictive* had landed at the commencement of the assault. They placed a couple of ladders, descended them, and then proceeded across the Mole, killing some Germans who were apparently making for the ladders. Demolition charges were placed in position, but not actually exploded owing to the presence of our own men in the vicinity. There is little doubt that the demolition parties would have been able to carry out considerable destructive work if more time had been available. Whatever the results of their efforts it is certain that Dickinson, Chevallier, and their men did all that was possible under the circumstances.

Iris had reached the Mole and dropped her anchor at the foot of

THE FIGHT ON THE MOLE.

Note the men coming down the outer wall of the Mole from *Vindictive*

the wall, about 12.15 a.m., her position being roughly one hundred yards ahead, *i.e.*, to the westward, of *Vindictive*. The heavy swell was tossing her about like a cork, with the result that the use of the parapet anchors was extremely difficult. After several failures to get these parapet anchors hooked to the top of the wall Lieutenant Claude E. K. Hawkings, one of the officers of the storming party, ordered some men to hold up one of the scaling ladders. They could not actually lean it against the wall; the rough nature of the latter and the surging of the ship would have combined to break the ladder immediately. The ladder was, therefore, merely sloping towards the wall without any support at its upper end. Hawkings ran up it and leaped to the top of the Mole, the ladder being smashed to pieces a moment later. He sat astride the wall for the purpose of fixing an anchor and appears to have been immediately attacked by some enemy on the parapet itself. He was seen defending himself with his revolver before he was actually killed. It was terribly sad that his great act should have cost him his life.

Lieutenant-Commander George N. Bradford, who was actually in command of the storming party in *Iris* and whose duties did not include that of securing the ship, climbed up the ship's derrick, which carried a large parapet anchor and which was rigged out over the Mole side of the ship. The derrick itself was crashing on the Mole with each movement of the ship, which, in turn, was rolling and pitching heavily; a more perilous climb can scarcely be imagined. Waiting his opportunity, Bradford chose the right moment and jumped to the wall, taking the anchor with him. He placed the latter in position, but almost immediately was riddled with machine-gun bullets and fell into the sea between *Iris* and the Mole. Gallant attempts were made to rescue his body, but owing to the darkness and the rush of the strong tidal stream he was swept away beyond recovery.

Nothing could have been finer than Bradford's efforts to secure the ship. He had been a splendid fighter in the "ring"; it was against his nature to give in as long as there was the remotest chance of winning through; his death brought us the great loss of a great gentleman. Really, one cannot conceive greater bravery than was shown by these two officers, who have set an example which will surely never be forgotten.

The anchor placed by Bradford had either slipped or been shot away, with the result that *Iris* suddenly surged out from the Mole. It was then obvious that the difficulty of securing to the Mole was insuperable, so Commander Gibbs very rightly decided to land his men across *Vindictive*. He therefore ordered the cable to be slipped and then steamed round the stern of *Daffodil* and came alongside *Vindictive*. This change of plan, necessitated by the unfavourable state of the sea, showed a highly creditable degree of initiative. It must be realised that these movements and proceedings of *Iris* had occupied over half an hour; it was about 12.55 a.m. before *Iris* was secured to *Vindictive*. By that time the order for the retirement had been given. A few men scrambled out of *Iris*, but that ship was almost immediately ordered to shove off. She therefore left *Vindictive* and shaped course to the northward. She had barely turned when she came under a heavy fire from some enemy batteries. Two large shell and several small shell hit her, and were closely followed by three more large shell. The lookout house at the port extremity of the bridge was destroyed and a serious fire was caused on the upper deck.

Valentine Gibbs, who had remained on the bridge throughout the operation, was mortally wounded. I had known "Val," as we had always called him, since he was a boy of thirteen. Even at that age he had shown himself to be absolutely fearless. Later in life he pad risen rapidly in his profession and would assuredly have been marked out for high command in due course. In peace days he had won the great race on the Cresta Run at St. Moritz, in war he had volunteered for every dangerous operation for which he had the remotest chance of selection. At last his opportunity had come and he lived for nought else than to put *Iris* alongside Zeebrugge Mole. I was told afterwards that in his short periods of consciousness after being wounded he asked and repeated but one question, "How are things going?" and he continued to ask how things were going until he died. I cannot write more of "Val"—words and phrases fail to do him justice.

The havoc in *Iris* was serious. From *Vindictive* she appeared to have been sunk, for she suddenly disappeared in a cloud of smoke and flame.

Major C. E. E. Eagles, D.S.O., in command of the Marine storming parties in *Iris*, was killed, and many of his men were killed and wounded at this period. Artificial smoke was emitted and a small motor boat also laid a smoke screen to shoreward of *Iris*—this probably accounted for her sudden disappearance from view.

The navigating officer had been seriously wounded. Lieutenant Oscar Henderson took command. Petty Officer Smith was illuminating the compass with a torch in one hand and steering with the other.

LIEUT. GEORGE N. BRADFORD, R.N.

LIEUT. CLAUDE E. K. HAWKINGS, R.N.

LIEUT. RICHARD D. SANDFORD, R.N.

COMMANDER VALENTINE F. GIBBS, R.N.

Able-Seaman F. E. Blake, having extinguished the fire on the bridge, employed himself in throwing overboard live bombs which were lying amongst the burning debris on the upper deck.

Iris had not received her share of good fortune. Nevertheless, although she actually failed to land her storming parties, there is every probability that her proceedings assisted to enhance the success of the diversion at the Mole and thereby materially assisted towards the safe passage of the blockships, *i.e.*, the attainment of our object.

CHAPTER 5

The Attack on the Railway Viaduct

In the previous chapter I mentioned that the explosion of the submarine took place shortly after the storming of the Mole had commenced.

The immediate purpose in destroying the railway viaduct connecting the Mole to the mainland was twofold: firstly, that of preventing the Germans from sending re-enforcements across to the help of the Mole garrison; secondly, that of augmenting the main diversion. There were, however, ulterior objects also. Firstly, the destruction in itself would be a valuable part of the general work of demolition designed to reduce the efficiency of the Mole as a naval and aerial base; secondly, the loss of the railway would deny to the enemy the use of the Mole as a place of embarkation for military purposes. If deprived of railway communication the Mole would lose a high percentage of its special war value.

Two old submarines, C1, commanded by Lieutenant Aubrey C. Newbold, and C3, commanded by Lieutenant Richard D. Sandford, were chosen for the purpose—each carrying a volunteer crew of one officer and four men in addition to the officer in command.

The submarines were provided with special control apparatus so that the personnel, after having set the apparatus to guide the vessel to its destination, could abandon their craft before reaching the viaduct itself.

For the purpose of abandonment each submarine was given motor-driven skiffs and special ladders. The latter might enable the crews to climb up the viaduct and escape before the explosion took place, the motor skiffs being supplied for escaping to seaward if that was found to be feasible.

Each submarine carried a heavy cargo of high explosive. This latter was fitted with time fuses and special instruments so that there would be sufficient delay between the ignition of the fuse and the final explosion. At a prearranged minute after passing position G, the submarines were to have slipped from their towing hawsers and then to have made the best of their way to the viaduct. Unfortunately C1 was so much delayed by the parting of a hawser that she could not continue her voyage to the viaduct without running the risk of hampering C3. The latter, exactly in accordance with the Plan, slipped from tow and proceeded under her own engines on the prearranged courses.

At midnight the submarine appears to have been sighted in the light of a star shell. Searchlights immediately picked her up and some firing was seen in their direction. Artificial smoke was immediately made use of, but the wind, having then commenced to blow towards the north, was found to be unfavourable. The firing was only of short duration and the artificial smoke was switched off. A few minutes later the viaduct showed up clearly against a glare in the background and course was altered to ensure striking exactly at right angles. Sandford disdained to use the control apparatus to take his submarine into her position.

The vessel was run under the viaduct, at a speed of nearly ten knots, immediately between two of the vertical piles. She charged against the horizontal and diagonal girders with such force as to penetrate the framework of the viaduct as far as her own conning tower, whilst being lifted bodily about a couple of feet on the frames. Firmly wedged under the railway in a position about fifty yards from the northern end of the viaduct the first part of the operation was completed. It is difficult to account for the small opposition offered to her approach by the enemy. Possibly they mistook her for a friend. Another suggestion is that they thought she was endeavouring to pass under the viaduct *en route* to the canal, and that, knowing this was impossible, they hoped to capture her intact. That suggestion sounds extremely unlikely. Possibly the diversion caused by our efforts at the other end of the Mole had distracted the attention of the defence commanders; the men may have feared to take unexpected measures on their own responsibility. Whatever the reason for the lack of enemy opposition, there was certainly no lack of difficulty. The darkness, suddenly giving way to the blinding glare of searchlights, the navigational difficulties, and the necessary care in handling such an awkward vessel combined to make their arrival a very fine feat. But finer was to follow.

Several of the enemy had appeared on the viaduct and commenced to fire on her with machine-guns from close range; the latter cannot have amounted to many feet! The crew lowered a motor skiff and Sandford ordered them to abandon ship. He then fired the time fuse and jumped into the boat. Their purpose was now to steam away to the westward at utmost speed so as to get well clear before the explosion took place. Unfortunately the skiff's engine was useless—the propeller had been broken! Oars had been provided for such an emergency and the crew pulled away from the viaduct for dear life. As soon as the boat was clear of the viaduct itself, the firing became intense, both from the viaduct and from the shore. The German searchlights were directed on to the boat.

Many miracles occurred that night, but none more extraordinary than the escape of this little boat with its two officers and four men. Presently Sandford himself and his petty officer were severely wounded; the stoker was also wounded. The boat was hit again and again, but fortunately the motor pump was working and the water could be rapidly ejected. Sandford was again wounded.

The skiff had managed to struggle about three hundred yards from the viaduct, when there was a deafening roar as submarine C3, the viaduct above her, the railway on the viaduct, and the Germans on the railway were hurled to destruction. It must have been a wonderful moment for Sandford and his crew.

The enemy searchlights were immediately extinguished and the firing died away. A few minutes later a picket boat—the ordinary type of steamboat carried by all large men-of-war—emerged from the darkness and hailed the skiff. The occupants of the latter were assisted into the picket boat, which then proceeded seawards and placed them on board the destroyer *Phoebe*.

The picket boat, under the charge of Lieutenant-Commander F. H. Sandford, R.N., brother of the commander of the submarine, had been detailed for this rescue work. She had made a great part of the overseas journey under her own steam and had arrived in the nick of time to effect the rescue. Sandford—the Lieutenant-Commander—had been largely responsible for working out the details of the attack on the viaduct in addition to the preparations for the demolition work on the Mole. His handling of the picket boat—incidentally she returned the whole way home again under her own steam—was excellent.

Submarine C1 saw what was probably the glare of the explosion caused by C3, but could not be certain whether the latter had reached her destination or not. They therefore waited until they considered

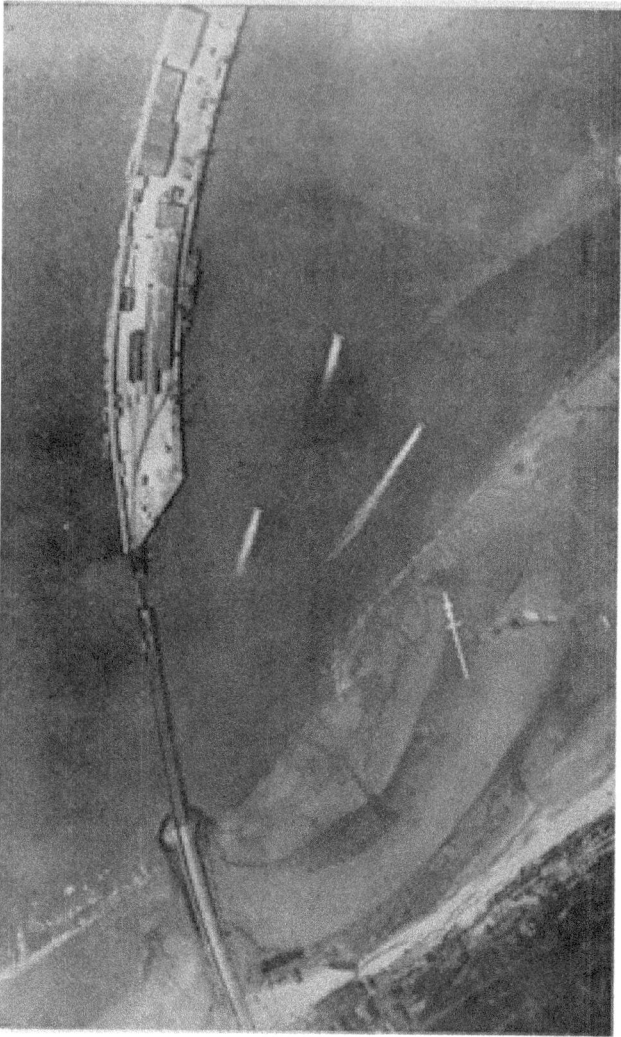

THE RAILWAY VIADUCT.
This aerial photograph shows the break in the viaduct planked over by the Germans. Three German seaplanes are rising to attack the photographer's plane

ample time had passed for C3 to have arrived at the viaduct if all had gone well. C1 then approached the Mole en route towards the viaduct and sighted *Vindictive* retiring to the northward. This appeared to signify that the forces were retiring and that the operation had either been completed or had been found impracticable owing to the change of wind. Lieutenant Newbold, therefore, had to decide as to whether he should continue for the sake of augmenting the destruction caused by C3 or whether he should haul off so as to be available for any further services required. It was a difficult decision to make. He chose the latter and earned the vice-admiral's commendation for doing so.

Those of us who were *au fait* with the details of all phases of the operation little thought we should ever see these heroic attackers of the viaduct again. The chances against manoeuvring a submarine into the viaduct were very considerable, the chances of any of the personnel being rescued were apparently nil. Nobody knew that better than the personnel concerned. The use of the control apparatus would have greatly increased their chances of being rescued, but they refused to consider preservation of life until the success of their undertaking had been assured. They cannot have expected to return. Yet there was no dearth of volunteers. The personnel had been selected in much the same way as those from the Grand Fleet. If the secret could have been made known beforehand and volunteers asked for in the ordinary way we should probably have had the whole submarine service begging to be allowed to take part.

The execution of this most difficult submarine operation was beyond all praise; it was, indeed, a miracle that the crew of C3 lived to witness the unqualified success of their efforts. Before the night was ended these gallant lives were again in jeopardy.

We heard afterwards that a German cyclist corps was hurriedly sent to re-enforce the Mole garrison, and, not knowing that the viaduct had been destroyed, they were precipitated into the sea and thus infringed the Gadarene copyright.

CHAPTER 6

The Smoke Screening

The author is particularly anxious that each phase of the operation and the work of each class of vessel should be clearly understood, so that the reader may fully appreciate the work of the blockships, the latter forming the crux of the whole operation. It will be convenient, therefore, to describe in this chapter the proceedings of those small craft whose work was not carried out in actual company of the blockships themselves.

The general idea of the smoke screens has already been described. A large number of small craft, including coastal motor boats, motor launches, and destroyers, were required for the purpose.

At given intervals after the force had passed through position G the several units left the force to carry out their various duties. The latter comprised laying screens shoreward of the main line of advance, further screens to cover the shore batteries on each side of Zeebrugge, others close off Blankenberghe for the purpose of hampering the German motor boats at that place, and a screen close off the German battery on the lighthouse extension of the Mole. The earlier screens were so efficient that they undoubtedly prevented the enemy from discovering our presence until we were close to our objective. When the wind changed, however, the ideal screening arrangements were no longer possible. Such an eventuality had been allowed for, and, in accordance with their instructions, the screening craft, regardless of the great danger, ran inshore close to the German batteries and did their utmost to ensure the attainment of our object.

The coastal motor boat (C.M.B.) detailed for "fogging" Blankenberghe was C.M.B. 16, Lieutenant D. E. J. MacVean, R.N.V.R. Owing to temporary difficulties with the engines, and uncertainty of position due to drifting while carrying out repairs, this boat accompanied *Vin-*

dictive to the Mole, which was first seen thirty yards away. MacVean then proceeded to Blankenberghe harbour. On arrival near the entrance he came under fire of a four-gun battery, but placed his smoke floats close to the entrance piers and kept renewing them at intervals until the whole operation had ceased, when he returned to harbour. This piece of work was typical of the C.M.B. flotilla, which, most ably commanded by Lieutenant A. P. Welman, R.N., established a new naval tradition.

Welman, himself in command of C.M.B. 236, found it necessary to undertake the duties of another C.M.B. in addition to his own, owing to a difficulty in communicating a modification in the orders. He was personally responsible for a very important part of the screening, namely, that close off the Mole batteries. In spite of the concentrated fire from the latter, and the difficulties due to the change of wind, this gallant officer, who had always allotted himself the most dangerous tasks, with the able assistance of two other C.M.B.'s, maintained a fog screen which must have been an important factor in our success. C.M.B. 226 steamed close in under the Mole battery and laid smoke floats within a few yards of the guns. It is remarkable that these coastal motor boats should have escaped. A single shell would be sufficient to send such a frail craft to the bottom.

Before *Vindictive's* arrival at the Mole two coastal motor boats had left the force for the purpose of attacking German vessels inside the Mole. They soon lost sight of one another in the fog and became separated. C.M.B. 7, Sub-Lieutenant L. R. Blake, R.N.R., first sighted the Mole about one hundred and fifty yards away and steamed close round the lighthouse at high speed. Having located the defence booms of barges and nets he followed down the line of the latter until close inshore and then stopped for the purpose of selecting a target. Observing an enemy destroyer alongside the Mole he steamed straight towards her at high speed and fired his torpedo at her. He then stopped to observe the result. The torpedo was seen to explode near the forebridge of the destroyer, but the conditions of visibility rendered it impossible to ascertain the definite result. During this time he was being heavily fired at by machine-guns on the Mole and by the shore batteries to the eastward of the canal.

Small enemy vessels suddenly appeared and engaged him, and he was further fired at from a dredger which had a machine-gun. C.M.B. 7 had other duties to fulfil in connection with smoke screening. Whilst proceeding at high speed for that purpose she collided with an unlighted buoy, which made a large hole in her bows. Speed was increased to lift the bows clear of the water. It soon became apparent that the damage which she had sustained precluded all further chance of being usefully employed, so course was set for home. An engine defect off Ostende necessitated stopping; this, in turn, brought them into imminent danger of sinking. Eventually one of our destroyers took her in tow and brought her safely to Dover.

The other, C.M.B. 5, Sub-Lieutenant C. Outhwaite, R.N.V.R., had found herself within fifty yards of the Mole and had immediately altered course to pass round the lighthouse. She then sighted a German torpedo-boat destroyer steering to the northeastward and at once increased to utmost speed with the object of attacking her. C.M.B. 5 was evidently seen in the light of star shell and the German switched on her searchlight and opened fire. As soon as the motor boat was sufficiently close she fired a torpedo, which struck the destroyer in the fore part of the vessel. By this time some guns on the Mole had taken up the firing. Under concentrated fire from two directions the motor boat was forced to haul off, and was unable to witness the fate of the destroyer or to search for survivors. This motor boat then proceeded to the eastward and rendered useful assistance to the smoke-screening vessels operating in that direction.

Three other coastal motor boats, Nos. 25, 26, and 21, had been detailed for yet another form of attack on the Mole, namely, that of dropping Stokes bombs on its western portion around the seaplane base. These three craft obtained many hits on the Mole from a range of only fifty yards, one of them actually remaining stopped opposite the seaplane sheds and pumping her bombs over the outer wall just as if there had been no enemy in existence.

C.M.B. 32 waited until the blockships had passed the Mole *en route* to the canal, and then, as soon as the moment appeared to be favourable, she dashed in at utmost speed and fired a torpedo at a German vessel berthed alongside the Mole. The torpedo was heard to explode, but the visibility prevented the actual result from being observed. This attack was carried out under extremely heavy machine-gun fire.

The work of the other coastal motor boats, in connection with the blockships' movements, will be described later.

Eleven torpedo-boat destroyers took part in the inshore operations; many others were utilised as supports to seaward and as escorts to the bombarding monitors. The destroyer flotilla was commanded by Captain Wilfred Tomkinson, under whose direction their work of preparation had been carried out; he accompanied the vice-admiral in H.M.S. *Warwick*.

Of the eleven destroyers, H.M.S. *Warwick*, flying the vice-admiral's flag, had a roving commission so that the vice-admiral could direct the whole operation and render assistance where necessary. The most favourable position from which to direct events was in the vicinity of the Mole lighthouse.

Two other destroyers, *Phoebe*, Lieutenant-Commander Hubert E. Gore-Langton, and *North Star*, Lieutenant-Commander Kenneth C. Helyar, were also detailed to operate near the lighthouse. These two vessels experienced a very anxious time. At the commencement of the attack they patrolled in company with *Warwick*, Commander V. L. A. Campbell, firstly with the object of preventing torpedo attacks by enemy vessels from being directed against the storming vessels at the Mole, and secondly for the purpose of assisting the smoke screening if required.

Just before the Mole was reached at the commencement of the attack these three destroyers, which had been stationed ahead of the main force during the approach, eased down to allow *Vindictive* to pass, and then commenced their patrol. They passed just inside an area of very heavy barrage fire and they frequently came under fire from the Mole. The smoke screens made it very difficult for them to keep touch either with the movements of other vessels or with each other. Very soon the *Phoebe* and *North Star* became separated from the *Warwick*; the latter continued her patrol until the attack was virtually at an end.

North Star, on becoming separated from the others, proceeded towards her patrol area, but had great difficulty in ascertaining her position owing to the smoke. Suddenly an enemy vessel was encountered and the track of a torpedo was clearly seen in the glare of the enemy's searchlight. *North Star* returned the compliment, but it is probable that her torpedo missed similarly to that fired by the enemy vessel; the latter was lost sight of almost immediately. Continuing her efforts to locate the Mole, she found herself close inshore to the eastward of the Mole. After putting her helm hard-over, some ships were seen right ahead, and were recognised as the blockships making their final run to the canal. The Mole was then seen to the northward and a torpedo was fired at a vessel alongside it. At this moment *North Star* was lit up by a searchlight and the German batteries opened a heavy fire upon her. She passed close to the Mole and fired three more torpedoes at vessels alongside it, but the conditions of visibility once more prevented the results from being observed. When passing the lighthouse *North Star* received several hits in the engine-room and boiler-rooms and was completely disabled. Her fate will be recounted presently.

H.M.S. *Phoebe*, after becoming separated from *Warwick*, commenced to patrol off the lighthouse in accordance with her instructions. Presently she fell in with the steamboat which had rescued the crew of Submarine C3. The latter, who were in urgent need of medical attention, were transferred to *Phoebe*, which vessel then continued her patrol as before. Later on *North Star* was sighted in a crippled state and *Phoebe* at once went to her assistance.

North Star was still being illuminated by searchlights and heavily fired at. *Phoebe* laid out a smoke screen to hide her and then took her in tow—a most difficult operation under the circumstances. Unfortunately the tow parted and the smoke screen drifted away before the wind. Once again heavy fire was directed at these vessels and they were being frequently hit. *Phoebe* again took *North Star* in tow, but the towing wires were cut by shell explosions; to make matters worse, the *Phoebe's* steam siren was hit and commenced to fill the air with its discordant shrieking, thus assisting the enemy to locate them.

Phoebe next endeavoured to push *North Star* bodily away from the batteries, but this proved to be impossible. The only other thing to be done was to save *North Star's* crew and to sink her to prevent capture. *Phoebe*, therefore, laid out another protective smoke screen and lowered her boat for the rescue work. Helyar in *North Star* very reluctantly had to order "abandon ship," and this was carried out by means of her boats and rafts. One boat unfortunately capsized, but the others were picked up and the whaler from *Phoebe* made several trips for survivors.

But *Phoebe* had not given up hope. She laid out yet another smoke screen and made another attempt to take *North Star* in tow, going alongside her for the purpose. Helyar and some of his crew had remained on board *North Star* and passed the wires to *Phoebe*. The *North Star* was still being hit repeatedly by shell and commenced to list over as a result of the damage. *Phoebe* then persuaded Helyar to leave his ship and took him on board after embarking the remainder of the crew.

On going astern to avoid the searchlights, another man was seen on board *North Star*. *Phoebe* at once returned alongside and ordered the man to jump across. During all this time *Phoebe* herself had been repeatedly hit, resulting in several casualties, but Gore-Langton considered that he ought to sink *North Star* before leaving her. His ship then came in for increased fire from the German batteries, and as a result of the smoke, was unable to locate *North Star* again—probably she had sunk, already as she had certainly been in a sinking condition when Lieutenant-Commander Helyar left her. (The wreck of *North Star* was afterwards located on the bottom to the northeastward of the lighthouse). For forty-five minutes the struggle to save *North Star* had been carried out within point-blank range of the German batteries, which had kept up an incessant fire almost throughout.

Phoebe herself had received considerable damage and it seems almost a miracle that she survived the ordeal. Anything finer than the conduct of the commanders of these two vessels, and of their ships' companies, cannot be conceived. Yet it was only typical of the destroyer service as a whole, this latter observation being perhaps the best commendation of all. The gallant crew of Submarine C3, previously transferred to *Phoebe* from the picket boat, had seen more than their share of the fighting.

The remaining destroyers, *Whirlwind, Myngs, Trident, Mansfield, Felox, Morris, Moorsom,* and *Melpomene,* all carried out their patrolling duties close to the northward of Zeebrugge without any incidents that require special mention here.

Captain R. Collins, R.N., in charge of the motor launches, was on board M.L. 558, commanded by Lieutenant-Commander Chappell, R.N.V.R. This motor launch rendered useful work in assisting the blockships to find the Mole before the latter vessels had penetrated the smoke screen, and also directed the picket boat towards the viaduct *en route* to rescue the crew of the submarine. Considering the dangerous locality in which M.L. 558 was operating, she was fortunate in being hit by only one shell.

M.L. 424, commanded by Lieutenant O. Robinson, R.N.V.R., was less fortunate. Soon after passing through the smoke screen she was badly hit—her captain and two men being killed and another man wounded. The second-in-command, Lieutenant J. W. Robinson, R.N.V.R., finding the launch was completely disabled, decided to abandon her. Having got the crew into the dinghy, he set fire to his boat and left her in flames; the occupants of the dinghy were picked up by M.L. 128. M.L.110, commanded by Lieutenant-Commander Young, R.N.V.R., was also unfortunate. She was struck and badly damaged by several shell, which killed her commanding officer and a petty officer, another officer and two men being wounded. The second-in-command, Lieutenant G. Bowen, ordered the crew to abandon the vessel in the dinghy. This was done after the launch had been sunk to prevent any possibility of its capture by the enemy. The survivors were picked up by M.L. 308.

The motor launches detailed for smoke-screening did splendid work, as did all the launches which took part in the operation. Some detailed stories of the remaining launches will be given presently.

CHAPTER 7

The Work of the Blockships

The blockships had eased down soon after passing through position G so as to drop astern of *Vindictive* sufficiently far to enable that vessel and her consorts to create the necessary diversion. The conning and steering positions in each ship were triplicated and fully manned so that, in the event of one position being destroyed, the handling of the ship could immediately be taken over by another party. Guns' crews were standing by their guns ready to defend their vessels against attacks by enemy craft or to retaliate against the batteries in the hope of reducing the latter's fire.

At about midnight heavy firing was heard close at hand, but nothing could be seen owing to the dense smoke screen which was then drifting slowly to seaward. During the first quarter of an hour after midnight the blockships passed through an area which was apparently being barraged with shell fire. They were steaming in the order *Thetis*, Commander Ralph S. Sneyd, *Intrepid*, Lieutenant Stuart S. Bonham-Carter, and *Iphigenia*, Lieutenant Edward W. Billyard-Leake.

At twenty minutes past midnight the Mole was sighted right ahead in the glare of the rockets fired from *Vindictive*; the blockships had just been hailed by M.L. 558, who gave the direction of the lighthouse.

Thetis increased to full speed and, passing round the end of the Mole, steered for the extremity of the barge boom. A fairly heavy fire was being directed at her by such guns of the Mole-extension battery as were still in action; as far as could be seen, nothing was fired by the three-gun heavy battery at the end of the broad part of the Mole. The ship's guns opened fire at the lighthouse, which was believed to be used as a signalling and observation station, and at the southernmost barge; the latter was sunk. At this stage *Thetis* was caught by the strong east-going tidal stream and was set towards the boom of entanglement

AERIAL PHOTOGRAPH TAKEN THROUGH THE CLOUDS A FEW
HOURS AFTER THE ENTERPRISE.
Note the blockships sunk in the entrance, the break in the
viaduct, and the southern barge missing from the boom.

nets. The ship passed over the latter between the two northern buoys and tore the nets away with her momentum. The piers at the entrance to the canal were then sighted, but the propellers were so badly fouled by the nets that the engines were brought to a stop.

It must have been at about this moment that the enemy first realised the true nature of the enterprise. The attacks on the Mole, the blowing up of the viaduct, the explosions of torpedoes on the inside of the Mole, the smoke, the rapid changes of visibility, and the terrific noise on all sides had combined to leave the enemy in a hopeless state of stupefaction as to our real intentions. We heard afterwards that they believed a forced landing on the coast was in progress. The impossibility of using one's defensive measures to the best advantage when the initiative lies in the hands of the attackers has already been referred to. Suffice it to say that the enemy do not appear to have discovered the real purpose of our operations until too late to make the best use of their defensive measures.

Thetis now came under extremely heavy fire both from the direction of the Mole and from shore batteries near the canal. Her six-inch gun on the forecastle was replying to the shore batteries. She appeared to have grounded about three hundred yards from the canal entrance. *Thetis* now appeared to be settling down. All chances of struggling into the canal entrance appeared to be hopeless. She had been hit again and again and was on fire in several places. She had taken the brunt of the firing whilst her two consorts were following comparatively undamaged. She could do little more now than assist *Intrepid* and *Iphigenia* to reach their objectives. Prearranged signals, therefore, were made to these other two ships guiding them to the canal. It must be remembered that it was now half an hour after midnight. *Intrepid* and *Iphigenia*, in that order, passed close to *Thetis*. Thanks to the latter's signals they were able to locate the entrance piers; the further movements of those two vessels will be described in a moment.

As soon as *Iphigenia* was clear Captain Sneyd in *Thetis* ordered the artificial smoke to be turned on, and had almost decided to abandon ship when Engineer Lieutenant-Commander Boddie succeeded in getting the starboard engine to go ahead.

The ship moved slowly forward for a short distance, but was apparently dragging her stern along the bottom. As far as could be seen she was not only in the dredged channel leading to the canal, but was lying across it. The ship was undoubtedly in a sinking condition, so her captain decided to blow the bottom out of her in accordance with the Plan.

The blockships had each been fitted with explosive charges inside the bottom of the ship. These charges had been connected electrically to a firing arrangement which could be operated from alternative positions in the ship. The petty officer in charge of the foremost firing keys had been killed and they could not be found owing to the fumes from bursting shell and those from the artificial smoke. The firing keys at the other end of the ship were, therefore, pressed after the crew had been ordered on deck. The charges immediately exploded. The bottom of the ship was blown out; in a few moments the vessel had sunk. The upper deck was now just under water. The ship's company abandoned the ship, which was still under incessant fire, in the only remaining boat and pulled away to the northward, where M.L. 526, which had followed the blockships, picked them up. The *Thetis'* boat was the cutter. It had been badly holed by shell fire and was crowded to its full capacity. Some of the crew were wounded; Sneyd and his second-in-command had been wounded and gassed. The proceedings of M.L. 526, which also rescued some of the crew from another blockship, will be described later.

Intrepid had experienced a certain amount of shell fire when approaching the Mole, having apparently passed through an area which was being barraged by the enemy. She passed the Mole without difficulty and navigated between the obstruction booms. The sinking of the southernmost barge and the tearing away of the entanglement nets by *Thetis*, with the resultant widening of the unobstructed channel, had greatly reduced the chance of *Intrepid* getting into trouble at this point. During the final run to the canal she had escaped serious damage from gun-fire because nearly all the German guns were concentrating either on *Thetis* or on the forces attacking the Mole. Having located the entrance pier, passing close to *Thetis en route, Intrepid* entered the canal and proceeded up the latter until just inland of the coast-line.

Having reached the exact position as signed to her, Lieutenant Bonham-Carter at once commenced to turn his ship across the channel. As soon as he found she could be turned no further—it must be remembered that the navigable channel at that position was exceedingly narrow—he decided to blow the bottom out of the ship. The crew had been previously ordered to take to the boats, but Engineer Sub-Lieutenant Meikle and three ratings had not been able to leave the engine-room when the charges exploded. Fortunately these four

THE THREE BLOCKSHIPS SHORTLY AFTER THE ATTACK.

INTREPID AND IPHIGENIA.
The former the nearer to the camera

individuals escaped destruction. The ship sank immediately.

One cutter full of men pulled out to seaward and was picked up by M.L. 526, which has already been mentioned as saving the crew of *Thetis*. Another cutter pulled out to sea, actually past the Mole, and was picked up by the destroyer *Whirlwind*. Lieutenant Bonham-Carter, Lieutenant Cory-Wright his second-in-command, Sub-Lieutenant Babb the navigator, and four petty officers were the last party to leave the sunken vessel. They launched a raft and proceeded to paddle it towards M.L. 282, which had followed the blockships into the canal. Whilst on the raft this party had a very trying experience. The Germans had a machine-gun on the shore within a few yards. This gun and many others had been pouring a hot fire into the ship. A lifebuoy light had been inadvertently left on the raft and automatically lit up on reaching the water. This gave away their movements. Every effort was made to extinguish the light; they even sat on it, but could not either obscure or destroy it for some time. The machine-gun bullets were cutting up the water all round them, and it was extraordinary that none of the party was killed. It is difficult to imagine any more awkward situation. By dint of great efforts they managed to reach the motor launch and all got into her in safety.

Iphigenia had followed *Intrepid* and had rounded the Mole with much the same experience as the latter ship. Having dropped somewhat astern she increased to full speed and made for the canal. By this time so many star shell were being fired and so many searchlights being used that there was not much difficulty in locating the entrance piers; she was also assisted by the signals from *Thetis*. Passing close to the latter, *Iphigenia* was twice hit by shell, one of which cut a steam pipe, with the result that the forepart of the ship was enveloped in steam. In addition to that she shortly afterwards ran into thick smoke and temporarily lost sight of the entrance.

Suddenly the western pier loomed up close ahead. Lieutenant Billyard-Leake ordered "full speed astern." The ship ran between a dredger and a barge; on going ahead again she pushed the barge up the canal. There appeared to be a gap between the bow of the *Intrepid* and the eastern bank of the canal, so *Iphigenia* was steered to close it. Turning his ship by going alternately ahead and astern, Billyard-Leake managed to get her round well across the channel and then grounded with his bows on the eastern side. He ordered the crew to abandon ship and exploded his charges. Exactly as had occurred in the other two ships, the bottom was blown out and the ship sank at once. The upper deck was still above water.

The entire crew, officers and men, got away in a single cutter, the other boat having been severely damaged. M.L. 282 was then seen close ahead of the ship. The cutter pulled up to her and most of the crew managed to get on board. The remainder turned the cutter and again pulled to the launch. All except about three men, of whom one had been killed, climbed into the launch at the second attempt. The cutter herself was secured to the bows of the launch, which, having just picked up the raft party from *Intrepid*, was still heading up the canal. The launch went astern and backed out of the canal, stern first, with the cutter in tow. No less than a hundred and one survivors from the blockships were on board the motor launch. Under ordinary circumstances such craft can carry from forty to fifty passengers with a bit of a squash; a hundred and one passengers, several of them wounded, must have crowded every inch of her deck.

M.L. 282, commanded by Lieutenant Percy T. Deane, R.N.V.R., and M.L. 526, commanded by Lieutenant H. A. Littleton, R.N.V.R., had followed the blockships, exactly in accordance with the Plan, during their perilous journey from the Mole. These officers had been specially chosen for the rescue work from the large number of volunteers for that dangerous task.

M.L. 282 had steamed straight into the canal and stopped between the two sunken blockships. She came under heavy machine-gun fire from close range, but was not in the least deterred from the work of rescuing the blockships' survivors. The fact that this motor launch was not sunk and that the crew survived was little short of a miracle. Lieutenant Deane, with his precious cargo, turned his boat round as soon as he was clear of the canal. Owing to the steering gear having been damaged, he was forced to steer by means of working the engines at unequal speeds. He passed as near to the Mole as was possible to escape the gun-fire from that direction—the reverse of the usual procedure being necessary under the peculiar circumstances in which they found themselves. After passing the Mole the launch was steered to the north-westward and fell in with the vice-admiral's vessel, H.M.S. *Warwick*. Many casualties had been sustained as a result of the continual fire which she had experienced.

M.L. 526 had steamed into the sunken blockships in the canal, embarking many of *Intrepid's* men from a cutter, and then proceeded to *Thetis*, where all the survivors from that vessel were also embarked from a cutter. The motor launch had come under heavy fire from the

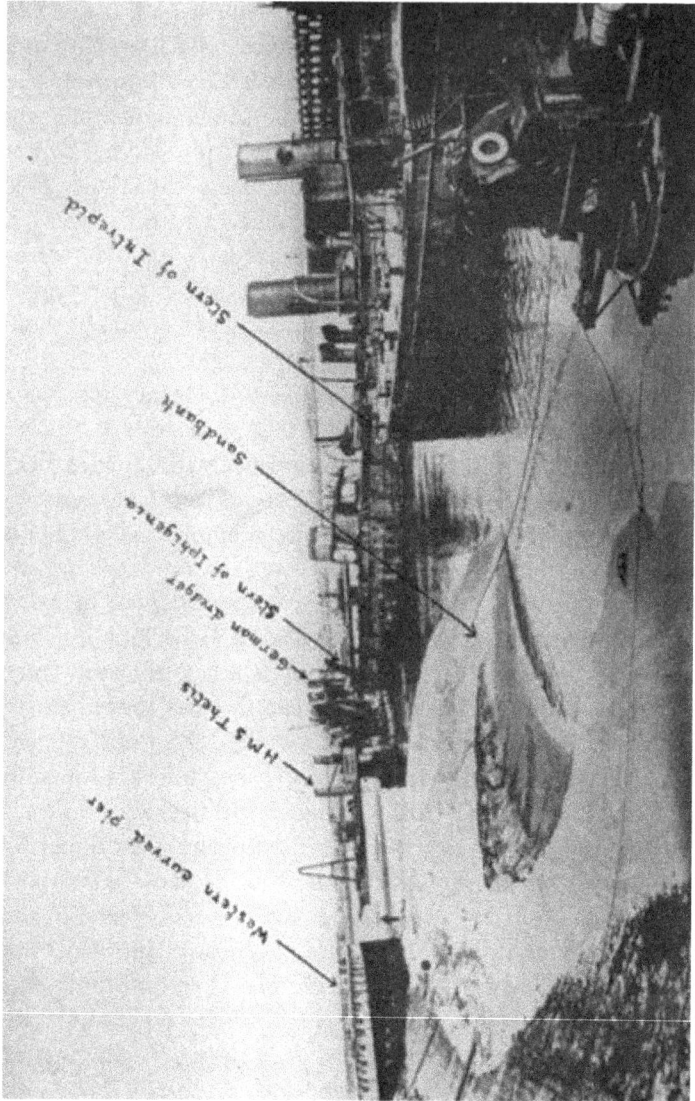

The WESTERN SIDE OF THE BLOCKED CHANNEL

Stern of Intrepid

Sandbank

German dredger

Stern of Iphigenia

HMS Thetis

Western curved pier

shore guns and her escape added one more item to the long list of miracles which took place that night. With sixty-five survivors Lieutenant Littleton steamed out to sea past the Mole and made the entire passage to Dover under her own steam, in spite of the gruelling which his frail vessel had gone through.

The rescue work, as carried out by these two motor launches, compels admiration. Their chances of success had seemed to be exceedingly remote. Yet, in spite of all the difficulties, they had rescued no less than one hundred and sixty-six men from right under the enemy's batteries. It will be remembered that *Intrepid* had not disembarked her surplus crew at position D on the passage across, with the result that she carried no fewer than eighty-seven officers and men into the canal. Of these, every single officer and man was brought back to Dover, although one petty officer had been killed and one officer mortally wounded whilst being rescued.

Of the crew of M.L. 282 one officer and two men (out of four) laid down their lives in this splendid achievement. Of all the blockships' officers and men not a single living soul fell into the hands of the enemy.

In a subsequent chapter I shall give a more detailed description of the results of the actual blocking.

There can be no two opinions concerning the handling of the blockships. The utmost that can be said of the diversions, from the point of view of their connection with the main object of the enterprise, is that they assisted the blockships to pass a danger point nearly a mile short of the canal entrance, and, to a lesser extent, diverted *some* of the enemy's attention during the final run to the blocking position.

From the vicinity of the Mole batteries to their final destination the blockship commanders had to depend almost entirely on their own efforts. Running the gantlet of modern batteries at point-blank range would ordinarily appear to be foolhardy in the extreme. Yet these officers made light of the task and showed that difficulties cannot always be judged by first impressions. The navigation alone was hazardous enough; concentration of thought in that particular direction must have been greatly hampered by the kaleidoscopic conditions of the situation. But perhaps the finest feat of all was the splendid display of seamanship in the face of extraordinary difficulty. The complete absence of local knowledge, the opposition of the enemy, and the unavoidable lack of practice in sinking vessels under such

THE EASTERN SIDE OF THE BLOCKED CHANNEL

conditions, all combined to make the task appear quite impracticable. Yet all difficulties were surmounted and the object of the operation was achieved.

Of all the happenings on that memorable night the outstanding feature, which turned success from a possibility into a certainty, was the magnificent handling of the blockships by Commander Sneyd and Lieutenants Bonham-Carter and Billyard-Leake. This fact cannot be too strongly emphasised, for, although it was naturally and fully realised in the navy, there were indications that it was not so well grasped by the man-in-the-street.

CHAPTER 8

The Retirement

It had been arranged that the storming parties on the Mole should have twenty minutes' warning of *Vindictive* leaving the outer wall. A maximum length of stay alongside had also been laid down so that, under certain circumstances, watches would provide some guide as to the amount of time available.

The warning signal for leaving the Mole was to consist of a succession of long and short blasts on the siren, or a particular method of waving the searchlight beams, or, if all other means failed, a message conveyed by runner.

At about 12.50 a.m., three-quarters of an hour after *Vindictive's* arrival alongside, the question of the length of stay was considered. The blockships had been seen passing the lighthouse *en route* to the canal, the viaduct had been blown up. The diversion on the Mole had throughout served to attract the fire of a large number of enemy batteries. From this followed the deduction that some chance of rescue work had probably offered itself to our motor launches. It was likely that in another twenty minutes these latter vessels would have definitely succeeded or failed in their object.

The primary object for which the attack on the Mole was designed had been attained. There remained the secondary object of demolition. The only guns in *Vindictive* which could have borne directly on the Mole had been put out of action. Her upper works were still being hit every few seconds with a continually increasing list of casualties amongst those in exposed positions. Owing to the failure of the Mole anchors no member of the storming parties could hope to return if *Daffodil* was disabled. That the latter vessel had thus far escaped destruction was little short of a miracle. The maximum period allowed for the operations of the storming parties would expire at twenty minutes past one. Thirty minutes remained. If the warning signal was made immediately, the storming parties would have their maximum time cut down by only ten minutes.

The question which arose out of the foregoing considerations was as to whether it was worth while to remain alongside during the last ten minutes for the sake of demolition work whilst risking, *at the least*, the loss of the whole of the storming parties then on the Mole.

Shortly after 12.50 a.m. the order was given to make the retirement signal. *Vindictive's* sirens had both been shot away. The starboard searchlight had received a direct hit from a projectile and had been hurled off the bridge down to the upper deck. The port searchlight had also been put out of action. An order was passed to *Daffodil* to make the retirement signal on her siren. The latter spluttered and gurgled whilst emitting a veritable shower bath, but presently began to show signs of being useful. A low groan developed into a growling note which in turn travelled gradually up the scale until loud enough to be heard at a distance. The signal was repeated several times and then came an anxious period of waiting.

At about this time a large stack of Stokes bomb boxes, containing fused bombs, was set on fire by a shell. All the fire-extinguishing apparatus in the vicinity had already been shot away. The chief Quartermaster, Petty Officer E. G. Youlton, whilst shouting to others to take cover, extinguished the fire by hauling out the burning boxes and stamping on them. A few moments later the fire broke out afresh. Youlton repeated his very gallant efforts and succeeded in saving a very awkward situation.

The storming parties commenced to return to the ship almost at once. Many of the ship's company, officers and men, assisted in carrying the wounded on board over the gangways, which were as rickety as ever. One marine carried a disabled man on board, placed his charge on the deck, kissed him on both cheeks and was heard to remark, "I wasn't going to leave you, Bill."

I have seen both statements and illustrations to the effect that our storming parties, before leaving, erected a staff on the Mole and hoisted a Union Jack upon it. It may seem a pity to spoil a good story, but this event was quite imaginary. A memento of our visit, however, was prepared in the shape of a board to which were attached our visiting cards bearing the letters P.P.C., but there is no very clear evidence as to whether this memento was left on the Mole, though I believe that was the case.

A shell burst just outside the conning tower whilst three of us were discussing the probability of any men being still on the Mole. Lieutenant-Commander Rosoman was shot through both legs; Petty Officer Youlton had an arm shattered; a very slight wound in the shoulder was my own share of the damage.

By the time that fifteen minutes had elapsed from the sounding of the retirement signal practically all the storming parties had returned. No more men were seen to come back, but I had given a definite promise that the full twenty minutes' notice would be allowed. After repeated assurances from other officers, backed up by my own personal observation, that no others were returning we decided to leave the Mole. The cable had already been unshackled ready for slipping overboard when no longer required.

Lieutenant-Commander Rosoman, in spite of his wounds, accompanied me to the conning tower. He absolutely refused to sit down, but remained standing so that he could keep a lookout through the slit in the armour.

The conning tower was of very small dimensions. Four wounded men had previously crawled inside and had died where they lay. Three or four other wounded men had crawled in later on and had collapsed. One of the telegraphs to the engine-room had been shot away, but the telephone was intact.

All the other compasses having been destroyed, we had to depend upon the conning-tower compass. The magnetic directive force on a compass needle is necessarily very weak in a conning tower of such small dimensions. The ship had received so many hard knocks that the magnetism on board was pretty certain to have undergone considerable change. Thus, whereas this particular compass was somewhat independable before, it was now exceedingly unreliable.

In spite of the many hundreds of times that I must previously have instructed young officers that no iron should be placed within five feet of the compass, I have my first lieutenant to thank for pointing out that the presence of so many steel helmets in the conning tower was inadvisable.

Daffodil was ordered to tow *Vindictive's* bow away from the wall. Lieutenant Campbell obeyed at once; our anchor cable was slipped overboard. Directly after the strain came on the *Daffodil's* hawser the latter broke, but it had served its purpose. "Full speed ahead" was ordered and the ship moved forward almost immediately. This was at 1.11 a.m.

A large steel boom—the original mainmast of the ship—had been rigged over the port side of the quarter-deck, jutting out rather further than the port propeller with the object of saving the latter from hitting the wall. When *Vindictive's* helm was put over to port, her stern swung towards the Mole, but the boom saved the situation as a result of a heavy blow against the wall.

As soon as *Vindictive* had moved a few feet the gangways slipped off the wall and fell overboard with a resounding crash. For a few moments the wreckage fouled and stopped the port propeller, but quickly cleared again without having done any serious damage.

It is not difficult to gauge the feelings of the enemy when they first noticed the ship moving off. We had taken them more or less by surprise on arrival and had managed to storm the Mole in spite of every effort to prevent us. The enemy could not have been over-pleased about that. The ship had been able to remain at the Mole for one hour and ten minutes without sustaining any vital damage. That fact was not calculated to engender a pleasant frame of mind amongst the enemy. But *they knew* exactly where we were. *They knew* we should endeavour to leave sooner or later; *they knew* that any attempt to do so would inevitably expose the vitals of the ship to their batteries at point-blank range; *they thought they knew* that our fate was sealed immediately we were clear of the wall; there could be no surprise about leaving. But all such matters had been carefully thought out beforehand. *Vindictive, Iris*, and *Daffodil* each carried several sets of artificial smoke apparatus for use on retirement. Immediately we started to go ahead orders were given for the smoke to be turned on. In less than a minute all previous fog records were beaten beyond comparison. Thus in place of a victim the enemy found a fog.

We steamed away to the northwestward at utmost speed. The flames were pouring through the holes in the funnels; the ship had the appearance of being heavily on fire. The wind being now offshore brought the fog along with us; fortunately for the navigation we had a clear lookout ahead. The enemy cannot have seen much more than the vivid glare of our funnel flames illuminating the upper part of the fog. From all accounts their batteries were far from idle. As the ship sped seaward we had the sensation of the ship jumping at irregular but frequent intervals. This may have been due to the concussion of heavy shell striking the water near the ship. Whether any shell hit us or not during the retirement is unlikely to be known. One could hardly see one's own feet. The ship had already been hit so often that any further damage of the same description would hardly have been noticed. Suffice it to say that no vital damage to the hull was received.

After steaming for twenty minutes the first lieutenant reported a light off the starboard bow. It was the Blankenberghe buoy, which we had passed during the approach. We altered course to pass close to the buoy and then for our line of retirement.

Presently the dark form of a vessel was sighted ahead. Our guns' crews were ready for any emergency, but the vessel proved to be H.M.S. *Moorsom*, one of the patrolling destroyers. All the bridge signalling lamps had been destroyed. With an ordinary pocket torch we flashed a signal requesting *Moorsom* to lead us as our compass was hopeless.

On the way across to Zeebrugge my anxiety with regard to accuracy of compass course had led me to criticise the steering of one of the quartermasters. Now, on the return voyage, I had become quartermaster, in the absence of Petty Officer Youlton, and am afraid the steering was execrable. That fact was officially recorded by the commanding officer of *Moorsom* who, knowing nothing about our amateur steersmanship, reported, "... *Vindictive* appeared ... steering a very erratic course!" Fortunately the services of another petty officer, as steersman, were obtained later on.

Lieutenant-Commander Rosoman combined the duties of lookout and navigator; his advice was most helpful. A visit from the stretcher parties relieved the congestion in the conning tower. Another memorable incident was the arrival of the paymaster with a jug full of a certain stimulating beverage which put new life into us; I shall *not* complete the testimonial.

Several signals were interchanged with *Moorsom* on the subject of shoals; it was a great relief when we eventually located a buoy marking a danger spot.

Vindictive was steaming nearly seventeen knots until daylight—a great achievement on the part of Engineer Lieutenant-Commander Bury and his department.

Soon after daylight a destroyer was observed to be racing up from astern at high speed. She quickly ranged up alongside and proved to be H.M.S. *Warwick*. The first signal from her, "Well done, *Vindictive*," cheered us up immensely, not because of its actual import, but because it looked very much as if the vice-admiral were alive. To make sure we enquired if that surmise was correct and, greatly to our relief, received a reply in the affirmative.

H.M.S. *Warwick* had continued throughout the operation to patrol in a central position, namely, near the Mole lighthouse. She had come under a heavy fire and altogether experienced a couple of hectic hours. Soon after one o'clock she had moved towards *Vindictive* and suddenly came upon the latter leaving the Mole. *Vindictive's* smoke screen made it impossible to keep touch, so the vice-admiral decided to search for *Iris* and *Daffodil* in case they should require assistance. Shortly after this M.L. 282 was met and transferred her blockship survivors to *Warwick*, who was also informed that *Iris* and *Daffodil* had left the Mole. *Warwick* then escorted some motor launches out of the danger zone, and, after rallying several other craft at a prearranged rendezvous, she steered for Dover and overtook *Vindictive* as mentioned above.

Admiral Keyes ordered *Moorsom* to lead *Vindictive* to Dover, to which place *Warwick* proceeded at high speed to land her wounded and to arrange for the arrival of the casualties from the remaining vessels.

The weather being misty, we did not sight Dover until within a mile or so. Our reception was wonderful, the result of the operation being already known at Dover. I think everybody cheered himself hoarse that morning. Presently we were ordered to proceed alongside the railway jetty. Within me there was some feeling of satisfaction at having berthed the ship at Zeebrugge, a place which I had never seen, in face of certain difficulties additional to the tide. Any feeling of pride, however, was quickly dispelled when, in accordance with the routine of the port, on my ship being ordered to proceed alongside Dover jetty in broad daylight, with no opposition from the enemy, and with every convenience in the way of hawsers and bollards, *a pilot was sent on board to handle her!*

On arrival alongside the wounded were disembarked into a Red Cross train, which immediately took them off to hospital. Those who had laid down their lives were then carried ashore; this, indeed, was a sad parting. Finally we moved out to a buoy to make room for other vessels.

After our arrival at Dover it was discovered that a large block of concrete was jambed between a fender and a ledge on the port side of the ship. Apparently a German shell fired from one of the heavy land batteries had struck the upper part of the outer wall and had torn away this block, which fell into the position mentioned. This concrete block, weighing nearly half a ton, was hoisted on board. A few pieces were taken as souvenirs. The main portion was presented to the Impe-

H.M.S. VINDICTIVE AT DOVER AFTER THE ATTACK.

A large piece of the Mole was found resting on the ledge shown at the bottom right-hand corner of the photograph

rial War Museum and formed rather a unique piece of evidence, not only of the fact that *Vindictive* lay alongside the Mole, but of the exact position at which the Mole was stormed. The illustration earlier shows the damaged portion of the wall from which this block of concrete was torn.

Daffodil was exceedingly fortunate in having escaped serious damage. Her hull had been exposed to the fire of the German batteries throughout the whole hour and the odd minutes during which she had been keeping *Vindictive* alongside the Mole. On the retirement signal being made everything was prepared for towing the bows of *Vindictive* away from the wall. Immediately the order was received, Lieutenant Campbell turned his ship and commenced to tow. The hawser had parted almost at once, but that was of no consequence. *Daffodil* then steamed away to the northward under cover of her own artificial smoke and eventually spoke H.M.S. *Trident*. The latter took her in tow and brought her safely to Dover, which was reached at 1 p.m. The enthusiastic reception commenced all over again. It must be realised that the fate of each vessel was unknown to the majority of the remainder until some hours after the completion of the operation.

It has already been described how *Iris*, after leaving *Vindictive* and suffering severe damage from hostile gun-fire, had been smoke-screened by a motor boat and had disappeared from view. This smoke screen, augmented by further smoke from their own apparatus, undoubtedly saved *Iris* from destruction. Under the directions of Lieutenant Oscar Henderson, R.N., who had assumed command after his captain had been mortally wounded, *Iris* steamed away to seaward and eventually proceeded to Dover under her own steam, whilst being escorted by other vessels met with in the small hours. She arrived at Dover at 2.45 p.m. and, once more, everybody cheered himself hoarse.

At intervals throughout the forenoon and afternoon of the 23rd the several vessels and craft arrived at Dover. We then had the opportunity of piecing together the information obtained from each unit and were thus able to gauge the probable results attained.

The air force had been requested to obtain new photographs of Zeebrugge as early as practicable, but the sky was so clouded over that no absolutely indisputable evidence was obtained until 2 p.m., when a photograph was taken through a chink in the clouds. This photograph showed the positions of the inner blockships and the break in the railway viaduct. The operation had been an unqualified success.

The operation at Ostende had unfortunately failed. The difficulties of navigation had been accentuated by the change of wind which brought the artificial fog back to seaward. The consequent obscuration of the harbour entrance made it necessary to place some dependence on a buoy which had, unknown to us and by the merest coincidence, just been moved a mile or so to the eastward by the enemy. In spite of the most gallant attempt by Commander A. E. Godsal in H.M.S. *Brilliant* and Lieutenant-Commander H. N. M. Hardy in H.M.S. *Sirius*, ably assisted as they were by their officers and men and by a large number of other craft, the blocking attempt had not achieved success. The vice-admiral decided, therefore, to make another attempt at the earliest possible moment. *Vindictive*, being the only suitable vessel available, was immediately prepared for this further service. Owing to a continuation of impossible weather conditions the operation could not be carried out until May 10th; thus it is clear that if our expedition had not started on their journey on April 22nd the operation at Zeebrugge could not have taken place during the allotted period.

Just one other reference to the further use of *Vindictive* cannot be omitted. Immediately on their return, after the failure to block Ostende, both officers who have been mentioned above as commanding the blockships at that place, begged to be given ships for a further attempt. They had failed through no fault of their own and had gone through some terrible experiences. Nothing could curb their ardour, and I believe they gave the vice-admiral no peace until he consented to give them another chance. Poor Godsal. Nothing could have been finer than his handling of the old *Vindictive* on the night of May 9th–10th, but he was killed at the very moment when complete success seemed to be assured; Ostende was partially blocked.

It was with considerable feelings of regret that, on April 25th, we made way in *Vindictive* for the new crew destined to take her to Ostende. It was a sad farewell.

The behaviour of the wounded had been splendid; their cheerfulness was unbounded. One poor fellow who had suffered severe internal injuries as well as the loss of both legs was asked if he was sorry that he went over to Zeebrugge. He replied, "No, sir, because I got on the Mole." That was all that mattered to him. There was practically no chance of saving his life, but "he had got on the Mole."

The spirit of all the men in *Vindictive* was fine. Nevertheless, I do not deceive myself into imagining that these men were exceptional. They only represented one small contingent of many which fought at

H.M.S. Vindictive on Her Return to Dover after the Attack

Zeebrugge and Ostende on St. George's Day; the combined crews of all the vessels in the operation only represented a trifling percentage of our total naval personnel; the behaviour of my men was merely typical of all those others.

Those of our survivors who had not been sent to hospital with wounds proceeded on a few days' leave before rejoining their depots or their ships in the Grand Fleet. What a piratical appearance the crew presented on their departure! Many of them had lost all their clothes, except those in which they stood during the action. Those others whose clothes had survived the fight were not much better off. The souvenir hunters had raided my ship, had "picked up" some of the men's belongings, and had even been inconsiderate enough to break into my cabin and make a complete clearance of the officers' handbags placed there for safety.

One last story of a personal nature. On receipt of the news at Dover a young officer, in his desire to do me a kindness, decided to wire the good news to my wife. He forgot that she would know nothing of the enterprise or even of its preparation, and he worded the telegram:

Operation successful. Husband quite all right.

The recipient's feelings may be easily imagined; she guessed it was appendicitis!

CHAPTER 9

The Material Results

The results of the operations on the night of April 22-23, 1918, were undoubtedly important. They can be classified under the two headings of "material" and "moral."

The degree of moral effect cannot usually be assessed until long after an operation has been completed. Recognisable evidence comes to hand very gradually. The actual results of moral effect may be early experienced without being recognised, especially in the case of effect on the enemy's morale.

Material results are more easily gauged. In this particular case photographic evidence was soon obtainable.

I must recall to the reader's mind the description of the entrance channel of the canal. It was shown in Part I, Chapter 2, how very narrow the navigable channel had become owing to the silting of the sand, and how rapidly the latter process would accentuate the obstructive quality of a sunken vessel. It was also shown why the channel at the shore end of the two curved piers was the ideal position at which to place the blockships. *Intrepid* and *Iphigenia* had been sunk by us exactly at their selected positions. Each vessel spanned right across the dredged channel, and therefore blocked it effectually. For the first time in naval history a blocking operation had been carried out successfully in the face of up-to-date defence measures.

Some of the photographs, taken at high tide, appear to show sufficient space through which vessels could pass on either side of the blockships. But the presence of water does not signify the presence of sufficient water to float such craft as submarines and destroyers even at high tide. Two other photographs show clearly that the ends of the vessels were practically on the edges of the sandbanks.

The Germans, as prompt in propaganda as they were unenterprising in sea-fighting, at once published a *communiqué* to the effect that the operation had utterly failed, adding that the blockships had been sunk by the German batteries before reaching their goal. Curiously enough, their official statements were strangely silent on the subject of prisoners. They also averred that the attack on the Mole had been driven back. Not content with these "terminological inexactitudes," they went so far as to take a photograph to prove their contention.

The photograph was taken with the camera pointed inland. The land was eliminated from the background in the original so as to give the impression that the camera was pointing out to sea. A line was drawn between, and parallel to, the blockships and marked "The line of the channel," whereas it was a line nearly at right angles to the channel. Words were added to the effect that the photograph proved clearly that the channel was not blocked, and copies of the photograph were circulated all over Germany and neutral countries. What wonderful liars!—but clumsy! The amusing part of it was that we knew the German naval authorities reported "Zeebrugge is blocked" to their craft stationed elsewhere, and, further, our airmen btained photographs day after day showing some twenty-three torpedo craft and twelve submarines bottled up at Bruges.

From the morning after the operation until the Germans finally evacuated Zeebrugge, our aerial bombers dropped, on the average, four tons of bombs daily on that place. Our special measures with regard to constructive work in each blockship, designed to hamper the work of salvage, must have presented the enemy with a formidable problem. The work of clearing the channel was certainly not assisted by the dropping of bombs upon the salvors. To what extent the Germans attempted to remove the vessels is unknown to me, but we do know well enough that none of the three was moved a foot nor were they cut away to allow vessels to pass over them. Thanks to our airmen, we knew, almost from hour to hour, what measures were being taken to dredge a new channel. I believe that no torpedo craft or submarines could use the exit for a considerable time, and that about five months elapsed before they could enter or leave the canal at any other period than the top of high tide.

Having contrived that each blockship should embody all the main obstacles to salvage work, we were more or less confident that, if once placed in position, these ships could not be easily removed. Subsequently, at the earliest opportunity, our own salvage service commenced their endeavours to clear the canal. In January, 1921, *two years and three months* after Zeebrugge was again in the hands of the Allies, the last of the three blockships was moved sufficiently to enable the channel to be used with freedom. A great amount of labour and money had already been expended, but still further efforts were required before the canal could be altogether freed from obstructions. One may certainly remark that the canal was "well and truly blocked."

Information reached us afterwards that the *Kaiser* personally visited Zeebrugge shortly after the operation so that he could discover the actual truth for himself. What his remarks were on arrival is not known to me, but a photograph in my possession, taken on that occasion, certainly does not give him an air of affability.

The main material result, then, was that the canal was blocked and that the services of twelve submarines and twenty-three torpedo craft were unavailable for a considerable period. As long as the canal remained blocked, German submarines detailed for operating against Allied commerce in the English Channel and other waters outside the North Sea were, for the most part, compelled to do so from the Heligoland Bight. This increased the length of voyage to and from their areas of operation and consequently reduced the duration of their stay in such waters.

But there were other material results. Firstly, the German High Command considered it necessary to send re-enforcements to Ostende in the shape of modern destroyers. Now vessels, like individuals, cannot be in two places at once. Those sent to Ostende had to be drawn away from the Heligoland Bight, consequently the forces in the latter area were weakened in strength *pro rata*.

The loss of German lives and vessels and the damage sustained during the action were by no means negligible.

Then again the efficiency of Bruges as a naval base was greatly lessened because the canal exit to Ostende proved to be too shallow for the larger craft. The fuel, dockyard, and stores at Bruges were also rendered comparatively useless as means of support for sea-going vessels.

The Mole, as a seaplane base, must have lost much of its value owing to the severance of the railway communication, heavy stores having to be transported to the Mole by sea-carriers. Finally, the work of "locking the stable door after the horse had been stolen," as practised by the enemy on this occasion, entailed extra mining at sea, mounting additional guns on the outer wall, and covering the floor of the Mole with such an abundance of barbed wire as to make the place exceedingly uncomfortable for themselves.

Our own losses consisted of one destroyer and two motor launches; no other vessel was rendered unfit for further services. Our casualties at Zeebrugge amounted to approximately one hundred and seventy killed, four hundred wounded, and forty-five missing; the majority of the latter were believed to have been killed. The casualties in *Vindictive*, including her storming parties, were sixty killed and one hundred and seventy-one wounded.

With regard to the loss of material we had not paid a high price considering the results achieved. The loss of personnel was small in comparison with losses sustained in military fighting, but was none the less keenly felt by those of us who had been in personal touch with these splendid fellows. They had all realised the danger and had been perfectly willing to lay down their lives in the attainment of the desired end. They did not die in vain.

CHAPTER 10

The Moral Effect

The moral effect on the enemy was shown, to a certain degree, almost at once. The fact that they thought it necessary to indulge in falsehood to appease their own countrymen, although they must have realised that the truth would inevitably become known, was clear enough proof that their morale was badly shaken.

Their earliest report stated that the attack had failed and that three British cruisers had been sunk at Zeebrugge. The latter portion of the statement was correct. The ships had, indeed, been sunk—by ourselves. All reference to the destruction of the viaduct was withheld until later. The fact of no prisoners being captured from any of the three British cruisers was never mentioned. As soon as our own reports had been circulated, the German authorities apparently considered it necessary to account for our success by stating that some Belgian fishermen had been arrested for piloting our vessels into position!

Imagine, for a moment, the effect on our own public if they heard that the enemy had attacked Dover, stormed the breakwater and remained in possession of it for over an hour, destroyed the railway jetty, and blocked the entrance. Even such a case as that would not be wholly analogous, for the blockships at Zeebrugge had sunk themselves nearly a mile *inside* the outer entrance. Imagine the outcry and the question, "What is the navy doing?" It is not difficult to conceive the downfall of highly placed personages and the feeling of insecurity that would pervade the atmosphere in our own country. Not only would the public be shaken by such news, but the loss of morale would be felt in the fighting services, firstly as a result of their own ineptitude, and secondly because of the visions of further enemy operations which would be conjured up.

Some such effect as described above was inevitable amongst both the German civilian element and their fighting services. We know that the operation caused a great scare at Bruges. Many of the German officials there hurriedly collected their effects ready for evacuating the city; it had been reported that the allies were landing an immense force on the coast of Flanders.

It is not generally known that friendship between the German Navy and Army was conspicuous by its absence. They had been at daggers drawn for some years; the crown prince himself was in the habit of being openly rude to naval officers of high rank. This antagonism was evidenced recently in a letter written by a certain German general to his brother-in-law, a young officer in our navy. Apparently the general hated the German Navy to such an extent that his letter remarked that there were two British officers with whom he particularly desired to shake hands—one was the officer in charge of our siege guns on the Flanders coast and the other was the officer commanding the attack on Zeebrugge; his friendly feelings arose from the fact that these two officers had "put it across" that section of the German Navy which had charge of the Flanders coast defences.

The German Information Bureau had never ceased to sing the praises of their navy; that fact was conducive to increasing the shock received by the enemy when they learned the truth. Many excuses have been invented in Germany to account for the fact that the final breakdown of morale which immediately preceded the ignominious flight of their War Lord emanated from the so-called High Seas Fleet, and that this breakdown coincided with the receipt of orders to try conclusions with our fleet. It can hardly be styled far-fetched if one suggests that the loss of morale was intimately connected with the situation at sea. It is also not outside the bounds of possibility that, in some measure, the events of St. George's Day, 1918, assisted towards the *débâcle*. A certain highly placed German official at Bruges certainly exaggerated when he averred that "the hopes of the Fatherland were buried at Zeebrugge," but such a statement as that clearly indicates the weakening of confidence.

The other aspect of the effect on morale may be worthy of mention. I refer to the effect on our own public, on our fighting services, and on neutral and Allied countries.

The great German military offensive, which everybody realised indicated the supreme effort on the part of the enemy, was in full swing in the month of April. The Allied troops were stubbornly contesting every inch of ground, but were being steadily pushed back on important sections of the main battle front. The British Fifth Army had suffered appalling losses. The Allies had their backs to the wall. The tension at home was apparent in all walks of life, and the extremely anxious days of 1914 were being repeated. Future generations will never be able to realise the depression and anxiety which pervaded the public mind. Everybody was wondering what the outcome would be, and there were days when one hardly dared to scan the morning paper. That very fact had provided us with an additional reason for wishing to register a success.

There is very little doubt that the success attained had a marked effect on the public; the latter fairly jumped at the opportunity to show enthusiasm. In addition to that, the public palate was tickled by the unusual and apparently spectacular nature of the attack.

This sudden rise of the "moralometer" served a good purpose. The pessimist changed his tune, the optimist earned the qualification "cheery." To those ignorant of naval matters the operation seemed to have bordered on the accomplishment of the impossible. "We always knew," they declared, "that our fighting men were invincible." Their old certainty of ultimate victory was re-born. That was all to the good. Modern war is national war. War is not merely a struggle between fighting forces, but between the opposing "crowds." The destruction of an enemy's army or navy is of primary importance as a means to an end, but the ultimate end and aim of each belligerent is to exert influence on the "crowd," to nourish the will to win amongst their own public and to bring about a feeling of hopeless despair, a complete loss of morale, throughout the enemy's country. It is for that important reason that the sentiments of one's own public must ever be borne in mind by the Higher Command.

The receipt of the news on the western front is reported to have been beneficial. Every fighting force must occasionally have its dark days; they are never so dark that news of success on another front will fail to bring a ray of light. Those of us in the fleet itself had often experienced such feelings of elation when our military brothers had brought off a "*coup.*" The navy and army, and the air force with them, are one at heart. The fighting services are interdependent. Our Navy cannot win a war unaided any more than our army can prevent Great Britain from being defeated by starvation. The waging of war, in the case of a maritime country which is unselfsupporting, cannot rightly be divided into naval warfare, military warfare, and combined naval and military operations, though the three types are commonly referred to and in that order. All war in which the British Empire is involved is in the nature of combined naval and military warfare. The actions of one arm are inevitably reflected in the other.

The Grand Fleet, from which so many of our officers and men were drawn for the operation on St. George's Day, was naturally elated at the result. Certainly the morale in the fleet had always been of a high order, but an extra touch of enthusiasm was not without value.

Of the effect in neutral countries I am not competent to speak, but I have some personal knowledge of the manner in which the news was received in the United States. The enthusiasm in that part of the world was genuine enough and undoubtedly assisted to cement the friendship between that country and our own Empire, a friendship which has a firm foundation even if the latter be occasionally hidden beneath a political superstructure which we are apt to mistake for the foundation itself.

CHAPTER 11

Some Remarks on the Enterprise

This book would be incomplete if I omitted to append some general remarks on the operation and on the factors which led to success.

First and foremost, it is necessary to indulge in comparisons. The enterprise described in this book attracted attention owing to its somewhat unusual type as far as the navy was concerned. Nevertheless, there are many points of similarity between the attack on Zeebrugge and the military trench raids which took place night after night on the Allied fronts. The preliminary bombardment, the advance under cover of darkness and smoke, the wild firing of star shell, the rush across No Man's Land, the encounter with barbed wire and other defence material, the leap down into the enemy's trench, the hand-to-hand fighting, the holding of the position whilst demolition work was in progress, and the final withdrawal when the object had been attained; such was a trench raid as carried out again and again by our brothers in the army. In their case the following day brought a two-line *communiqué, e.g.*:

> Last night in the Ypres salient our troops carried out a trench raid; they captured seven prisoners.

In our case the *communiqué* and unofficial reports filled many pages. I would warn the reader not to be misled into thinking that the military raids were any less hazardous than our own.

The story provides just one more illustration of the fact that, however large may loom the difficulties with which one is confronted, the means to overcome them can usually be found if one possesses the "will to win through."

The fundamental principles of war demand the Offensive and

221

Concentration. The all-important element of strategy to be utilised against a strongly entrenched enemy is that of Surprise. From the latter spring Diversion and Mystification.

An attempt has been made to describe the manner in which the seemingly impossible was accomplished without very great difficulty.

The plan was built up on the foundation of surprise—not surprise in the sense that something would suddenly occur where all had been quiet up to that moment, but surprise in that the real object of the enterprise would be concealed up to the latest possible moment, the concealment to be brought about by mystifying the enemy and diverting his attention.

Whilst concentrating all available powers of offence against the enemy, and allowing nothing to divert us from our main object, we took every step to bewilder the defence and to shift the weight of the difficulties upon the shoulders of our opponents. But that was only the foundation. The material brought into use was the best available at the moment; it is not suggested that, given further time, it would have been incapable of improvement.

Earlier in this book a few remarks were offered on the importance of the personnel. Many further remarks could now be added after the story has been told. I only propose, however, to deal with certain aspects which, by their nature, are less likely to be realised by the man-in-the-street.

It has already been mentioned that a considerable percentage of the vessels and craft engaged in the attack were commanded and manned by officers and men of the Royal Naval Reserve and Royal Naval Volunteer Reserve. The majority of the smoke-screening craft and rescue craft came under that heading. Without the smoke the operation must have failed. Without the rescue work the price paid for success would have been excessive. These representatives of the auxiliary naval services earned a full measure of admiration. Their daring in the face of danger, their coolness in situations which lacked nothing in excitement, their initiative when confronted with the unexpected, and their perfect co-operation with the remaining forces engaged in the enterprise, were worthy of the best traditions of the navy. The more that one considers the dependence upon seamanship, the practical use of technical knowledge, the mental and physical strain, the value of perfect discipline, and the initiative called for on such an occasion, the greater is one's admiration for these fine fellows of whom the majority had seen comparatively little of sea life and had lacked that severity of training which is inseparable from the naval profession.

The reports of all commanding officers contained one particular similarity—I refer to the behaviour of the men. The cynic who might be inclined to discount such unqualified praise, on the plea that the men were specially chosen, could easily be silenced. The specially selected personnel were certainly picked with difficulty, not because the desired qualities were rare, but for exactly the opposite reason. The Grand Fleet and naval bases contained many thousands of such men; the embarrassment lay in deciding who of these thousands should be taken to make up the seventeen hundred and eighty personnel required. But the latter were only required for some ten vessels out of one hundred and sixty-two; required because those ten vessels were out of commission and therefore had no crews. The remaining one hundred and fifty-two vessels and craft took part in the operation with their ordinary crews, and I repeat that the behaviour of the crews of *all* units was exemplary.

But co-operation between units, and efficiency of individuals, are not alone sufficient to ensure success. Absolute confidence and perfect co-operation between officers and men, founded on true discipline, is of vital importance. Without these, little or nothing can be achieved in war. The seeds of these vital requirements were sown by our forefathers. Those of our predecessors who, although too old to serve in the Great War, were still in the land of the living had reason to feel proud at the success attained by their pupils.

There is one other human aspect which cannot be omitted without leaving a serious blank in these pages. That aspect is the one of leadership.

Leadership has been defined as that power in a man which causes others to follow him irrespective of the direction in which he leads.

It would be a presumption, almost amounting to an impertinence, for me to endeavour to measure out the praise which is due to the vice-admiral in command of the enterprise, now Vice-Admiral Sir Roger Keyes. The reader will understand my difficulty. In past history, again and again, it was manifest that some of the outstanding factors which led to success were the personality of the leader, the supreme confidence in him held by all ranks, his realisation of the powers and limits of his subordinates, his personal courage, and his intensity of purpose. The outstanding factors which brought success on the particular occasion described in this book have served to repeat and illustrate these old historical lessons.

A few more words and I shall have finished.

I venture to suggest that this particular exploit provides just one more example, such as are recorded again and again in the histories of most civilised countries, of what can be accomplished in the face of difficulty. Unfortunately, when hostilities cease, we are prone to forget, not only the sacrifices by which successes were achieved, but also the principles which guided us in the achievement. We are all ready enough to admit that confidence and co-operation are of prime necessity for the preservation of our lives and our interests when danger threatens us in war, but, somehow, when the welfare of communities is threatened in days of so-called peace, by international suspicions, by revolutionary doctrines, by economic difficulties, by unemployment, and by political schisms, we weaken ourselves as a result of deconcentrating into numberless camps, one against the other, in direct opposition to those fundamental principles which are the root cause of our existence.

It is all very strange, and, I suppose, very human, for nothing is stranger than humanity. How many of us realise that our superiority over the rest of the animal world is directly attributable to the fact that human beings, alone, have sufficient understanding to combine when danger threatens? Having successfully combined for the greatest of all causes, are we now to revert to the instincts of the inferior animals? Are we to persuade ourselves that co-operation merely results from paper treaties rather than from a common spirit, forgetting that officers and men, armies and navies, needed no signed agreements between them for the overthrow of the greatest menace to civilisation that the world has ever seen?

The Great War is over; is a Great Peace to follow?

What is our object? Surely it is the welfare of civilised communities and the progress of those who are less enlightened.

There will always be secondary objects calculated to divert us from our purpose. There will always be individuals who, for their own ends, will endeavour to sow discord and confuse the issue. It is of paramount importance that we keep our object in view, and that we cultivate intensity of purpose and wholeheartedness, without which our object is unattainable.

We know that the right spirit exists, but it is of little value if we keep it locked away within us until disaster is imminent; the mere fact of its existence cannot keep us free from danger any more than the existence of medicine stored at the apothecary's can protect us from infection and illness.

Let each one of us, each class, each sect, each nation, each group of nations, do all that is humanly possible to foster that spirit, to further mutual understanding, to breed confidence in one another, and to co-operate for the weal of all.

Without such confidence and co-operation success is impossible; with them, our well-being is assured.

Appendix

THE following vessels and craft took part in the simultaneous blocking operations at Zeebrugge and Ostende.

THE ZEEBRUGGE ENTERPRISE

(a) *Special services during the oversea voyage*

Aerial Escort —
  61st Wing of Royal Air Force.
Other services —
  Special service vessel *Lingfield*. Motor Launches Nos. 555, 557.

(b) *Offshore forces*

Outer Patrol —
  Scout — *Attentive.*
  Destroyers — *Scott, Ulleswater, Teazer, Stork.*
Long-range Bombardment —
  Monitors — *Erebus, Terror.*
  Destroyers — *Termagant, Truculent, Manly.*

(c) *Inshore forces*

Flagship —
  Destroyer — *Warwick* (Flag of Vice-Admiral R. J. B. Keyes).
Blockships —
  Light Cruisers — *Thetis, Intrepid, Iphigenia.*
Storming Vessels —
  Light Cruiser — *Vindictive.*
  Special vessels — *Iris, Daffodil.*
Attack on Viaduct —
  Submarines — C 1, C 3, and one picket boat.
Aerial Attack —
  Aircraft — 65th Wing, Royal Air Force.
Other Operations —
  Destroyers — *Phœbe, North Star, Trident, Mansfield, Whirlwind, Myngs, Velox, Morris, Moorsom, Melpomene.*

Motor Launches — Nos. 79, 110, 121, 128, 223, 239, 241, 252, 258, 262, 272, 280, 282, 308, 314, 345, 397, 416, 420, 422, 424, 513, 525, 526, 533, 549, 552, 558, 560, 561, 562.
Coastal Motor Boats — Nos. 5, 7, 15, 16A, 17A, 21B, 22B, 23B, 24A, 25BD, 26B, 27A, 28A, 30B, 32A, 35A.

THE OSTENDE ENTERPRISE
(a) Bombarding forces

Monitors —
Marshall Soult, Lord Clive, Prince Eugene, General Craufurd, M. 24, M. 26, M. 21.
Destroyers —
Mentor, Lightfoot, Zubian.
Motor Launches —
Nos. 249, 448, 538, and three others.
French Destroyers and Torpedo Boats —
Lestin, Roux, Bouclier, and Torpedo Boats Nos. 1, 2, 3, and 34.
French Motor Launches — Nos. 1, 2, 33, 34.
British Siege Guns in Flanders.

(b) Inshore forces

Blockships —
Light Cruisers — *Sirius, Brilliant.*
Destroyers —
Swift, Faulknor, Matchless, Mastiff, Afridi, Tempest, Tetrarch.
Motor Launches —
Nos. 11, 16, 17, 22, 23, 30, 60, 105, 254, 274, 276, 279, 283, 429, 512, 532, 551, 556.
Coastal Motor Boats —
Nos. 2, 4, 10, 12, 19, 20, 29A, 34A.

COVERING SQUADRON FOR BOTH ENTERPRISES
Forces from Harwich —
Light Cruisers, seven.
Leaders, two.
Destroyers, fourteen.

The Zeebrugge Raid

By Arthur Hungerford Pollen

ZEEBRÜGGE

In the course of the night April 22-23, an attack was made on the two Flemish bases Ostend and Zeebrügge, with a view to blocking the entrances of both by the familiar method of sinking old cement-filled ships in the narrow fairway. At Ostend the block-ships were grounded slightly off their course, and a few days later a second attempt was made. The Zeebrügge blockships got into their chosen billets and are safely grounded there. The latter port, in spite of official denials, was for many months made almost useless to the enemy, and it is probably safe to assume that the value of Ostend, where *Vindictive* lies across the fairway, is considerably diminished. Material results, therefore, of high importance were achieved by this enterprise.

The operations are worth examining on three quite independent grounds. First, what is the strategical value of their objective? How, that is to say. would the naval activities of Great Britain and her Allies gain by Zeebrügge and Ostend being, for some months at least, out of action? And, conversely, what would the enemy lose? Unless we are satisfied that the gain must be substantial—apart altogether from the moral effect—we should obviously have a difficulty in justifying, not the losses in ships incurred, which were trivial and easily replaced, but the losses in picked men, which were irreparable. Secondly, the incident is clearly worth examining for its tactical interest. What were the difficulties the vice-admiral in command had to overcome? By what weapons, devices, and manoeuvres did he attempt to effect his purpose? Third, what was the moral effect?

STRATEGICAL OBJECT

There is now only one theatre of the war, and in this the issue of civilisation or barbarism must be decided by military action. The event depends upon the capacity of the sea power of the Allies to deliver in France all the fighting men and all the war material that Allied ships can draw from Asia, from Australia, from South America, from the United States, and from Canada, and then deliver either directly into France, or first into British ports, and then from Britain into France. To beat the German army is ultimately a problem in sea communications. The whole of these have to pass through the bottle-neck of the Western end of the Atlantic lanes. Into an area south of Ireland and north of Ushant, a hundred miles square, every ship that comes from the Mediterranean, from the Cape, from Buenos Ayres, Rio, the West Indies, or the Gulf of Mexico, from the Atlantic seaboard of America, must come.

Secondary only to this are the areas that feed ships into it, or into which the ships that pass through it are dissipated on their way to the several ports—the Mediterranean, the Bay of Biscay, the English Channel, St. George's Sound, the Irish Sea. It is in these, when it is driven from the main funnel point of traffic, that the submarine must do its work. The defeat of the submarine, when at large, turns upon three factors:

(1) the underwater offensive—that is, minefields, that will tend to keep it within certain areas;

(2) the efficiency with which ships liable to attack are protected by convoy; and

(3) the skill and persistence with which submarines, once on their hunting grounds, are in turn hunted. To maintain a cross-Channel barrage, the enemy surface craft must be handicapped in every possible way. The second and third factors of anti-submarine war make heavy demands on material, on personnel, and on skill, judgment, and organisation. Here the decisive material factor is the number of destroyers available for both forms of work.

When it comes to a close-quarters fight, no craft that has a speed of less than thirty knots, that cannot maintain itself in any weather, that does not possess a large cruising radius, can be of the first efficiency. The larger petrol-driven submarine-chasers and the many special craft which are built for various purposes in connection with the defensive campaign, all have their field of utility. But for the final power to rush swiftly on to a submarine, if it is momentarily seen afloat, and for covering the area into which it can submerge itself, while the destroyer approaches, with depth bombs, the destroyer, if only from its superior speed, stands supreme is the enemy of the U-boat. From the very earliest days of the submarine work it has, then, been axiomatic that every measure which will put a larger number of destroyers at our disposal should be taken at almost any cost. How does the work at Zeebrügge and Ostend help us, both in this respect and in a mining policy?

At these two ports our enemy was able to maintain a very considerable destroyer force. Its activities were necessarily mainly confined to work in darkness or in thick weather. But in such conditions its efficiency was of a very high order. The public only heard of its activities when it shelled some point of the coast of Kent, or raided our trawlers or other patrols, and, in all conscience, it heard of these activities often enough. Yet we were inclined to suppose them unimportant because their material results were insignificant. The news that a cross-Channel barrage was in course of establishment gave them a new value. But their value to the enemy should not be measured by the casualties they inflicted on our light craft, nor by their occasional excursions into the murder of civilians on shore. It lay in the fact that the enemy's force permanently withdrew from the anti-submarine campaign numerous destroyer leaders and destroyers which had to be maintained at Dover to cope with it.

From Zeebrügge to Emden—the nearest German port—is, roughly, three hundred miles by sea; and it does not need elaborate argument to show that if Zeebrügge and Ostend were permanently out of action, the problem of dealing with enemy craft in the narrow seas is totally and entirely changed. With these gone, the East Coast ports became the natural centres from which to command the waters between Great Britain and Holland. They are fifty miles nearer Emden than is Dunkirk. If any German destroyers got west and south of Dunkirk, and the news of their presence were cabled to an East Coast base, destroyers could get between the enemy and his ports without difficulty. Thus, enemy surface craft, based upon German ports, would practically be denied access to Flemish waters altogether, and this by the East Coast and not by the Dover forces. In other words, the Dover patrol forces would, by the closing of Ostend and Zeebrügge, be set free for the highly important work of aiding in the anti-submarine campaign—and there is certainly no naval need that is greater.

The strategical objective, therefore, which Admiral Keyes put before himself in his expedition was, so far as he could, to set back the enemy's naval bases by no less than three hundred miles. Its importance as setting free new forces, both for the direct attack on submarines, and for saving the minelayers from attack, cannot be exaggerated, for it was a step—and a great step—forward in making sure of the sea communications on which all depends. It must be conceded, then, that the results Admiral Keyes had in view amply justify a very considerable expenditure both of material and men. Let us next ask ourselves what kind of material he chose, and how he proposed to use his forces with utmost economy and maximum tactical effect.

SIR ROGER KEYES' TACTICS

The purposes of the expedition, as we have seen, were to block the exit of the canal at Zeebrügge and the entrance of the small, narrow harbour at Ostend with old cruisers filled with cement, the removal of which would be an operation of a lengthy and tedious kind. Incidentally, the plan was to effect the maximum destruction of war stores and equipment at Zeebrügge and to sink as many as possible of any of the enemy vessels found in either port, and, finally, to inflict on the enemy the maximum possible losses of personnel. By blocking the canal the value of Zeebrügge was reduced from being an equipped base to being a mere refuge. As there were two points of attack, the expedition naturally resolved itself into two distinct, but simultaneous, undertakings. The simpler, the less dangerous, the less ambitious, but, as the event showed, the more difficult operation of the two, was the attempt to block Ostend. The larger, more complex, and infinitely more perilous undertaking, but because of its very complications, ultimately easier, was the attempt at Zeebrügge.

In its broad outlines, the scheme was to get the ships as near as possible without detection, and then to trust to a final rush to gain the desired position. Concealment up to the last moment was to be secured by smoke screens. At Ostend the problem was simply to run two or three ships into the entrance—that is, to get them into position before the enemy's artillery made it impossible to manoeuvre. If the Ostend attempt failed, it was largely because a sudden change in the weather conditions robbed the smoke screens, which were to hide the ships, of their value, so that the operation of placing the blockships accurately was made almost impossible. The operation of blocking such entrances has, of course, long been familiar. The exploit of Lieutenant Hobson in the Spanish-American War is fresh in the memories of all sailors. This failed through the steering gear of the blocking-ship being destroyed by gunfire at the critical moment. The Japanese attempted the same thing on a large scale at Port Arthur, but with anything but complete success. If the first Ostend effort, then, fell short of finality, we have the experience of these earlier precedents to explain and account for it.

I have dealt with Ostend first because, after the preliminary bombardment, nothing more could have been attempted than to force the ships into the harbour entrance and sink them there. But at Zeebrügge a far more intricate operation was possible. Zeebrügge is not a town. It is just the sea exit of the Bruges Canal, with its railway connections, round which a few streets of houses have clustered. The actual entrance to the canal is flanked by two short sea-walls, at the end of each of which are guide-lights. From these lights up the canal to the lock gates is about half a mile. A large mile protects the sea channel to the canal from being blocked by silted sand. The mole is connected to the mainland by five hundred yards of pile viaduct. The mole is nearly a mile long, built in a curve, a segment amounting to, perhaps, one-sixth of a circle, the centre of which would be a quarter of a mile east of the canal entrance, while its radius would be three-quarters of a mile. It is a large and substantial stone structure, on which are railway lines and a railway station, and has been turned to capital military account by the enemy, who erected on it aircraft sheds and military establishments of many kinds.

The general plan was to bombard the place for an hour by monitors and, under cover of this fire, for the attacking squadron to advance to the harbour mouth. Then, when the bombardment ceased, *Vindictive* was to run alongside the mole, disembark her own landing party and those from *Iris* and *Daffodil*, who were to overpower the enemy protecting the guns and stores while the old submarines were run into the pile viaduct to cut the mole off from the mainland, thus isolating it. Meanwhile, other forces were to engage any enemy destroyers or submarines that might be in the port. Finally the block-ships were to be pushed right up into the canal mouth and there sunk. The success of the latter part of these operations turned upon the extent to which the enemy could be made to believe that the attack on the mole was the chief objective.

To ensure success against the mole, several very ingenious devices were brought into play. The main landing parties were placed in *Vindictive*. This cruiser—which displaced about 5,600 tons, and had

233

a broadside of six 6-inch guns—was fitted, on the port side, with 'brows,' or landing gangways, that could be lowered on the mole the moment she came alongside. All the vessels of the squadron were equipped with fog or smoke-making material, which would veil the force from the enemy until he sent up his star-shells and, in the artificial light, would conceal the character, number's, and composition of the force as completely as possible. It seems that a shift of wind at the critical moment—here, as at Ostend—robbed this plan of some of its anticipated efficiency. At some point of the approach, then, apparently just before *Vindictive* rounded and got abreast of the lighthouse, the presence of the invaders was detected, and they were saluted first by salvoes of star shells, and next by as hot a gunfire as can be conceived. *Vindictive* lost no time in replying. Her six 6-inch guns—and no doubt her 12-pounders as well—swept the mole as long as they could be fired, and, once alongside, the 'brows'—only two out of eighteen seem to have survived the heavy gunfire—were lowered, and officers and men 'boarded' the mole.

The earlier accounts stated that this landing was effected in spite of the stoutest sort of hand-to-hand fighting, that the enemy was overcome and driven back, and that the landing party then proceeded to the destruction of the sheds and stores. The plans had included the blowing-up of the pile viaduct, which connects the stone mole with the mainland—by means of one or two old submarines charged with explosives, and so virtually converted into giant torpedoes. These did their work most effectively, and had the enemy been in occupation of the mole, his force would have been isolated. But, as a fact, the mole was not occupied, and the enemy relied upon machine and gunfire organised from the shore end of the mole for making the landing impossible. In spite of a withering fusillade, a considerable landing party of marines and blue-jackets got ashore, though Colonel Elliott and Commander Halahan and great numbers of their men were killed in the attempt. Those that got on the mole proceeded to destroy, as far as possible, the sheds, stores, and guns, and then turned their attention to the destroyers moored against its inner side.

Meantime, the only enemy destroyer that seems to have had steam up tried to escape from harbour, and was either rammed and instantly sunk or torpedoed. Others, less well prepared, were either boarded, after the resistance of their crews had been overcome, and, it must be presumed, sunk also. Others, again, were attacked by motor launches, which preceded and helped clear a way for the blockships. Whether an attempt on the lock gates was made or even contemplated, we have not been told; but the main purpose of the expedition, the sinking of at least two out of the three old *Apollos* in the right place, was achieved with precision. The moment the block-ships were in place, the purpose for which the mole was occupied was gained, and the order was rightly given for an immediate retreat. The work had been done, and there was no knowing what new resources the enemy could have brought to bear had time been wasted. Many of the vessels, including *Vindictive*, had been holed by 11-inch shells. But *Vindictive's* damages were not of a serious kind, and the whole force was able to withdraw in safety, with the exception of one destroyer and two motor launches. The destroyer is known to have been sunk by gunfire. The successful withdrawal of the expedition is conclusive evidence that the enemy was demoralised.

For such close-quarters work Admiral Keyes, naturally enough, armed his forces as for trench fighting. *Vindictive* carried howitzers on her forward and after decks, and her boarding parties were liberally armed with grenades and flame-throwers as well as with rifles, bayonets, and truncheons. Machine-guns also seem to have been landed, so that hand-to-hand fighting was prepared for in the full light of the most recent war experience. The plan, it should be noted, was to have included aeroplane co-operation to supplement, if not to assist, the work of the monitors; but the change in the weather appears to have interfered with this part of the programme, and may quite easily have made any accurate work by the monitors impossible also.

It is, first of all, patent that the expedition was thoroughly thought out in all its details, and therefore closely planned. An accurate study of the enemy's defences had been made, and suitable means of avoiding his attack or overcoming his defences had been elaborately worked out. It is equally clear that almost to the moment when the attack was made, the weather conditions were those which the plan contemplated as necessary to success, and that it was only the sudden, unexpected change in the wind that threatened the Ostend part of the operations with partial failure and made the Zeebrügge operations more costly in life than they should otherwise have been.

When it is remembered that the approaches to Ostend and Zeebrügge are commanded by very formidable batteries, armed with no less than 120 guns of the largest calibre, and that the mole and the sides of the canal bristled with quick-firing 12-pounders and larger pieces, it will be realised that, to the enemy, any attempt actually to bring an unarmoured vessel, with her cement-laden consorts, right up either to the mole or to the actual mouth of the canal must have appeared an undertaking too absurdly harebrained for anyone but a lunatic to have attempted. It was just because Sir Roger Keyes had evaluated the enemy's defences with exactitude and had thought out and adopted, first, methods of evading his vigilance and, next, manoeuvres that would *for the necessary period* make his weapons useless, that it was possible not only to make the attempt, but to realise the very high degree of success that has apparently been won.

The essence of the matter, of course, was to take the enemy by surprise. At first sight it may appear a curious way of putting him off his guard, that he should for an hour be bombarded by monitors and aeroplanes. But the vice-admiral probably reasoned that this would lead, as it often does, to the crews of the big guns taking shelter underground until the attack is over. If the monitors were placed at their usual great distance from the ports, and were concealed by smoke or fog screens, the enemy gunners would know that it was merely idle to attempt to reply to their fire. If nothing was to be possible in the way of response until daylight, the gunlayers were just as well in their shell-proofs as anywhere.

Under cover, then, of this long-range bombardment, and concealing his squadron by the ingenious fog methods invented by the late Commander Brock, Sir Roger Keyes made his way within a very short distance of the veiled lights at the end of the mole. It was at this point that the wind shifted and the presence of the squadron was revealed to the enemy. There was a brief interval before the big guns could be manned, and it was doubtless owing to this that *Vindictive* got alongside before more than one 11-inch shell had struck her. Once under the shelter of the mole, she was safe from the larger pieces, and only her upper works could be raked by the smaller natures.

ATTACK ON THE MOLE

The policy of attacking the mole and making that appear to the enemy the central affair, was a fine piece of tactics. The engagement which developed there was, in fact, a containing action, which left the execution of the main objective to the other forces, and its purpose was to prevent the enemy from interfering too much with them. Nelson, it will be remembered, cut out a block of ships in the centre of the enemy's line at Trafalgar, occupying them so that their hands were full, and preventing both them and the van from coming to the succour of the rear. The main operation was the destruction of the rear by Collingwood. Here it was *Vindictive*, her landing-party, that played the Nelson role while the vice-admiral, in *Warwick*, himself directed the crucial operation, namely, the navigation of the block-ships to their billets. The moment they were blown up and sunk the purpose of the expedition was fulfilled, and *Vindictive's* siren recalled all those from the mole who could get back to the ship. The actual fortunes of the fight on the mole itself, while of thrilling human interest owing to the extraordinary circumstances in which it was undertaken, were of quite subsidiary importance. The primary object, it must be borne in mind, was not the destruction of the mole forts, or of the aeroplane shed, or of whatever military equipment was there, or even of killing or capturing its garrison. These were only important in so far as their partial realisation was necessary to relieving the block-ships from the danger of premature sinking.

This is a matter of real capital importance and of very great interest, for it is, I think, not difficult to realise that, had similar circumstances existed at Ostend—had it been possible, that is to say, to occupy the defenders and distract their attention on some perfectly irrelevant engagement—the requisite time would have been given to those in command of the block-ships to make sure of getting them into the right position. As things were, they were threatened by the fate which made Hobson's attempt at Santiago a failure. With the whole gun-power of Ostend concentrated upon the blocking-ships, there was not a minute to be wasted. But with the enemy's fire drawn there would have been the leisure which alone could make precision possible.

Moral Effect

The attack on Zeebrügge and the two successive attacks on Ostend, carefully planned and boldly and resolutely carried out, achieved a very high measure of success. It was natural enough, on the first receipt of the news, that we should all have been carried away by our wonder and admiration at the astonishing heroism that made it possible to carry through so intricate a series of operations, when every soul engaged was seemingly aware of the desperate character of the enterprise, when no one could have expected to return alive, when the enemy's means seemed ample, not only for the killing of everyone engaged, but for the immediate frustration of every object that they had in view, and so made most of the astounding gallantry and daring of all concerned. For over four years now we have had a constant recurrence of such feats of courage, and repetition does not lessen their power to intoxicate us with an overwhelming admiration of those who are the heroes of these great adventures. But we should be misconceiving the significance of these events if we were to measure their importance either by the ordered daring of those engaged, or by their successful execution, or by their immediate military results, great and far-reaching as these were.

The thing was more important as affording conclusive evidence that the British Navy, as inspired and directed from headquarters, had now abandoned the purely defensive role assigned to it by ten years of pre-war, and three and a half years of war, administration. It meant that the fleet had escaped from those counsels of timorous—because unimaginative and ignorant—caution which had checked its ardour and limited its activities since August, 1914. The effect may be incalculable. The doctrine that every operation which involved the risk of losing men or ships must necessarily be too hazardous to undertake, was thus shown to be no longer the loadstone of Whitehall's policy. The navy was at last set free to act on an older and a better tradition.

It is indeed on this tradition that on almost every occasion the navy has, in fact, acted when it got a chance. When *Swift* and *Broke* tackled three times their number of enemy last year, and *Botha* and *Morris* six times their number this year, the gallant captains of these gallant vessels did not wait to ask if the position of their ships was 'critical' or otherwise; but, with an insight into the true defensive value of attack—which, seemingly, it is the privilege only of the most valorous to possess—went straight for their enemies, fought overwhelming odds at close quarters, and came out as victorious as a rightly reasoned calculation would have shown to be probable.

Similarly, on May 31, 1916, Sir David Beatty, when his force of battle cruisers, by the loss of *Indefatigable* and *Queen Mary*, had been reduced below that of the enemy, persisted in his attack upon von Hipper and, by demoralising the enemy's fire, provided most effectively for the safety of his own ships. Losses did not make him retreat then, nor, when Scheer came upon the scene with the whole High Seas Fleet, did he withdraw from the action—his speed would have made this easy—though the odds were heavy against him. He kept, on the contrary, the whole German Fleet in play, drawing them dexterously to the north, where contact with the Grand Fleet would be inevitable. And, when the contact was made, his last effort to break up the German line was to close from the 14,000 yards, a range he had prudently maintained during the previous two hours, to 8,000, where his guns would be more certainly effective, realising perfectly that no loss of ships in his own squadron would signify, if only the entire destruction of the German Fleet were made possible by such a sacrifice. It would not be difficult to give scores of incidents in which individual admirals and captains have shown the old spirit under new conditions.

But, save only for the crazy attack on the Dardanelles forts—and this was hardly a precedent we should rejoice to see followed—we have looked in vain for any sign of naval initiative from Whitehall. The explanation lies in the fact that we had no staff for planning operations, nor the right men in power for judging whether any proposed undertaking was based on a right calculation of the value of the available means of offence and defence. The events, therefore, of the night of the 22nd and the early hours of the 23rd were of quite extraordinary importance, for they marked an undertaking needing long and elaborate preparation, and one which could not have been brought to a successful issue had it not enjoyed from its first inception the enthusiastic support of the Admiralty. But this is not all. Not only was this an Admiralty supported undertaking, it was one that, unlike the Gallipoli adventure, was carried through on right staff principles. There was a definite, well-thought-out plan—careful preparation for every step in the right selection of men and means for its execution.

I think it is right to put this forward as the most important aspect of a significant, stirring, and successful enterprise. It is the most important because the news meant so very much more than that Zeebrügge was blocked, that Ostend was crippled, and that an expedition—at first sight perilous beyond conception—had been carried through with losses altogether disproportionate, either to its dangers or to the results achieved. The news meant that a new direction either had been, or certainly can, and therefore must, now be given to our naval policy. In the spring of 1917 sceptics were asking if the army could win the war before the navy lost it. Why, they said, if our land forces can force a way through what we were told were impregnable fortifications, should the greatest sea force in the world be impotent against an enemy who slinks behind his forts with his surface craft, while devastating our sea communications with his submarines?

Is naval ingenuity, they asked, so crippled that we can neither protect our trade against the submarine at sea, nor block the enemy's ports so that the submarine can never get to sea? The critics replied that all was well with the navy, but that all was sadly wrong with its official chiefs. The reorganisation of the Admiralty was immediately followed by the adoption of the convoy principle—and submarine losses were reduced to half. This long-advocated measure, the recently inaugurated barrage at Dover, and now the events of the morning of April 23, have justified the critics and the changes in method and men which they urged. Zeebrügge had been in the enemy's hands since September, 1914, and it took us three and a half years, not to discover a man capable of attacking it, but in developing an Admiralty capable of picking the man and giving him the right support before the attack could be made. If a similar spirit had actuated a properly constituted Admiralty all these years, what might not the navy have accomplished?

In the previous year the emancipation of the navy had gone forward apace. And not the least significant of the stages in the process were first the appointment of Admiral Sir Roger Keyes to be head of the Planning Division at the Admiralty, next his removal from the Admiralty to Dover, next the inauguration of the Channel barrage, and finally his surprising and masterly stroke at the Flemish ports. The enumeration of these stages is worth making, for they mark the genesis of the plan we have seen achieved. It was, if I am correctly informed, quite understood when Admiral Keyes went to Dover that his mission was temporary. If he was sent to do the things which he has done, and now that he has done them is taken back to Whitehall, then it might seem as if we might look forward to an aggressive policy at sea more worthy of the superb force which we possess, and more consonant with its glorious heritage than anything which we have witnessed in the past.

And if Sir Roger cannot be spared from his new command, so auspiciously inaugurated, then we must trust that some other of equal brains and spirit has already taken, (as at time of first publication), or will take his place. Zeebrügge and Ostend, then, will figure in naval history, not only as the names of achievements unique and splendid in themselves, but more famous as the harbingers of still greater things to come.